ST...

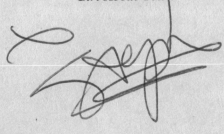

By the same author

VISIONS OF ANOTHER WORLD
The Autobiography of a Medium

VOICES FROM HEAVEN
Communion with Another World

IN TOUCH WITH ETERNITY
Contact with Another World

ANGELS BY MY SIDE
The Psychic Life of a Medium

A GIFT OF GOLDEN LIGHT

A Heart-warming Life-story
that covers Twenty Years of a
Medium's Psychic Experiences

Stephen O'Brien

**PO BOX 8
SWANSEA
SA1 1BL - UK**

For a Mail Order catalogue
and further information, see page 376

A GIFT OF GOLDEN LIGHT

Set in 10pt Linotype New Century Schoolbook by Phoenix Typesetting, Ilkley, West Yorkshire.

Printed and bound in Great Britain.

PRINTING HISTORY
Bantam edition published 1995
Voices edition published 1998

Acknowledgement and Dedication

With undying gratitude to the Golden Light
that shines through every soul,
and burns brightest in the darkness . . .

Contents

PART ONE
The Dissolving Veil

PART TWO
The God-Power Within

PART THREE
Bright Shining Lights

PART ONE
The Dissolving Veil

Are you sleeping?
No, I'm wide awake.
Then why can't you feel
what I can feel?

Are you dreaming and unconscious?
No, I'm fully aware.
Then why can't you see
what I can see?

Tell me: what can you see?
Many wond'rous things,
there for the viewing . . .

1

Prophecy Fulfilled

An invisible presence shivered the psychic atmosphere in the dusty room that served as a church, but only one of the fifty people present was aware of the arrival of this ancient spirit being – the slim young man in the light-brown jacket and trousers, who was seated on a raised platform in front of the crowd.

The young man's nervous system shuddered when he sensed the nearness of his spirit guide. 'I knew you'd come tonight,' thought the dark-haired youth, with eyes tightly closed, 'I prayed that you would, and I'm ready. Go ahead . . . but please, be gentle . . .'

So much apprehension filled the twenty-year-old lad that he felt his heart pounding against his ribs as the invisible sage drew closer to him in the spirit; the young man had only experienced being entranced by his guide on a few previous occasions so these odd sensations were still new to him, strange, and thrilling, and he wondered what on earth would happen to him next.

Suddenly the lad gasped when he caught sight of his inspirer: standing next to him, a six-feet tall American Indian shimmered into his psychic vision. He was a magnificent warrior: bare-footed, and wearing only a tan leather loincloth, the spirit man's bronzed and muscle-corded body gleamed like burnished copper in the ethereal light; his kind face radiated wisdom and dignity; his full lips were parted by a wise and knowing smile; his powerful shoulders were immensely strong; and his long black hair, as sleek as a raven's wing, complemented his dark brown eyes which shone with compassion.

Privately, the spirit warrior's deep thought-voice told the lad, 'I bring you my peace. My love for you is stronger than the sunlight.' The youngster smiled, feeling now more safe and secure in the midst of this unusual experience, while – unseen by the people in the dusty room – his spirit guide began the mysterious psychic process of blending two minds together as one.

But suddenly the twenty-year-old became nervous because he sensed the crowd's expectations: they wanted him to succeed, and he thought, 'The people demand so much from me, from us.'

His guide's response was quick. 'Never fear those whom you are called to serve. Just open your mouth and deliver what the Spirit gives you to say. My friend, our work is just beginning. In the years that lie ahead you will face much greater challenges than this.'

The lad frowned. 'Then I'll need your help.'

'Your soul is strong, young man, and guidance will always be given.'

Silently, the seated congregation watched as the young medium's chest expanded and his breathing deepened, but they were unaware of the warrior's wisdom that was being secretly conveyed to the youngster on the platform. 'You were born to

4

deliver the message of the Spirit,' echoed the voice in the lad's mind. 'Your life has a purpose, and together we will sow spiritual seeds in the minds of others; and they shall bear fruit, and the harvest will feed many.'

The youngster shuffled uneasily in his seat then replied awkwardly in thought, 'I understand . . . and I place my trust in you.'

'And also in God,' added his guardian. 'Never forget, you are about your Father's business, teaching and healing, revealing the truth of eternal life, and encouraging man to become more aware of the spiritual part of himself.'

'I've promised to help you,' replied the medium. Then he became conscious of a great soul power flooding into his being, and it seemed to him that two minds, two separate personalities, were gradually mingling, blending, as if trying to become one individual.

But all this passed unnoticed by the crowd, who obeyed the chairman of the meeting when he commanded them to, 'Stand up, and sing hymn No. 360.' Pages rustled; wooden chairs scraped along the dusty floor; and the medium opened his eyes for a few seconds to gaze at the fifty people. He knew that soon the air would resound with their rich Welsh voices, warm as the evening sunlight that was streaming through the windows of the humble church – humble because this temple was no golden-pillared edifice hung with priceless jewelled tapestries, nor did it display any of the pomp and grandeur of a magnificent cathedral; no, this small House of God was just a sparsely decorated hut.

The young man noticed its thin-planked walls that let in the brisk winds through their cracks; its floorboards that creaked under a scattering of worn-out mats; its rusty tin-sheeted roof that bravely battled to keep out the rain which usually succeeded in joining the services; and on its walls he saw only two religious texts: *God is Love*, and *To Serve is Noble*.

In one damp corner a wizened vulture of a woman was hunched over an upright Edwardian piano, banging her hands on the yellowed keys so vigorously that she appeared to be bouncing the music out of it. Her bony talons clawed out the Twenty-third Psalm which sounded as old and as crotchety as herself, while some faded red roses in a cracked vase on the piano's lid quivered in time to the melody.

'The room is small,' thought the young medium, 'but the welcome is big.'

> *The Lord's my shepherd, I'll not want.*
> *He makes me down to lie*
> *In pastures green: He leadeth me*
> *The quiet waters by . . .*

Silently, the youngster psychically scanned the full-toned congregation. They were a happy crowd, comprising a cross-section of ages: the elderly, whose bodies ached but whose hearts thanked God for the many blessings they'd received in their long lives; and the young, whose bodies glowed with strength but whose eager minds craved spiritual guidance which they hoped would lead them safely into their futures.

But within each mind the medium registered one dominant thought: a desire for contact with departed loved ones whom death had claimed. At the beginning of the service he'd already prayed that God might grant this request, and that peace might reign on Earth; and he'd ended his invocation by assuring the people that, 'Beyond the veil, eternal life waits for everyone: there is no death. We shall exist in the next world as complete persons in every way, whether we believe in the hereafter, or not,' he had said.

'For this knowledge, Great Spirit, we are grateful. And tonight,' he'd continued, 'we hope that we can generate in this temple enough of the psychic power of love, which will enable me to hear clearly the voices of those who have gone before us and to relay precisely their evidence of survival.'

And the final comforting words of his prayer had been: 'Death is an illusion: we are forever alive.'

Now, as he gazed at the singing crowd he felt his prayer had receded a million miles away from him and the room seemed to shiver and shake . . . He felt drowsy, sleepy under the influence of the spirit energies that were gathering around him. Slowly, his eyelids closed over his green-brown eyes, while fifty velvet voices echoed through the church:

Yea, though I walk in death's dark vale,
Yet will I fear no ill;
For Thou art with me, and Thy rod
And staff me comfort still . . .

The lad's breathing deepened further, and because he knew his spirit guide's personality would soon

7

overwhelm his own he slid his hand along the bench where he was sitting and pressed the 'Record' button on a portable tape-recorder nearby – just in time, for his awareness began to fade away – and the singing blurred and thickened, as though he were hearing it through sound-proofed glass . . . Time danced, and turned, and pirouetted— then ceased to have a meaning, as the spirit guide embraced his mind with an ancient personality that was both compassionate and benign.

The youth's last clear vision was of the Indian's bronzed body shimmering as it clothed itself in long and flowing lilac-coloured robes that had suddenly materialized around it; they seemed to be 'alive', as though they'd been crafted out of some kind of self-luminous light.

Goodness and mercy all my life
Shall surely follow me:
And in God's house, for evermore
My dwelling-place shall be.

Feet shuffled, chairs scraped along the creaky floorboards, people coughed and sat down, then the room became quiet.

The young lad's final impressions were hazy and vague – but startling: suddenly he felt much older than his twenty years; behind tightly shut eyelids his eyes rolled upwards and viewed the black darkness inside his head which was momentarily lit by bursts of golden light; then his voice-box was pulled downwards by invisible forces, after which he became aware of his body as it stood up of its own accord, walked forward, clasped its hands around the wooden altar-rail, and drew itself up to its full height. But the youth was no longer nervous, for he was now filled with a depth of confidence and maturity that was clearly not his own. And in that moment he knew that he and the Shining Being had become one – and his consciousness faded out . . .

There were thirty seconds of silence.

Then out of the twenty-year-old's mouth boomed the resonant voice of an entirely different personality. In place of the lad's quiet tones there came the deeper guttural sounds of a man twice his size who surprised the public by raising the medium's right hand to shoulder level, palm forward, and asking in his native Cherokee Indian dialect that the Great Spirit might bestow His Spiritual Blessing upon the meeting, after which the guide revealed to the listening congregation the purpose of his presence:

We, whom your world thinks of as 'dead' – but who are, in fact, far more alive than those who question our existence – are much closer to you than you know: Heaven and the Earth are not separated at all; nothing more than a fine ethereal mist stands between them. We contact you because we are charged with an important mission: with us we bring spiritual truth and knowledge that will release mankind from the bondage of ignorance and fear.

If man embraces our teachings he will illuminate his soul with the realization that he is an integral part of the Great Eternal Spirit of the Universe; and that, like his all-powerful Creator, he is deathless.

Our world interpenetrates your world; we are near to you all, but more especially to those whose hearts are lit by the light of compassion, whose minds are tolerant, whose desires are powerful enough to lift up and liberate the souls of the oppressed.

Those who feed the hungry and clothe the naked, and befriend the lonely, already know us. Those who, for the sake of Love, heal the sick and guide the lost out of their despair and into new hope are already aware of us, for our minds are linked with many souls who were born into your world to serve these spiritual causes.

It has never been easy for us, and never will be easy for us, to spiritualize the mind of man, but victory will be ours because we represent the mightiest power in the universe: God, the Great Spirit.

Millions on Earth have already joined our ranks, and one of these was a young woman who was dismayed by the cruelty and selfishness which was being expressed in the world around her. This woman believed in a God who cared for His children and, even though she did not understand the mysterious way in which He governed them, she *felt* His goodness, *knew* His presence, and loved Him in secret.

At twenty-nine years of age her body carried within it her second child; and one night she knelt in silence beside her bed, closed her eyes and prayed, 'May my child be healthy, and may he bring a little joy into this world, if it be Thy Will, Lord.'

Many invisible watchers heard this prayer; and when her time was due, the woman birthed a healthy boy who, when he reached adulthood, became a medium for the world of spirit, after his mother's death.

This woman's son is the man through whom I am now speaking; and the spirit form of his mother stands nearby at this moment, witnessing the answer to her prayer . . .

For a further twenty minutes the gentle Indian spoke about the spirit world and its Plan to bring peace to mankind, after which he withdrew his mental influence from his young medium, who immediately regained normal awareness and then tried hard to meet the expectations of the fifty people in the room by nervously relaying spirit messages to them.

An hour later the service ended and everyone thanked the new young medium; then they went home, leaving behind them the sound of happy laughter and the scent of best perfume and spicy aftershave floating in the air.

Alone in the damp church the youngster pulled on his blue plastic anorak, picked up his tape-recorder, and strode to the door where the President who had chaired the meeting was waiting for him. He shook the medium's hand. 'And what do we owe you for tonight's service, young man?'

'Oh, nothing,' said the lad brightly. 'Put it into the New Roof Fund.'

The President positively beamed. 'Thank you *very* much. And don't forget: I'll be dropping you a reminder shortly because you've got another booking with us soon. You're up there on the notice-board. See!' – and he pointed to the Speakers' List on

11

the wall – 'Five Sundays from now: Mr Stephen O'Brien.'

I was, indeed, the nervous young man whose spirit guide had entranced him in that dusty Spiritualist church in the 1970s, and who had revealed to the congregation that his medium's future life and work had been known to the world of spirit even before he'd been born.

What now follows is the story of my eventful psychic journey through those two enthralling decades; a journey that has been full of joys and pains, heartaches and laughter, and has contained some incredible revelations about mediumship, life after death, and the nearness of the spirit world to the earth . . .

Outside the little church, long ago on that frosty winter's evening in the 1970s, I shouted 'Cheerio!' to the smiling President and shivers went up and down my spine when the sharp night air penetrated my thin plastic coat.

As I stepped through the church doors my heels clicked onto cold cobblestones and I strode off purposefully down the path and into the empty Sunday-night streets.

I raised my collar against the gusty breeze, zipped up my anorak, and smiled eagerly at the thought of listening to the tape of my spirit guide's trance address later that night; White Owl's talks were so fascinating.

Clutching the tape-recording I was so anxious to hear, I crunched over frosty grasses, and quickly made my way home.

2

The Medium's Apprentice

Mrs Palmer's wrinkled fingers switched off the tape-recording of White Owl's talk that we'd been listening to, then pushed her blue-tinted spectacles back onto the bridge of her pointed nose. In the palpable quietness that followed, her grey eyes twinkled then stared at me.

Silence fell in folds around Mrs Palmer's cosy Welsh kitchen where we sat opposite each other, resting our arms on her spotlessly white tablecloth. For a few minutes the only sounds in the warm room were the loud ticking of the mantel clock and the crackling of sticks in the blazing fireplace; and the only movement was the flickering light of the bright coals that were burning in the grate.

My elderly host pulled her dark blue cardigan more tightly around herself. 'Now then,' she said at length, in soft Welsh tones, 'it's wonderful that White Owl can overshadow you so closely, Stephen.'

'It's been happening for a while now,' I returned, watching while she took off her glasses and became thoughtful again. Her old grey eyes seemed to sparkle as if they were psychically peering deep into my soul, reading the secrets of my mind, my motivation; but her face was quite relaxed.

She cleaned her spectacles with a lace handkerchief

13

during a deafening silence that magnified out of all proportion the ticking of the clock. Mrs Palmer was an excellent medium and I sensed that she was carefully assessing my clairvoyant abilities.

My awareness told me something else, too: many invisible eyes were studying us and they made the hairs on the back of my neck stand on end. I wondered what they, and Mrs Palmer, could see within my mind, but my thoughts were soon quietened by the bright coal fire that glowed and wrapped me in a homely warmth that obliterated the bleak winter night outside; and for the first time since my mother had died of cancer, a few months back, I felt warm and secure, here in Mrs Palmer's kitchen-cum-living-room. Everything around me was snug and comfortable and my host's hospitality seemed powerful enough to melt the cold fingers of ice that clung to the dark windowpanes.

Mrs Palmer's voice broke my reverie. 'Now then,' she said as she stood up to close the curtains; then she switched on a lamp that bathed the room in soft yellow light, left the table, and snuggled her small frame down into her cosy armchair next to the fire. I smiled to myself because she often had that endearing habit of saying 'Now then' before she launched into her speech proper; it was a homely turn of phrase, and I liked it very much.

'Now then,' she said. 'Last week you asked me to advise you on how to develop your clairvoyance, because you kindly said you respected my mediumship. Remember?'

My voice was quiet. 'Yes.'

'So— in effect, Stephen, you've asked me to instruct you. Is that right?'

I hadn't thought of it that way, and never for a moment had I even dreamt she would 'apprentice' me, so to speak. But yes, what she'd said was right: I'd asked for help, so I nodded my head anxiously.

'Well . . . I've given it a great deal of thought and I've also consulted my spirit friends because psychic development isn't something to be trifled with, it requires serious study and mediums must be very dedicated to their work.'

'I understand.'

'Anyway, what I've decided is—'

The next five seconds felt like five minutes, and I clasped my nervous hands in my lap.

'—I'll teach you everything I know, love.'

'Oh, thank you,' I said. 'That's very kind of you, Mrs Palmer.'

'Not at all. You were born with your gifts and your heart's in the right place. I've watched you struggling to improve your mediumship at the Open Circle meetings in the church over the last few months and I think you deserve some help. We older ones have a great responsibility to pass on our knowledge to the promising youngsters that are coming up. That's the least we can do.'

My apprenticeship as a medium had begun – and the spirit world made immediate contact. From the framed picture just above my head on the wall there came a repeated *tap tap tap tap tap*, like the sound of a coin clicking on the glass. I raised my eyebrows and looked up.

Mrs Palmer smiled warmly. 'Oh, that's Ahmed, I expect: my Arab spirit guide,' she said. 'He's a proper Nosy Parker and he's been listening in again.'

I glanced quickly around the room, but of course I saw no-one.

'Now then. I've only known you for a short while, Stephen, since that night you walked into the Spiritualist Church meeting after your mother had died. You told me she'd returned to you in a vision—'

'It was a wonderful experience,' I affirmed.

'Yes I've no doubt about that. What's more I've a feeling your mam guided your feet towards the church, too. I'm certain she loved you very deeply, and it's this love that will have given her the power to inspire your thoughts and to point you in the right direction. Don't you think so?'

'Yes, I do.'

'I know you've told me you've been psychic since you were a child, but I've no doubt that your mother's spirit-return was the start of a new and important phase in your life.'

A sudden spiritual warmth seemed to embrace me. 'Yes.'

'Now then, I've given our friendship a great deal of thought and I've also consulted my spirit guides about how to proceed with your training. First of all, remember you're only twenty and the thrill of working your mediumship is new and exciting to you, but it'll take many years for your psychic powers to unfold to their full potential, you know. You'll need bags of patience because a medium's road is one of the hardest to walk, mind,' she said, wagging a cautionary finger. 'Oh, there's no doubt we're privileged to help people in such a wonderful way; God's called us to serve, to do our best to prove survival, and there's a tremendous joy in bringing a little comfort to others, but I've known many sensitives and not one of them's had an easy life, mind.'

Drinking in her wisdom, I nodded my head.

'Yes, it's a tough old road, Stephen, spiritually and physically.' She leaned forward in her seat. 'It's a lonely path, too, and there'll be many difficulties strewn along it. Can you cope with hardship?'

My answer was immediate. 'My back is young, and I'm strong,' I said, sitting up straight. 'I'm not so sure about the patience, Mrs Palmer, but I want to learn as much as I can, and I've got plenty of determination.'

'Well, you'll need it, God only knows.' Mrs Palmer settled back in her armchair again, rested her hands comfortably in her lap, and sighed thoughtfully. 'You see, sensitives sometimes experience a feeling of Great Aloneness. It's a soul sensation. And many mediums are rejected by their own families, too. You see' – she gathered her words carefully – 'people who can't see the wonders of Spirit like we can, don't understand us. And what they don't understand, they're frightened of.'

'Yes.'

'And what people are afraid of, they try to hurt,' she warned.

We both nodded in silence, then I heard myself say, 'But I won't let the Other Side down. I promised I would help them, Mrs Palmer. I've given them my word.'

She pressed her lips together and then released them. 'You'll need loads of tolerance, then, especially with the public.'

As if to emphasize her advice the spirit people clicked the picture-glass above my head again: *tap tap tap*.

Mrs Palmer's creamy skin glowed orange in the dancing firelight; she gave her head a little shake then her face took on a thoughtful expression. 'It's such a tough world for sensitive people. I'm in my seventies now, but do you know, last week I trudged through snowdrifts to take a meeting and no-one at that church offered me a lift home, or even a cup of tea. I stood for forty-five minutes in a snowstorm, waiting for a bus that didn't come. By the time I got in I was frozen to the marrow.'

My voice was low and sympathetic. 'People can be very unkind,' I said, recalling that last week, at home, my father had gone out for his daily drink and left me on my own, shivering and 'dying' of a 'Red Flu' virus. Shakily I'd dressed and dragged my quaking body through deep winter snowdrifts to the nearest telephone box, but the harridan at the health centre had refused to send out a doctor. 'If you can get to a payphone you can crawl to the surgery,' she'd snapped like the dragon she was.

A piece of coal shifted in the grate and the noise brought me smartly back into the room. Mrs Palmer was fumbling for the poker with which she so vigorously riddled the fire that I wondered if she were venting her anger on it. An acrid taste of smoke was in my mouth. She laid the poker back on the hearth and sat up straight. 'Aye, you're right enough there, Stephen: people can be very unkind. I tackled my spirit guide about it, you know, during one of my daily meditations. I asked Ahmed, right out, why I'd suffered so much in my life, and do you know what he said?'

I shook my head.

'He told me, "Those who lead must be stronger than those who follow."'

There was a long pause while she allowed this spiritual truth to brand itself indelibly upon my mind, and this was followed by another *tap tap* on the picture-glass overhead.

She then touched a sheaf of foolscap papers next to my tape-recorder on the table and I knew exactly what was coming next: it would be 'Now then'.

'Now then,' she said matter-of-factly, 'I've studied these inspired writings on the Development of Mediumship that White Owl had dictated to you, and they're very interesting. His teachings are sound and educational. But this tape-recording of your last service' – she patted it pointedly – 'proves he's much too strong a trance personality for your slight frame. Have you sent him thoughts to ask him to blend more gently with your mind?'

'Yes, I did that last night.'

'Good, because thoughts are living things, you know. See that drawing up on the wall? The young girl's face with a bouquet of flowers in the right-hand corner?'

'Yes.'

'That's a psychic portrait which proved to me that thoughts can be seen and answered by the spirit world. A psychic artist sketched it years ago and that little girl is one of my three children. None of my babies lived, of course; I lost all three of them just after they were born. Something to do with my blood, the doctors said . . .' Her eyes became still for a moment, then she gave her head a little shake and continued more brightly, 'There's some wonderful evidence in that picture.'

I scrutinized the sketch, which had been drawn with white pastels on jet black paper and showed the profile of a beautiful girl's face.

'Now then. I'll explain. When my daughter was born I wasn't allowed to see her because she'd already died.'

A lump came into my throat.

'It was a terrible experience, to birth a stillborn baby. And I felt so sorry for Bill, my late husband, because he had the heart-rending job of taking her little body down to the cemetery . . . it wouldn't happen today, of course, but we were very poor, and those were very tough times . . .' Her voice trailed off in sad reflection before she continued, 'We were both devastated, as you can imagine.'

I certainly could.

'Our hearts were broken and I cried my eyes out when he wrapped her tiny premature body in a white shawl, ready to take her away. But as he was leaving I looked up through my tears and just caught sight of one of my daughter's tiny hands, clenched in a little fist, that had fallen free of one of the folds . . .'

I swallowed hard.

'It was one of the saddest days of my life . . . But Stephen— take a closer look at those flowers in the

20

corner of the portrait. Under the pink ribbons, can you see what's holding up the bouquet?'

And there, clutching the flowers, was a small child's hand, clenched in a little fist. I was more than impressed. 'That's wonderful,' I said.

'And my daughter's hand's been drawn at exactly the same size, shape and angle as I saw it on the day she died. What's more that psychic artist and I were total strangers, you know: we'd never met. She sent me the drawing by post, and it was very comforting to receive it because I'd prayed so hard to God to allow the spirit world to bring me evidence of my child's survival, and that picture was the answer to my prayers. So you see, thoughts *are* living things.'

She smiled poignantly, then rose on awkward legs and from the scuttle tipped shiny black coal onto the fire which immediately crackled and spat and sent yellow-blue flames soaring into the chimney, drawn up by the winter winds. 'That'll keep the chill out,' she said, wiping her hands on her flowery apron; then she cricked the pains out of her old back. 'Now then: I'll fetch the tea – and after that we'll talk about your mediumship and how you might receive your spirit messages.' She tottered out into the tiny adjoining scullery and turned up the gas on the stove.

My eyes winked in the bright firelight, and the mantel clock struck a hollow seven. As I smoothed out the creases on the snowy tablecloth I realized that Mrs Palmer's place wasn't just a house – it was a home, a home that radiated a peaceful atmosphere that was so unlike that of my father's house where the air was charged with our daily personality clashes. I sighed deeply. Dad and I lived together and there had been nothing between us but senseless arguments and icy silences since my mother had died of stomach cancer, a few months back.

A gust of wind down the chimney blew firesmoke into my nostrils and made me aware again of the kitchen and I heard the pleasant clicking of knives and forks in the scullery. When the acrid smell cleared, it was replaced by the delicious aroma of Mrs Palmer's cooking that wafted through to me. Through the open door I watched as she brushed from her forehead some strands of short curly hair, the colour of which perfectly matched her twinkly grey eyes; then she shook the chip basket, and turned out the food onto warmed plates.

How strange it was to see this sensible, five-feet tall pensioner cooking a meal. Tonight she was just an ordinary Welsh housewife, an elderly widow taking care of herself, but at the Spiritualist Church she was a quite different person altogether: there, Mrs Palmer was a respected President and a brilliant medium – the best medium in South Wales, I thought, and I felt privileged to know her.

Tap tap tap went the picture-glass; I gave it a smiling glance then turned my eyes back towards the scullery.

Mrs Palmer buttered two thick slices of bread, and light glinted off her energetic knife as she softly sang to herself one of her favourite hymns to God: 'Open my eyes that I may see, glimpses of truth Thou hast for me. Help me to set the Higher Self free, so shall I serve and worship Thee.'

She was such a lovely soul, so homely and

thoughtful, and she'd drastically changed my way of thinking: I'd begun to believe there was little or no kindness left in the world since my mother had died, but Mrs Palmer had proved my youthful assumption wrong.

Supper smelled delicious. My mouth watered and I swallowed in anticipation; I hadn't been eating regularly and I was famished. My hostess lifted the heavy tray, gave a huge smile that stretched high over her rosy cheekbones, ambled back to the kitchen table and, much to my delight, plonked the steaming food right under my quivering nose. My eyes widened and I licked my chops.

'Now then,' she said, sitting down, 'I know grief makes people lose their appetites, but you've hardly eaten at all by the look of you since your mother passed over. You're as thin as a rake.'

I lowered my gaze. She was quite right. I'd lost a stone in weight since the funeral and hadn't looked after myself properly: my black denim jeans were faded and torn over the knees; there was a hole in the baggy white jumper my mother had always called my 'Sloppy Joe'; and I hadn't shaved. I must have looked like a scarecrow.

Greedily, I eyed the hot cheese pie, the pile of chips, and the bright green peas that glistened with yellow butter on my plate. After setting out the cutlery Mrs Palmer sat down at the table. 'I enjoy cooking two square meals for you each week, Stephen: that's the least I can do.'

'Thank you,' I said, self-consciously prodding my pie with a fork and thinking how kind she'd been to me – as thoughtful as any mother would have been.

'Well, tuck in then, before it gets cold.'

'Thank you,' I said, lifting a shaky forkful of chips to my mouth and politely nibbling at them, when what I really wanted to do was gulp the whole lot down in one heave-ho! But I couldn't. I'd always been shy with strangers, ever since I was a toddler. I remembered the time I couldn't touch a schoolfriend's scrummy birthday cake because I'd felt all the other children in the room were staring at me.

Mrs Palmer's knife and fork clicked while she busily polished off three fish fingers in batter and, when she wasn't looking, I wolfed down two thick slices of cheese pie.

Our plates were soon cleared, and with full bellies we settled down again in front of the glowing fire.

'Now then,' she said as she riddled the fire, then straightened her blue cardigan, 'Now then, never forget that a spirit message is a mind-to-mind communication, Stephen, and when you're starting out as a medium, you might not always hear the communicators' voices clearly. Sometimes reception is good, sometimes it's bad: it varies because of the psychic conditions inside the meeting place, and in the minds of the sitters, and in your own mind, too. The more peace and love there is in the atmosphere, the better the mediumship functions. So never get anxious and frustrated; always stay peaceful and give whatever you get, even if it's only symbolic pictures.'

I clasped my hands in my lap and listened attentively, grateful for her wise instruction.

'. . . Because some spirit messages are given to mediums in thought-pictures, just like that image

24

of my daughter's hand holding those flowers in the psychic portrait.' We both glanced up at the drawing. 'It's your job as a medium to relay faithfully what the Other Side gives to you; the information might seem trite and banal, but it could be very meaningful to your recipient. Your function is not to judge it, but to act as a channel for its transmission.'

I nodded thoughtfully.

'So when you next work, watch out for these thought-images because they can pop into your mind as quick as *that*' – and she clicked her fingers. 'As a matter of fact I received a symbol from the Other Side earlier on when I was in the scullery.'

Intrigued, I asked, 'Did you?'

'Yes, I was shown a picture of the church full to capacity for tomorrow night's Open Circle; so I hope you're coming.'

'Of course. I wouldn't miss an Open Circle for the world. I want to develop my mediumship by practising it.'

'That's the sign of a good apprentice. Now, when you're giving out your messages tomorrow, try to be more aware of the symbols in them.'

Tap tap tap went the picture-glass and Mrs Palmer chuckled good-heartedly. 'All right, Ahmed! We know you'll be there, too!'

And the following evening – he was. Furthermore, his prediction proved perfectly correct: Oxford Street Spiritualists' National Union Church was packed to the rafters . . .

3

Pictures in the Mind

Buzzing voices charged the air with expectation;
seventy wooden chairs had been arranged in three
concentric circles in the small upper room that was
Oxford Street Spiritualist Church and every seat
was occupied; the crowd was eagerly awaiting the
start of the Saturday Open Circle, a public meeting
where experienced mediums could work and also
'fledgling' clairvoyants could try their wings, so to
speak, to strengthen them and to see if they could
fly solo.

I gazed around me at the light-blue painted
walls, the mid-blue carpet on the brown linoleum
floor, then looked up at the high white ceiling.
Most small Spiritualist churches up and down
the country were similar to Oxford Street, so
Mrs Palmer had told me, comprised of a single
room with perhaps a tiny cupboard-like kitchen
just big enough to accommodate a sink and maybe
two washers-up, if you were lucky.

The Spiritualist Movement was certainly not
wealthy and neither were its mediums – at least,
not in the things of the material world. Like the
rest of the seventy people, I sat on a hard wooden
chair obtained from a Junior School, but I was at
one end of the inner ring of a horseshoe of chairs,

and Mrs Palmer, wearing her dark-green winter coat and close-fitting hat, sat at the other end. In the gap between us stood a calor-gas fire which completed the Open Circle and did its best to keep out the chilly winter weather.

The congregation fell quiet and then started the service by trembling its way through one of Mrs Palmer's favourite sacred songs, 'It Is No Secret What God Can Do', while I remembered the first time I ever set foot inside the church: it had been three months after my mother's death, just after her spirit-self had miraculously appeared to me in a blaze of golden light at the top of our staircase at home. I'd been stunned and startled by the vision but also profoundly moved; and then my heart had sung because I knew for certain that my beloved mother had survived the grave. It was her spirit-return that had made me realize there was a definite purpose behind the many strange psychic visions and voices that had come to me intermittently throughout my childhood.

After this I found myself 'inspired' by the invisible world to enter Oxford Street Spiritualist Church; and now here I was, watching my new friend Mrs Palmer singing with gusto opposite me. I was glad she'd befriended me and apprenticed me as a medium.

Suddenly the hymn-singing finished and Mrs Palmer stood up and delivered a beautiful spontaneous prayer, given straight from her heart, then she began to relay impressive spirit messages while I struggled to get a mental contact with the Other Side. It would be my turn next and, as usual, I was quite nervous even though I'd sensed the incredibly

27

strong spiritual presence of my spirit guardian,
White Owl, standing next to me; and next to him
stood Ahmed, Mrs Palmer's guide.

Mrs Palmer gave some remarkably accurate
messages, and my nervousness intensified and
I wondered how anyone could possibly surpass
her detailed survival evidence: she'd relayed an
incredibly emotional link to a woman whose sister
had 'fallen to her death from a cliff', and she'd even
named the seaside town where the accident had
occurred, followed by the 'dead' sister's birth-date.
This was breath-taking mediumship – brilliant
stuff.

True to her excellent teaching methods (which
required mediums to deliver survival evidence, a
personal message from communicators, and *a reason*
for their spirit-return) Mrs Palmer had completed
the contact by telling her recipient that her sister's
death *was* an accident. She'd fallen, and hadn't been
pushed, as some of the family had thought.

The sister was overjoyed at the news and was
further delighted to receive from her relative, 'Please
tell my children that I love them, and I'm very near
to them.'

Mrs Palmer thanked the woman, smiled, then
confidently declared to the public, 'Now then, young
Stephen will demonstrate clairvoyance.'

She sat down, and I stood up and looked at the
crowd. Every face in the congregation had turned
towards me and was full of expectation, I felt,
and more than eager to criticize my inexperience.
Apprehension swept through me because I was just
a raw beginner who hoped he'd be successful, but who

knew he couldn't possibly equal his tutor's excellent work.

Nevertheless, I gritted my teeth and was determined to give whatever impressions I received from the Other Side. I'd promised the spirit world I'd help them to serve the people – and I would.

All at once I received a strong impression to speak to a frail old man who sat hunched up in a chair directly opposite me. For all the world he looked like a ninety-year-old miniature wax doll wrapped in a huge grey overcoat that had seen much better days; I noticed there was a dried gravy stain on its lapel. 'I feel very drawn to you, sir,' I said.

He cupped a shaky transparent hand round one of his ears and leaned forward slightly in his seat; his thick Yorkshire accent quivered in high tones, 'Aye, lad,' and his trembling fingers brushed back the sparse white hairs around his ear, 'Ah can hear you.'

Cautiously I continued, 'I feel you have a very strong spirit, sir, that you're a fighting-man, but I think there's been an upset or a family row. Is that right?'

His eyelids drooped and the wrinkles on his shiny forehead multiplied. Answering barely above a whisper he said, 'That's right. Ah've been through hell with me family; and Ah *am* a fightin'-man. Ah were a soldier, an' proud o' it, an' all.' Then his small form issued a hoarse, chesty cough.

'Well, I feel your loved ones in Spirit know all about your difficulties,' I added, hoping this would comfort him, 'and I believe they're sending healing energy to you, to help you over your distress.'

29

'Champion,' he replied, and his chest rumbled again.

Inwardly I began to panic because the female spirit voice I was so desperately trying to hear was maddeningly fading in and out of my consciousness. How I wished I could register it more clearly – but I was just a struggling beginner.

Then I was made suddenly aware of his communicator's identity. 'It's a lady, sir, sending you this message. I think she's your wife. She's a tall woman who's in perfect health now but before she died she suffered dreadful pains in her head. And good Lord!' – my voice rose in surprise when I saw some vivid symbolic pictures – 'could she cook? She's showing me dozens of hot pies, and bowls of steaming jam puddings with thick custard on them.' My mouth watered.

'Aye . . .' whispered the old soldier, 'aye, she were a first-class school cook was me wife . . .' His light voice trailed away and he seemed lost in special memories.

More symbols flashed across the mirror of my mind, clear thought-pictures of this elderly man locked inside a huge metal cage; he was rattling the bars with all his might and, although he screamed out at the top of his voice, there was no sound, which made the vision all the more disturbing. Then I watched as his image dashed frantically round and round the cage like a wild animal, desperately seeking an exit – but he found none.

Should I tell him what I'd seen? It would be awful if I gave it to him and it was wrong. I'd feel so silly. But I'd have to deliver it; I'd promised.

In a mighty effort I overcame my shyness and bravely decided to describe these detailed pictures to the man, but out of my mouth came a surprising spirit-interpretation: 'You feel trapped,' I said, 'and your wife knows you've tried everything to escape from your situation. But I feel impressed to say, "There's no way out".'

He blinked his bloodshot eyes, and I hoped I hadn't upset him. 'Aye . . .' he said weakly, 'Ah do feel like that,' and his dry cough rumbled again, which caused a matronly pensioner next to him to pat his doll-like hand. The old man nodded his sad white head. 'Ah've thought as much meself – there's no way out o' it at all.'

Then, incredibly, I heard the distinct voice of his spirit wife say, 'I'll ease his chest complaint,' which I gladly reported to him.

'Aye, she always did 'ave the magic touch.' A gentle smile rippled through the congregation. 'But this old brown-chitis o' mine is a killer, lad. Once the frost's on the ground it cripples me summat chronic. Some mornin's Ah can 'ardly breathe wi' it,' he rasped, and heaved his ribs for air.

Half under her breath the compassionate Mrs Palmer murmured, 'God bless him,' and the matronly pensioner squeezed his delicate hands.

But my own smile was overshadowed by another startling symbol: in my mind's eye I saw images of this man's bony frame strapped and bound to a medieval wooden rack, and I was taken aback by the horrific scene. Could he have been captured by the enemy during war service at some time and then tortured in this terrible way, I wondered? I didn't know. And had I picked up the message properly? As a new medium I'd made so many silly mistakes in the last few months, I'd have to be careful now. And the public – I knew they'd all be watching me and expecting me to succeed.

Although I wasn't sure of this vision's meaning I did know one thing instinctively: I felt the man's soul had cried out for help to the Great Spiritual Master, Jesus, whom I sensed he dearly loved and followed. But were my psychic impressions correct?

When my eyes sprang open they met those of an observant Mrs Palmer who said, 'Right then, Stephen – out with the rest of it.'

But I struggled with my reticence to speak of such personal matters. I wouldn't have wanted someone to describe that awful scene to me in public. Would the frail man's heart be strong enough to withstand these unpleasant memories? All at once I was again the shy toddler who couldn't eat anything at his friend's party because every child's gaze burned a hole in his head. But this time my shyness was brushed aside by the kindness in Mrs Palmer's face, which inspired me with confidence.

I would tell him.

Hoping that the correct interpretation would be given through me by the spirit people I took a deep breath and addressed the man.

'Sir, you feel as if you've been "tortured" because of your beliefs,' I heard myself say. 'And your wife knows the mental agony you've suffered because you stood firm against prejudice and refused to renounce your faith.'

Why on earth had I said that?

But whatever it meant, it certainly had the right effect; the symbols had been unravelled by words with such a ring of spiritual truth about them that everyone was spellbound – and the man didn't move a muscle.

'I can also hear a name that sounds like "Boyce", or is it "Joyce"?' I asked, uncertainly. 'And I see the number 65, and I'm told you're to take no notice of the kids . . . Your wife also suffered with head pains, I feel, and for some strange reason I sense that she's standing beside me and drawing a big circle in the air with her hand.'

More confusing images – but the hotchpotch of symbols wasn't refused by the old soldier. In the stillness that followed I watched his muscles tense, then he held back his emotions so admirably that not one glinting teardrop spilled from his eyes. Pursing his trembling lips together he stuck out his fine-boned jaw, his white hands clutched unknowingly at his overcoat, and it took him a while to find his voice; but when he did, he spoke quietly and with great dignity, as if he were a solitary soul whispering a prayer in a chapel of rest.

'Bonny lad, me dear wife's name was Joyce, and she's been dead these past fifteen years. She were only sixty-five . . .' He straightened his thin spine. 'An' Ah miss her awful. A finer woman you'd nivver find on God's Earth.'

You could have heard a pin drop in the upper room.

'But after she died – it were a brain haemorrhage – Ah saw her again – twice. She were stood in a big circle o' silver light, as plain as day. She were

33

"dead", you understand, but Ah saw her. An' after that Ah became a Spiritualist.'

His face relaxed a little.

'Oh, Ah believe in God all right,' he said with conviction, 'an' more so since Ah saw Joyce. Ah follow the teachings o' Jesus. But me family . . . Eh, lad' – and he faltered while his cough rumbled again – 'me daughters 'ave cut me soul to ribbons. They nivver come near now, but whenever they do Ah'm accused o' losing me mind, because Ah know me wife and me will be together again after me death. An' Ah can't wait, bonny lad. Ah can't wait to be with 'er again . . .'

Everyone maintained a respectful silence.

'. . . Me daughters 'ave mentally tortured me because me faith is different from theirs, y'see, because Ah've seen their mother, an' they 'aven't.' He cleared his throat. 'Still, the Lord was killed because 'e loved God an' spoke the truth; so, the girls can hurt me as much as they like. Ah'm too old to fight back. Me body aches and me chest's got the brown-chitis. But Ah know what Ah know – and no-one can take that away from me.'

Mrs Palmer, who'd been a Christian before becoming a Spiritualist medium, and who had experienced her own family's prejudice in the past, quietly reminded the man, '"Forgive them, Father, for they know not what they do". God sees everything, my love,' she said gently, 'and He always sends a Comforter to the lonely.'

The man's eyes shone. Lifting up his chin he fought back the water that was gathering in his eyes with all the pride of a disciplined soldier, and not one of his teardrops fell. The Spiritualist lady next to him, who was a nurse, reached out and held his slender hands, and didn't let them go until an hour later when the service had ended.

While the public were milling to and fro, gossiping about their messages, I watched the old gentleman smile broadly when Mrs Palmer handed him a piping hot cup of tea. 'This'll keep you warm,' she said, and he clasped the hot cup in both of his cold hands and thawed them out before pulling deeply at the brew. He finished it just as I arrived with a plate of chocolate digestive biscuits for him.

'It's bitterly cold out tonight,' I said, tidying his woolly muffler – then he placed a trembling hand over my own, and whispered, 'Thank 'ee, lad. Ah'm grateful.'

We smiled at each other and he shivered, no doubt at the thought of battling against the cutting winds and negotiating the slippery ice outside; he obviously didn't relish the thought of returning to a lonely house, full of memories.

I raised my voice a little. 'I've 'phoned a taxi for you,' I said, 'and don't worry about the fare – it's all settled.'

Then two kind Spiritualists, one of them the matronly nurse, helped him to stand on his shaky legs and to button up his outsize greatcoat. He was ready to go now. 'Ah'll remember you in me prayers, young 'un,' he said to me, shaking my hand.

I thanked him and followed the elderly threesome slowly across the upper room. They eased their way down the steep staircase that led to street level where they were met by a bitterly cold wind. I drew my thin plastic anorak around me, but my bones were soon chilled.

A loud taxi horn split the night, and the three pensioners were driven away through a curtain of light snow. I watched them go, and thought to myself, 'Yes . . . God does comfort the lonely.'

Back inside the bustling church I found Mrs Palmer busily washing dishes in the tiny kitchen that was no bigger than a cupboard. There were soap bubbles on the sleeve of her dark-green coat but she didn't seem bothered; in fact, she looked quite pleased about something. 'You did very well, tonight, Stephen,' she said. 'I could see you were shy about giving that old gentleman his message, but you overcame it and delivered the link with tact.'

'I saw most of it in symbols,' I informed her.

'Yes, I know – I was tuned in to your spirit helpers as they projected the images to you. Your mediumship's developing nicely; it's coming on a treat.'

There was a small *click* on the windowpane, and we both laughed out loud. I rolled up my sleeves, picked up a tattered dishcloth, and tackled the sticky chocolate-stained plates that she handed me.

'Yes,' she added, 'I was very pleased with the way you handled that link.' She turned to face me. 'After all, it was such a personal matter, and not easy to give out in public.' She replaced the soggy tea towel on the draining-board, then asked brightly, 'How would you like to share the platform with me next Sunday, at one of my services up in the Welsh valleys?'

I simply looked at her.

'It'll be your first demonstration miles outside of Swansea, but it'll be excellent practice for you. You need as much experience as you can get, you know. Practice makes perfect. Besides, the spirit people told me tonight that you're ready to branch out. What do you say?'

My eyes opened wide.

'I take it that means "Yes"?'

I grinned.

'Very good,' she said, then she turned her attention back to the work surface, grabbed a cloth and scrubbed it with a vengeance.

I couldn't believe my luck.

'Now then' – soap-suds were flying everywhere, popping right, left and centre, and she wasn't even looking at me – 'I hope you won't have second thoughts in the week, then get a bit nervous and chicken-out!' – and she polished the metal until it gleamed.

Seconds thoughts? Was she joking? As far as I was concerned, Sunday couldn't come quickly enough.

4

Suicide, Accident, and Murder Victims

Just a few minutes before the Sunday church service in the Welsh valley started, Mrs Palmer and I were relaxing at a table that was heavily laden with delicious cakes and refreshments, set in a smart medium's room next to the public platform.

The flat-roofed church was one of the few in Britain that had been purpose-built: it had a large carpeted hall, a well-equipped kitchen, two small rooms used for spiritual healing and psychic development classes, three toilets, and a swish medium's room where we were now waiting for our call to take the meeting.

Outside, deep crunchy snowdrifts lay thick on the ground, but inside, everything was snug and warm, spick and span, and well-organized, which made me all the more nervous because Mrs Palmer hadn't yet asked the Chairman if I could work with her.

Beyond the medium's room door, a hubbub of excited voices filled the hall. 'Sounds like a full congregation,' my tutor said.

I was all fingers and thumbs and spilt the dregs from my teacup over the white tablecloth; there was a tight band of tension around my forehead.

'Now then, Stephen, try to relax. Don't look so

worried,' she said patting my knee. 'Just do the best you can.'

'Yes,' I said, mopping up the stain with a serviette, and breathing deeply at the same time.

'As long as you're doing the work for the right reasons – to help people – the Other Side'll never let you down, love. Trust in their guidance. You'll be all right.'

'Yes,' I said, but my stomach turned over at the thought of a full church waiting for us out there.

The door opened and the white-haired Chairman came in, and Mrs Palmer explained the situation to her old friend. 'Young Stephen, here, is a promising new medium.'

'Nice to meet you,' he said, vigorously shaking my hand.

'I hope you don't mind if he shares a little of the service with me? It'd be good experience for him.'

The Chairman gave a hearty chuckle. 'Is he any good, then?'

(At that moment, 'he' felt dreadful.)

'Oh yes. Stephen came to Oxford Street not long after his mother died, and his natural psychic abilities started working. He's done very well, too, haven't you?'

My cheeks burned hot, but I gave a weak smile.

'He's a regular at the Open Circle now, and he's quite popular. He does some spiritual healing at the church, too, on a Wednesday afternoon; and last month he took his first solo demonstration of clairvoyance, in place of myself. He did very well and they want us to book him again!'

The Chairman laughed. 'I'm only joking, Mrs Palmer! Any friend of yours is a friend of ours. Of course he can take the service with you.'

I straightened my light-brown jacket and trousers – my one and only 'platform rig-out' – and Mrs Palmer smoothed her navy-blue two-piece suit and adjusted her matching close-fitting hat; and before we knew it we were seated on the platform, facing a crowd of strangers wrapped in thick coats, fluffy scarves, and woolly hats. Some of the older ones had steam rising from their damp clothes and they were rubbing their hands, and seemed to be sizing me up, or so I thought.

After the usual opening prayer and a few hymns Mrs Palmer delivered an uplifting spiritual address on The Power of Love which was very well received. There was another hymn and then she launched into a confident display of excellent mediumship.

'I have a tragic passing here,' she announced to the crowd. 'So sad . . . I'm in touch with a man who was only twenty when he died. It was a car accident that happened, I should say, about six years ago; and he gives me the name of Trevor. I believe he wants to reach his wife. Is she here tonight?'

A surprised young woman at the back of the church raised a hand. 'Yes. I understand.'

'Now then: first of all, I have to say that no matter how we pass over, the spirit body cannot be damaged and it functions perfectly in the next world; so, your husband isn't injured any more. He's all right now. Can you follow me?'

'Yes,' she said, then murmured half under her breath, 'thank God.'

'And he's well aware of how much you miss him. But he says you've met another gentleman since his passing. Does the name of Fitzpatrick mean anything to you, my lovely?'

'Yes, it does. That's the gentleman's name.'

'Then we must be on the right connection. Now, your husband is very happy about Mr Fitzpatrick, and it's his wish that you should marry again. "Settle down," he says, "don't sit on the shelf! You're young; you've got your whole life in front of you – so enjoy it. Have kids, and don't worry about me any more: I'm OK." Can you accept this, my dear?'

The woman's lips were trembling. 'I can,' she said quietly. 'Thank you very much.'

'"Build a new life for yourself. All I want is for the two of you to be happy, *cariad*," he says. *Cariad*'s Welsh for *darling*, isn't it?'

'He always called me *cariad*.'

'Well, I hope that message has brought you some comfort. Thank you, my dear. God bless you,' said Mrs Palmer to the grateful woman. Then she turned to me. 'Stephen, come along, you're next,' and knowing I was nervous she touched my hand as she sat down.

I stood up and she whispered to me, 'You'll be fine, love,' and I moved to the altar-rail and tentatively launched into my first message, bits of which I'd been receiving over the last few minutes – but not very clearly. In fact, my psychic reception was maddeningly faint. But I made a start.

'I think,' I announced to the congregation, 'there's a gentleman with me tonight who, when on earth, was blind.' I closed my eyes and tried so hard to listen

41

to his voice. 'I don't know who he is; he doesn't tell me. But . . . whether or not . . . I wonder . . . did he have any connection with a "St Joseph's Church"? I get those words. I can't see the blind man, but I feel he wants to link with someone here . . . is it Ron?'

When my eyes opened they saw thirty-odd people sitting in abject silence, as if they were afraid to move. A smell of damp clothes filled the air and the people seemed stony-faced.

'I . . . Does anyone . . . Can somebody understand this message?' I asked again, quietly but hopefully.

More silence.

The room was full of eyes . . .

Because there were no takers I glanced over my shoulder at Mrs Palmer to see what I should do, but she simply inclined her head, as good as to say 'Carry on'. So, feeling rather embarrassed and acutely aware of the pulse throbbing in my neck, I said, 'Well, I'm sure he was here, ladies and gentlemen, and . . . should you remember him later, please send him a kind thought.'

Not a movement. Just silence. If someone had dropped a pin it would have sounded like a clap of thunder.

Then something clicked inside me and my old fighting-spirit returned as a sudden surge of determination rose within me. I decided to defy those dozens of staring eyes. They weren't going to upset me, and to prove it I launched bravely into another link – but this time with more confidence.

'Very well . . .' My voice gained volume. 'Now I sense a sad passing . . . a tragedy involving a lady called Sandra, I think . . . I can see an empty medicine bottle, so I think she took an overdose of tablets. But she wants to give a message of reassurance to a young man.'

All at once an eighteen-year-old lad at the right-hand side of the church waved his hand. 'I know this,' he said anxiously. 'She could be my mum.'

The tight band around my head immediately slackened and I felt so relieved that someone had responded. Thank God. But before I could proceed I sensed White Owl's powerful spiritual presence and his thoughts that clearly inspired me to 'Take care with emotionally-charged messages. Present them sensitively,' he cautioned. 'Don't upset your recipient.'

Heeding his words I looked into the fresh face of the lad, who was just a few years younger than me, and relayed to him, gently, 'I must tell you that your mum is happy now; so please don't worry. And is she Sandra?'

'Yes.'

'She's very close to you tonight,' I said. But then I faltered because the mental link was fading in and out. Then I lost it. Owing to my inexperience I'd failed to finish the contact and supply the *reason* for his mum's return which, according to Mrs Palmer's teaching, was the most important part of any spirit message. Rather frustrated, and secretly annoyed with myself, I politely thanked the lad, then quickly sat down.

Knowing I wouldn't feel in the least offended Mrs Palmer immediately stood up, expertly re-connected with the sad boy and completed his mother's link. With dignity and experience shining through her every word she told him, 'Your mother loves you dearly, son.'

His eyes filled up with tears.

'She's often beside you, and still cares for all the family. And she's giving me a road name here . . . "Park Place". Can you understand this?'

'We lived there,' he replied in a choked voice, 'before she . . . died.'

'Now then, my lovely, your mother wants me to pass on a very important message to you. She says, "Don't be ashamed of me, son, or my memory; I wasn't thinking straight when I took the tablets . . . I just felt I couldn't cope. But I've survived and I'm in the Light. And know this: I love you, Simon – and I'm much happier now." '

The boy was visibly moved, and the silent wall of tears in his eyes overflowed.

'"Don't grieve any more," your mum says. "And find it in your heart to be as proud of me as I am of you. I will always love you, son – you are mine."'

The youngster made no reply, for he was too overcome by his mother's comforting words. But after the service he walked to the platform, shook my hand, and kissed Mrs Palmer's cheek; then, without a word, but with a happy expression on his face, he slowly walked out of the church.

How I wished I could have worked like Mrs Palmer: she gave so much relevant information and her messages were always so spiritually meaningful.

After we'd had tea and sandwiches in the medium's room a kind soul was gracious enough to offer Mrs Palmer and me a lift back home to Swansea – fifteen miles away down icy roads and open snowy countryside. We accepted gratefully, and sitting in the back of the steamed-up car as it sped past snow-capped fir trees and glistening fields Mrs Palmer spoke about the spirit world, and my work.

'There were a few tragic deaths mentioned in the meeting tonight. Some people think those who die in those circumstances are in a kind of darkness, you know, or that they get punished in some way. Have you heard that before, Stephen?'

'Yes,' I answered.

'Well, they're not in the dark, love; they're in the light, and they're well cared for by their family and relatives Over There. What they need more than anything else is the love and kind thoughts from their people because it helps them to know that they haven't been forgotten, you see.'

'Yes,' I replied, grateful for her teaching.

'Those who commit suicide, of course, will have a great deal of adjustment to make in Spirit – because they haven't achieved what they set out to do. As soon as they realize they're still alive, they often feel sorry for what they've done, and for the distress they've caused to those who love them on earth. But they soon settle down: eternal progress is open to every soul – that's one of Spiritualism's Seven Principles, upon which this great religion was founded.'

The car sped on, and Mrs Palmer became thoughtful.

'Stephen, you'll go far – because you're eager to learn. That's a good sign. We're always spiritually evolving and progressing, you see. Progression is the Law. And nobody knows it all, love; and no medium is ever fully developed – ever. There's always room for improvement.'

I nodded in the darkened car, but she saw the sadness in my eyes. 'You're thinking about that message from the blind man, the one you couldn't place tonight.'

She was correct.

'Did I get it all wrong?'

'No, only a bit of it. We're human, love – we all make mistakes, especially when we're just starting out. I tuned in while you gave it, and you misinterpreted the link. The man had *failing eyesight* before he died, but you said he was blind.' I coloured up red. 'That's why no-one claimed him. His loved one was no doubt sitting there but afraid to accept him because one piece of information was wrong.'

I was taken aback. 'Just *one* mistake and they won't accept their messages?'

'Oh yes, the public are very demanding, you know; you'll have to get used to that! They want it all in black and white, thank you very much; and they expect perfection from us every time. It doesn't enter their heads that we're fallible and we can have our off-days!' She chuckled with experience, and somehow my burden lightened and I joined in.

As the car drove on past rows and rows of tiny white-roofed miners' cottages that lined the road into Swansea I gazed out through the misty windows and marvelled at the shapes of stark black trees set against the lilac evening sky; they looked like great lungs stripped of flesh, silent, unbreathing . . .

Lost in thought, I wondered if I'd ever master my mediumship . . .

Mrs Palmer tapped my knee. 'Now then, Stephen. Don't look so serious. It's very much a hit-and-miss affair when your gifts are first developing; but with patience and plenty of practice, your sensitivity and awareness will increase, and then you'll receive your messages more clearly and more accurately.' She smiled, and I thanked her for giving me the opportunity of sharing the platform with her.

Soon the lights of Swansea town came into view and our driver dropped us off outside Mrs Palmer's home in Cecil Street, Manselton. The frosty night air coaxed clouds of steam from the car's exhaust as it left us standing in the pale snow on her doorstep. We waved our thanks to the man for his kindness.

When I commented, 'It's bitterly cold,' Mrs Palmer's response was, 'One day, they'll find you frozen to death in that thin plastic coat.' She opened her large handbag, took out a key, turned it in the lock, and opened the oak door. 'Will you come in for a hot cuppa?'

'Oh thank you very much, but no. These days I try to be in bed before my Dad comes home from the pub – anything to avoid a slanging-match.'

'Fair enough,' she added, flicking on a hall switch that flooded the snowy steps with yellow light; then she opened her handbag again and took out something else. 'Here,' she said. 'I want you to have these books. They're full of spiritual wisdom and they'll help you a great deal.' And she presented me with three volumes of spirit-teachings about mediumship and the nature of the soul, recorded by the famous spirit guide of the Hannen Swaffer

London Home Circle, who was an American Indian known as 'Silver Birch'.

Embarrassed, I muttered, 'Oh, I couldn't possibly—'

'Now then, no nonsense, Stephen – it's late and I'm tired. You've had a grammar school education and there's a good head on your shoulders – I know what I'm doing. Silver Birch's spirit teachings will help you to understand the meaning of your life and how your psychic gifts operate. So, no nonsense, now; I'm old and I'm cold' – and she gently shook the books in her outstretched hand. 'Read as many good books as you can; and learn from other people's experiences. Please take them.'

I did, then I shivered and pulled my thin anorak more tightly around me, saying, 'Thank you, Mrs Palmer. You're very kind.'

'You're welcome,' she replied, standing in the doorway and facing me with her back towards the hall. 'And let me give you another piece of advice before you go: study the art of platform presentation. The more you use your mediumship the more it'll strengthen and deepen, but *you've* got to master the skill of delivering it sensibly to the people.' She smiled. 'God gives us the gifts, but it's up to us to develop them. Do you see?'

I nodded and thrust my hands into my coat, seeking warmth.

'You can learn a lot about how best to deliver your messages by studying other mediums when they're working. You can determine *why* their messages get accepted or rejected. You'll probably find they interfere with their communications by letting their own minds colour them or misinterpret them – like you did with the blind man's link tonight.'

'That's a great idea – and I'll do it,' I promised, looking forward to my investigations.

'Well, I'll see you soon for another chat and a hot cooked meal. We'll need it to keep this chill out!' Then she laughed and we said good night.

Sliding on the packed snow I slithered my way home to Lion Street, about a mile away in Waun Wen district, where I dived into the chilly bed just in time to hear my father slamming the front door behind him.

In the months that followed I gladly took Mrs Palmer's advice and learned a great deal about mediums by carefully analysing their work.

Winter turned into Spring and, with all the skill and concentration of an accomplished pathologist, I visited the churches several times a week and dissected every scrap of evidence their mediums gave there. I systematically sifted through their information to discover how much of it had been meaningful; how much of it had sprung from a paranormal or psychic source; how much of it had originated in the demonstrator's own subconscious mind; and how much of it had been pure imagination, guesswork, or – worse still – how much of it had been born of delusion.

I found that some mediums were very accurate, while others were not; and many promised more than they were able to deliver and their standard of work disappointed me. After making a thorough investigation over several months I began to wonder if true mediumship – which should always contain survival evidence and a message from an identified communicator – was a rare commodity.

Yet thousands of people a year were comforted by these gifted Spiritualist sensitives who all shared one saving grace: they really did believe in the next world and they wanted to share its presence with everyone they met; furthermore, like myself, a great many of them served without thought of any financial reward.

And platform exponents, I found, came in all shapes and sizes and possessed differing characteristics: some were intelligent and articulate, others were ignorant and unread; a number were eccentric and extrovert, but the majority were spiritually inclined. Most of them were elderly, or else in their middle years, and a great many of them were women.

I also discovered that because church committees had the right to make their own decisions about whom they would invite to work for them, their platforms seemed open to anyone who showed the least flicker of psychic potential, or possessed 'the gift of the gab'.

No written qualifications were necessary in order to serve, and when church secretaries were criticized for booking some of the undeveloped mediums they justified their choices by saying things like, 'Jesus and the prophets didn't have letters after their names!'

One dry-witted old dear who was a lifelong Spiritualist told me she was enraged by what she called 'the dreadfully poor standard of public mediumship' she felt she had to endure each week, and wryly declared to me, 'It seems the only qualifications people need to stand on today's Spiritualist platforms are two legs and a voice, young man!'

Although I didn't feel her opinions were shared by the majority she had a point, and I did agree that while most mediums presented valuable and satisfactory work, there were some demonstrators who should never have been unleashed upon the public.

I recall being horrified by the antics of one such dubious 'medium' on a warm Spring evening in a tiny local church which was nothing more than a rented wooden room (about the size of a small bedroom) above what used to be a tumble-down stables, hidden in a back lane. Although I'd spent many happy hours there, experiencing some excellent clairvoyance and imbibing a great deal of spiritual philosophy from the services, one medium's 'performance' really upset me.

On the night in question I sat among thirty-five other people who were packed like sardines into the drab, half-decorated upper room; there was barely enough space left for the tin tea-urn that rested on a small rickety table in one corner, and the air was sticky and claustrophobic.

The very noisy congregation was silenced only by the booming voice of an ample chairlady who commanded them to 'Be silent!' Then she welcomed the medium by announcing her full name – but I shall call her Nettie.

The cadaverous Nettie grinned in her seat and shook her large-boned shoulders when she chuckled.

Then she proudly patted into place her dark, springy hair. When the congregation started singing a hymn, I didn't join in with them because I was fascinated by Nettie, who glanced furtively around the crowd; there was something hideous about her eyes – they were as black as coal and had sunk deeply into their sockets. Like two pieces of hard jet, they peered out from beneath her thick lowered brows.

Smoothing the floral-print dress that made her look like an overgrown schoolgirl, Nettie frowned – but even then those glittering eyes couldn't keep still: they glowered out of a death-mask face that, to my psychic senses, had Ignorance stamped firmly upon it; and beneath them was a long bony nose above a mouth so thin that it looked like a purple line a child had drawn across her jaw.

I shuddered all over – little wonder some people thought Spiritualists were a peculiar lot.

After the singing stopped, Nettie mumbled her way through a prayer in a hollow 'Holier-than-Thou' voice, then those beady eyes darted from side to side, taking in the faces of her public, and giving me the impression that we were not a congregation – but a captive audience.

And then she started.

With amazing insensitivity she delivered such a deeply tragic link from a murdered girl who wanted to speak with her father. The message didn't contain a scrap of survival evidence but Nettie took immense pleasure in dramatizing what she believed to be every gruesome and gory detail of the youngster's death. In harsh and confident tones she insensitively blurted out to the girl's trembling father:

'This foul act was done by a knife, slitting across the throat – like this!' And she supplied the necessary Long John Silver actions.

My insides turned over. 'Dear God,' I thought, 'no wonder the sceptics criticize the Spiritualist Movement.' I was thoroughly incensed, but the girl's father was in a much worse state: stunned beyond words, he visibly shook with grief and shock.

But the black-eyed Nettie set her tight mouth in a grim line and mistook the man's pain for nervous apprehension and she stupidly trumpeted at him: 'Never be afraid of death!'

How I left that church at the end of the service without screaming my disgust at the top of my voice, I'll never know. And on the way home the more I thought about what I'd witnessed the more angry I became, until I spoke my disgust out loud to my spirit friends, right there in the clammy street, 'If Nettie isn't a genuine medium, why don't you take away her psychic gifts?'

Mrs Palmer shared my distress when I reported to her the manner in which Nettie had spoken to the man about his daughter's death – but I didn't tell my tutor about my asking the spirit people to remove Nettie's gifts if she wasn't genuine, or about my sending out a prayer to that effect when I'd got home after Nettie's service – for my thoughts on that score were private.

Mrs Palmer and I had just eaten another of her scrumptious cooked meals and we were sharing a pot of fragrant tea in her cosy kitchen when she tut-tutted and shook her head at Nettie's disgraceful antics. Her voice was as flat as a pancake when she raised her eyes heavenwards and commented, 'Unfortunately, Nettie's been like that for years. She's never read a book on mediumship, hasn't been trained properly, and certainly doesn't get booked at Oxford Street.'

I was so glad to hear that last statement.

Her grey eyes looked across the kitchen table into mine. 'I just can't understand these mediums who fail to realize they're often working with people who are in grief, and that their messages should be delivered with compassion,' she added.

Nettie's poor conduct steered my tutor's thoughts into the realm of training. 'And that reminds me. Now then, I think it's time you had some more disciplined instruction, Stephen, to help you to deepen your mediumship. Unlike Nettie you want to learn and your motivation's right, so I'd like you to join my private home circle for psychic development, if you're willing.'

It was a good job my teacup was resting on the table because if it had been in my hand I'd have dropped it! I was speechless.

'Well then, what do you say?'

For a few moments no answer would come because to me Mrs Palmer's private psychic awareness class was like the inner sanctum of a Temple of the Spirit – the Holiest of Psychic Places.

Unable to believe my good fortune I accepted with a quiet 'Thank you.'

'Good. We sit on Tuesdays at seven o'clock sharp. If you arrive one second later the doors'll be locked and you won't be able to get in. We sit in the front parlour for two hours. There'll be about eight of us, all freshly bathed and wearing comfortable clothes, all with peaceful and calm minds, ready to contact the next world.'

A quiet 'Thank you' was all I could say again. I was thrilled, and this sensation heightened as circle day rapidly approached.

But I had no idea on my first Tuesday night at her class that my secret and unkind request to the Other Side asking them to remove Nettie's psychic gifts had paved the way for the invisible world to teach me a powerful spiritual lesson that I would never forget.

5

Thought-Forms and Telepathy

'This awareness class is run on disciplined lines,'
Mrs Palmer explained to the eight sitters, as she
gently pushed her spectacles back to the top of her
pointed nose. 'And there are some important rules
which must be observed.'

We shifted slightly in our seats.

'Try not to think of any bad thoughts before, or
during, the circle. Talking about aggression and
wars, conflicts, politics, differences of religious belief,
murders, or about any other fearful or distressing
events is strictly forbidden.'

'Why is that?' asked a shy young woman.

'Because we must attract the minds of higher
intelligences from the world of spirit and they have
only love in their hearts,' she wisely instructed. 'Like
attracts like – so keep your thoughts as pure as
possible whenever you sit here for development,
please.'

We nodded and willingly accepted her tuition.

'Now then – if anyone has the least bit of psychic
potential it'll make itself known in the silence.
Tonight we're giving our spirit friends a wonderful
opportunity to approach our minds and to get to know
us, to try to blend with us, and to make contact with
us. But no-one is to break the stillness, mind' – she

was wagging a cautionary finger – 'and no talking. Please be considerate to your fellow sitters and remain silent. There'll be plenty of time at the end to tell us what you've received.'

A man wanted to know how to 'blank' his mind during the hour's silence that was to follow.

'You can't blank it,' Mrs Palmer replied. 'Just try to keep it still. Mediums must learn to relax their bodies *and* their minds. The mind is full of thoughts that jump around and constantly disturb its peace; they spoil the quietness of the spirit. Mediums must learn to *still* the mind. If the mind is stilled it can then receive the gentle thoughts and subtle influences which the spirit people are projecting towards it, you see.'

The questioner said he understood, just as the mantel clock in Mrs Palmer's neat front parlour started chiming.

'Now then, everyone – it's seven o'clock, and we shall sit in the silence for one hour,' she said, turning off the central light, which left the room bathed in a dim orange glow that was cast by the electric fire in the grate. 'That's much easier on the eyes,' my tutor mumbled, adding just as the quiet-time began, 'or you can close them, if you wish.'

Liquid Silence

Sink into liquid silence
wherein all answers dwell
in swirling pools of
pure tranquillity . . .

Bathe in the liquid silence
that smoothes the mind, and makes it well
with watery fingers of
clarified velvet . . .

Drink of the liquid silence
and anxieties will dispel
in quivering waves of
flowing peace . . .

Swim in the depths of liquid silence,
a never-ending Well
that heals your soul
and sends your troubles hence—
then revel in their absence . . .

For sixty minutes the eight of us were wrapped
in what seemed to be a solid wall of absolute peace
and stillness; yet it was also a strangely vibrant
and 'living' atmosphere that, for me, was filled with
inexplicable soft murmurings and inner soul-sounds.
Yet no-one in the room had spoken or had stirred
from his seat. Once or twice someone had only gently
cleared his throat, re-positioned his hands in his lap,
or brushed away an imaginary cobweb from his face;
so I was certain that the whispering voices I'd heard
hadn't reached me from this world, but from the
next.

I'd loved the wonderful sense of serenity I'd
experienced and felt as if my spirit had been
washed clean by surging waves of golden light.
Time was meaningless and I was quite surprised
when the clock struck out eight hollow chimes.

Feet shuffled as people stretched the blood back into their legs and I thought we'd all soon be 'coming back' to normality, but I was wrong. Everyone in the room had 'returned' but Mrs Palmer resembled a rigid stone statue – incredibly still, her chest didn't seem to be moving at all. But then her breathing deepened, and I heaved a grateful sigh.

We waited for a few minutes in respectful silence and our patience was rewarded when a subtle transformation occurred in the psychic atmosphere around our tutor. Mrs Palmer's eyes were tightly closed, and her personality was somehow 'altered' and she seemed to 'become' someone else; I sensed she'd allowed her spirit guide, Ahmed, to blend his mind so closely with her own that this was why her body was now able to raise one of its arthritic hands, under his mental direction, and point one of its fingers directly at me.

I was fascinated.

Suddenly Ahmed reproduced the deep masculine tones of his own voice through Mrs Palmer and declared to me, 'My brother, I am charged to tell you something of great importance. *Send out only thoughts that are good.*'

My face felt hot.

Ahmed spoke again. 'Do you understand?'

I stammered back, '. . . Well . . . I . . .'

'The mind is a very real power,' he continued through his medium, 'and each thought causes an effect, either for good or ill. Do not degrade your soul by holding negative thoughts which stem from the darker forces of arrogance and aggression.'

There was a murmur of agreement from the eight

sitters and I wondered if he was referring to the nasty thoughts I'd had about the unkind way my Dad had been treating me at home.

'My brother,' his deep voice said, 'there is nothing wrong with making personal judgements about your fellow beings' conduct – this is natural – but condemnation is a spiritually unhealthy act. You asked us, did you not, to remove the psychic gifts from a local medium's mind?'

My God! He was talking about my wicked request concerning the deluded Nettie whose remarks had upset a grieving man at a Spiritualist meeting. But how could he possibly have known about them? 'Yes, I . . . I did . . .'

His voice was full of authority and compassion. 'My friend, send out only thoughts that are good.'

'I will,' I sheepishly promised. 'Thank you, Ahmed.'

I considered myself well and truly spiritually corrected – and rightly so. Ahmed had also proved to me that telepathy was a fact: my youthful and unkind thoughts about Nettie had been clearly received by him, and probably many others, on the Other Side.

While Ahmed withdrew his influence from Mrs Palmer's mind and she returned to waking consciousness, I chided myself for being so arrogant and unfair to Nettie; after all, she believed she was doing her best to help people; and I realized that I still had a great deal of growing up to do.

Gently, the circle's quiet-time was ended with a sincere prayer of thankfulness to the Great Spirit given by Mrs Palmer, and then we had our tea and biscuits and discussed our psychic experiences while Mrs Palmer offered us her wise guidance.

But my own spirit guide must have heard Ahmed's well-deserved reprimand to me because I was amused to catch White Owl's thought-voice telling me: 'Don't speak ill of the "dead", for we might be listening!'

I smiled, but my lessons in telepathy were far from over because a few days later I was unexpectedly challenged to test my own powers of mind-to-mind psychic reading at an impromptu after-dinner seance that was held in a friend's house.

Five Spiritualists and I were seated on comfortable sofas and armchairs in a swish dining-room when I suddenly received a vivid psychic vision of a woman's phantom form dancing around the floor. Right in front of my eyes appeared this gorgeous waltzing lady, exquisitely dressed in a pink crinolined evening gown; and as she swirled round and around, her ghostly image shimmered in the psychic light surrounding her.

I watched this lovely young belle from the 1800s as she swayed her pink full-skirted ball-gown back and forth; and peeking out from underneath it I saw masses of expensive white lace petticoats. Her perfectly arranged hair was light brown and thére were soft copper highlights glinting in her ringlets which gave her an air of sophistication as they bounced over her slender white shoulders. I was also aware that she carried with her a marked psychic feeling of 'America', even though she was visible for only a few moments.

Then she vanished – and everything in the swish

dining-room was back in its rightful place. But my eyes must have glazed over with surprise because my hostess wriggled to the edge of her armchair and became curious.

'And what have you just experienced, Stephen O'Brien? Come on, I've seen that paranormal expression before! Spill the beans!'

Interest crackled in the air, and the dinner-guests goaded me into describing this dancing apparition, which amazed all of them – but one of them especially.

Our male host gave an embarrassed cough. ''Tis a funny old world, ain't it? You mentioned a waltzing girl' – we leaned forward in our seats – 'Well . . . this afternoon' – and he coughed self-consciously again – 'I was just sitting here minding my own business when I started to daydream about the ballroom scene from *Gone with the Wind*. You know the one: where Scarlett O'Hara danced and stole all the men's hearts.'

He glanced awkwardly at his captive audience and smiled when he noticed the big grin spreading across my face. Although, in his visualization, Scarlett's gown had appeared much darker than the pale tones of the dress worn by the beautiful Vivien Leigh in the film (which indicated that his own mind had coloured the thought-form) his projected image had left a clear imprint in the psychic atmosphere of the room – and I'd seen it.

To use the vernacular, he was gobsmacked.

'Right then, clever-dick!' cried our hostess in high spirits. 'If thoughts can be seen, Stephen O'Brien – I challenge you to give us a practical demonstration!'

I groaned miserably. 'Oh no, please. Look, it's my night off!'

But the guests would have none of it. 'Aw, go on, Stephen,' they chorused, eager for a bit of fun; and so, for the sake of peace and quietness I weakly gave in, moved to the edge of the sofa I was seated on, and conducted an experiment by trying to look into the psychic atmosphere of the mind of our hostess: I stared into the space just above her head, and my clairvoyant powers revealed something.

Pointing into the area I announced, 'I can see a thought-form hovering about nine inches above your forehead, just to the left of you,' I said, startling her because she hadn't realized that in issuing the challenge she'd automatically selected herself as my guinea-pig.

But her voice was full of disbelief. 'Oh yes? Describe it, then.'

'Well, it's a set of figures – some money. I can see £1.10p formed out of grey cloudy light, and I don't feel very happy about this amount. Does it make sense?'

'No!' she replied sharply. But then she slapped her hand to her mouth and nearly jumped up off her armchair. 'Well, good Gawd Almighty!' We all turned to face her. 'My usual bus fare to work is £1.00 but from tomorrow the price goes up by ten pence; so this morning I told myself to put an extra 10p in my purse each day because having the correct fare ready saves time.'

An eerie feeling prickled up and down my spine, and we were all astonished.

'Right!' declared our hostess. 'We'd better stop this

nonsense *immediately*, before he tells everyone what colour bloomers I'm wearing!'

The laughter that burst into the room thankfully ended my party-piece, but the memory of this experience haunted me much later that night, in bed.

I turned uneasily under the sheets because my mind was restless, full of new and challenging ideas that I had to consider. The results of that telepathy experiment had astonished me and taught me that sensitives could receive thoughts not only from the 'dead', but also from the living – and they could even be picked up from the psychic atmospheres surrounding buildings and objects.

If I wanted to be a reliable medium, I reasoned, then I'd have to learn to recognize which thoughts were coming to me from the next world, and which impressions were reaching me from this world. No doubt it would prove to be quite confusing at first, but I'd have to learn the technique.

My mind boggled at the immensity of these new concepts, and serving my apprenticeship, I decided, wasn't going to be easy. There were so many new psychic laws to discover, to understand, and then to master. Then there was Ahmed's reprimand. And was it just a coincidence that I'd explored the world of telepathy so soon after Mrs Palmer's guide had proved its existence to me? There were so many questions that needed answering.

It was a warm and sticky night and I pulled the sheets up over my ears, and made up my mind to ask my tutor's opinions when I next saw her.

And I didn't have long to wait, for the next evening I bumped into Mrs Palmer on a crowded smoke-filled bus that would take us both to Oxford Street Church.

'Stephen! What a coincidence – I was just thinking about you,' she said brightly, wafting away the cigarette smoke from some very rude passengers who shouldn't have been puffing away on the lower deck. We both coughed, then I took my chance to ask about Fate.

'I don't believe in coincidences,' I said above the din of the noisy passengers. 'Everything in my life has seemed to fall into a pattern, like the pieces would in a jigsaw puzzle. And the more I think about it the more it all seems so well planned and thought out. What do you think?'

'It certainly does,' she said, waving smoke away from her face.

'And especially so, when I try to avoid people I don't want to see!' I added. 'If I whizz into a supermarket and shoot out of the back door to avoid them – I usually turn the next corner and walk right into them!'

'Me, too!' and we laughed.

Above the chattering racket in the hot bus Mrs Palmer then confirmed for me my own belief in the force of Destiny.

'We're fated to meet certain people in our lives, Stephen,' she said. 'I'm sure of it. And when you look back, it's all been for some greater purpose, don't you think?'

I nodded.

'I think you and I were meant to meet, you know, because my spirit friends asked me on that first night when you walked into the church to give you as much help as I could.'

We smiled, and I thanked her for meeting their request.

She continued pensively, 'When something really important comes along in our lives, like a birth, or a tragic accident, or a death, perhaps – you know the kind of thing I mean: an event that brings a great change into people's lives and is full of emotion – have you noticed that it seems to happen in slow motion, as if you're powerless to stop it occurring? Know what I mean?'

'Yes,' I replied, thinking of my mother's three months of pain and suffering which followed her operation for stomach cancer, and then her tragic death at just forty-nine years of age.

'I don't think we can escape our Fate, lad. The way I see it, people and events are drawn together by very powerful but invisible spiritual and psychic forces that have often been generated by themselves. There's a Plan working somewhere, I think, somewhere outside of our immediate vision.'

I pondered on this, above the noisy talk of other passengers.

'Now then, I'll tell you something. I saw my future husband's face, you know; I saw Bill's face in my mind, as clear as day, *years* before I met him and we got married.'

'That sort of thing's happened to me, too. I've met people for the first time and yet it feels as if we'd known each other for centuries.'

'Perhaps you had,' she grinned. 'Yes, I've often had strange feelings about the future, as if I *knew* what was going to happen. And more often than not, my thoughts were right.'

The smoke had thickened, and she gave a little cough.

'I remember, years ago, just after Bill and I had settled down, I had such a strange presentiment, an odd feeling that any children I might carry would never survive birth . . .' She became still for a moment, then said chirpily, 'This is our stop.'

We got off the crowded bus, gratefully gulped great lungfuls of clean air and walked up the church stairs.

'Now then, I've advertised you for next week's service as "Mr Stephen",' Mrs Palmer told me as we arrived in the upper room, 'because we don't want to aggravate your father's temper, should he see the announcement in the newspaper.'

'No we don't,' I replied. 'That's a good idea.'

After this, Mrs Palmer advertised that 'Mr Stephen' would take many more church services in the months that followed; and she also faithfully kept the promise she'd made when she'd 'apprenticed' me, and she taught me as much about mediumship as I could assimilate.

Naturally, on the big nights when I was to demonstrate alone I was nervous, but the spirit people didn't let me down. Just like Mrs Palmer they also kept their promise that 'guidance will be given'; and as the seasons tumbled over one another and time moved on, they did their best to spiritually comfort and uplift the public through our two-worlds' partnership.

I loved working for them, and each hour-and-a-half service seemed to fly by in less than five minutes. And every time I demonstrated, my confidence increased and my mediumship strengthened and, month by month, I gradually accustomed myself to hearing the sometimes faint psychic voices that spoke to me within my mind; they weren't as clear as I would have liked but Mrs Palmer assured me that in time they would be:

'You must have patience, Stephen, to be a dedicated servant of the spirit,' she told me. 'And you must stay humble at all times, and get in as much practice as possible. Mediums must work their abilities in order to develop them, and nothing comes easy, you know – progression must be earned.'

And earn it I did, through hard work, diligent questioning and studying, and through the rendering of service whenever I could. Then one cold winter's evening, after my tutor and I had conducted a very happy Open Circle together, we walked towards the bleak bus-stop. 'Winter's here again. The wind is bitter tonight,' I said.

'Aye, it is. Good job I'm well wrapped up,' she replied, pressing her blue cloche hat firmly down over her grey curls.

Our footsteps clicked on the hard pavements, and a rising breeze caught Mrs Palmer unaware and irritated her chesty cough, which made her wheeze for a few minutes after we'd reached the deserted bus-stop.

'Now then, Stephen,' she rasped, while we waited patiently, 'I've got a surprise for you.'

My ears flapped.

'Next week, when you call around for a meal and a chat, I thought we might conduct a little psychic experiment?'

My eyebrows rose. What an excellent idea. 'That sounds great,' I replied.

'Good. You're always eager to learn.' She shivered in the chill night air. 'Well then, next Friday we'll try to communicate with the spirit world but in a slightly' – she inclined her head towards me – 'different way. See you at seven?'

'On the dot!' I said.

We got on the bus and I was so excited that for once I didn't even notice the choking cigarette smoke on the journey home; I was thrilled to be included in any of Mrs Palmer's psychic investigations. The noisy passengers didn't bother me, either – I just sat there, wondering what on earth my tutor had in mind.

6

'Knock, Knock: Who's There?'

'Now then, it's seven o'clock, on the dot.'

Mrs Palmer's mantel clock agreed by striking out the hour as she put her hands together in prayer and closed her eyes. I joined her and listened while she sincerely requested that the powers of Truth, Light and Love would surround us and bless our efforts to contact our loved ones on the Other Side.

After whispering 'Amen,' she opened her eyes and rose to her feet, saying, 'I'll put the big light off,' which she did.

In her cosy Welsh kitchen, lit only by soft yellow lamplight and the warm glow from the fire that was crackling in the grate, we sat at either side of her table and lightly placed our forefingers on a heart-shaped wooden pointer which was resting on a polished wooden rectangle with black letters of the alphabet carved into it – a Ouija board.

We waited patiently for the spirit world to make its presence known.

'There's a lot of nonsense spoken about the Ouija board, Stephen. Granted it's the slowest, most cumbersome means of communication with the Other Side but it isn't dangerous – not really, not if you know what you're doing; you've got to treat the exercise with reverence and respect.'

'Do you mean its success depends on who's operating it, and why they're conducting the experiment?'

'Exactly,' she said, as we waited in the hope of detecting any movement of the pointer. 'Fearful people work themselves into such a frenzy over nothing sometimes, especially if they receive a silly communication through the board; they let it worry them without ever questioning it.'

The pointer gave a tiny shudder.

'Now then, the spirit power's building . . .' and we watched the heart-shaped pointer for further flickers of movement; three small felt pads that were glued to its underside would allow it to glide smoothly over the board's polished Formica surface if the experiment was successful.

But the pointer was as motionless as a tombstone, and stayed so while we waited for another ten minutes, trying not to press down too hard on it.

A fire-stick cracked in the blazing heat, and the smoke from it wafted into the room and tickled my nostrils.

Mrs Palmer's face was a picture of patience. 'You see, it isn't easy for the spirit people to blend their own energies with ours, but that's what they've got to do if they want to move this pointer.'

'I understand.'

'All mediumship's like that – it's a blending of minds and psychic energies. The medium must be in a state of attunement with the minds of his helpers on the Other Side. That's the vital link.'

'I see.'

The clock ticked and ticked, and twenty minutes

71

had now passed since we first sat down at the table.

'Mrs Palmer? Someone asked me at the church the other day if it was safe for anyone to try the board. What do you think?'

One of her eyebrows rose, then lowered itself. 'What did you tell them?'

'Well, I said that as a general rule no-one should dabble with things they don't understand—'

'Good lad.'

'—in my opinion they should leave it to the experts: the trained mediums.'

'I quite agree. In matters of the spirit, always apply common sense. If something went wrong with the electricity in your house, you'd call a skilled craftsman to deal with it, wouldn't you?'

'Of course.'

'Experienced sensitives'll do the job properly; they know all the pitfalls.'

A short silence fell between us, and a dog barked outside in the icy streets. Mrs Palmer winked her eyes in the firelight and gathered her thoughts.

'People who do the Ouija board for a lark or a thrill, or to be shocked, often receive *exactly* what they want, because like attracts like. Then they frighten themselves and get hysterical when their own imaginations run away with them.'

'Aren't people peculiar?' I commented wistfully.

'They don't understand that spirit communication is just like a telephone link and anyone can come in "on the line". This isn't a toy, you know,' she warned, tapping the board with a fingernail. 'Communicators should be questioned to see if they *are* who they claim to be.'

72

'Evidence,' I emphasized.

The pointer gave a little shake, and then it was still again.

Flickering coals cast dancing shadows on the walls around us, and the oak mantel clock marked out the long silence that followed with rhythmic, unhurried ticks. The coals sank down a little into the fire-basket.

I couldn't help smiling to myself when I remembered other Ouija board sittings I'd witnessed as a teenager where daft messages such as *Don't leave Maude on her own: she'll be coming over to us next Tuesday* had been received – and I hoped that tonight's communications would be more sensible.

An imperceptible psychic shiver rippled through the kitchen.

'Did you feel that power-surge, Stephen?'

'Yes,' I replied excitedly, and the pointer immediately started whizzing around the board at top speed as if an invisible hand were propelling it.

'Here we go!' said Mrs Palmer with a smile – but the pointer suddenly slowed down to a sluggish pace and slid around the alphabet like an injured dog dragging a broken leg behind him. Slowly, letter by letter, it spelt out a name:

Mam Wise

'Oh, that's my mother. Hello, Mam,' said Mrs Palmer.

Hello

'I haven't heard from you for such a long time. How are things?'

Not too bad

'Is Dad with you tonight?'

73

Yes

'How is he?'

Same as ever

The letters were being touched a little more confidently now. 'It's lovely to hear from you. What have you come to say, Mam?'

Suddenly the pointer stopped, as if the communicator were either thinking or gathering power before spelling out:

Tell Leslie I visit him often

'Who's Leslie, Mrs Palmer?'

'My brother.'

His legs are bad

'No, not these days, love; but they used to be, years ago.'

Yes . . . When I was alive

'But you're alive now, Mam.'

So I am

Mrs Palmer's brow furrowed slightly. 'Tell me, Mam, what was the matter with Leslie's legs?'

There was a very long pause, and not so much as a shudder from the pointer. My tutor looked at me and winked.

'Can't you remember?'

. . . They were poorly

'Aye, they were. But what was it that made them ill?'

. . . So long ago . . .

'About twenty years, I think. But can't you remember, love?'

. . . Blodwen's legs will be OK

'Who's Blodwen, Mrs Palmer?'

74

'One of my sisters; she's got varicose veins,' Mrs Palmer informed me.

Yes

I was quite impressed but Mrs Palmer seemed uneasy. 'I'm not happy with this communication.'

'But your mother's given evidence.'

'Those facts could have been seen in my mind, in my memories. Some spirit people find that easy to do.'

Yes

'Very well, then. If you really *are* my mother, spell out the address where I was born.'

The pointer faltered on the board; it moved one way then the other, then it slid back to the centre. It moved towards the *Yes*, but didn't quite touch it. Then it stopped. Then it spelt out:

. . . *Can't remember, dear*

Mrs Palmer raised her eyebrows until they met her hairline.

'Oh, can't you?'

. . . *No*

She relaxed her face again. 'But your spirit memory should be much clearer Over There than ever it was Over Here, Mam.'

. . . *Sometimes, dear*

My tutor's lips curled up at the edges, and she winked at me. 'My mother never called anyone "dear"; and she certainly knew where I was born. Very well then' – she was addressing the communicator again – 'here's another test question for you, Mam: what was Dad's second name?'

The pointer was rigid with silence. Then it jiggered back and forth a little, almost as if it were expressing anger. Butting in, I asked it, 'What's the answer, please?'

. . . Stupid questions

Mrs Palmer's grey eyes sparkled with suspicion. 'Now then, "Mam Wise", temper, temper. You're not my mother at all; she'd never be so rude to a guest. The game's up. Who are you?'

Gentle "Mam Wise" then vigorously spelt out on the board:

We've got a couple of clever buggers here

I looked at Mrs Palmer. Mrs Palmer looked at me. We both looked at the board and simultaneously removed our fingers from it.

No-one spoke, but the picture-glass above my head went *tap tap tap*. 'We've got a joker with us, Stephen. Put your finger back on the pointer with mine, and I'll handle this.'

We resumed the sitting and Mrs Palmer's stern voice took charge and asked the questions.

'Who are you, my friend?'

. . . None of your business

'That's a funny name. Now be sensible.'

Ha ha . . . I am Jack

'Oh aye?'

Yep

'Well then, Jack, do you belong to either of us?'

No

'Have we met before?'

No

'Then who are you?'

I'm wonderful

'Answer sensibly. Why are you here?'

. . . Followed the boy's light . . . up the road and into the house

My tutor looked up at me. 'He means the psychic lights in your aura; everyone has them but a medium's are usually brighter.' Then she looked back to the board. 'Did you come through the wall?'

Can't walk through walls! Came through doorway, behind the young man

Mrs Palmer commented to me, 'He must be an earthbound entity: someone who's bound himself to the earth by his desires, instead of wanting to travel across to the spirit world. The spirit body can pass through our walls because it vibrates at a much higher frequency than the atoms of the wall. He must be a newcomer Over There who still believes that bricks are solid objects.'

Einstein

'No, just an experienced Spiritualist medium, Jack – and you didn't fool me for a minute. Now then, Stephen and I would like you to leave the board because we want to communicate with our loved ones. You're being impolite.'

No woman gives me orders

In annoyance I called out to him, 'You're an uninvited guest in a lady's house. Now come along – let go of the pointer, there's a good man.'

No

'Why not?'

I'm a persistent swine

'Now *then*! That's enough of that! Take your finger away, Stephen, and that'll stop his fun.' I instantly obeyed and the pointer stood still.

A little peeved, Mrs Palmer rose from her seat and stretched the muscles of her elderly back. 'Fancy trying to impersonate my mother! Of all the cheek!' she said, casting a sharp glance over her shoulder at the table, and thrusting her spectacles to the top of her pointed nose. 'We'll leave it for ten minutes while we have a hot drink.' Then she tottered out on awkward legs into the scullery to boil the kettle.

By the time we'd drained our Ovaltine to the dregs and Mrs Palmer had rinsed out the sticky cups then wound up the mantel clock with a big iron key, at least fifteen minutes had passed. 'Perhaps we'll have more luck this time,' she said, as we lightly placed our fingers back onto the pointer. It moved straight away.

Hello

'Now then, who's that, please?'

Who the hell do you think?

We instantly removed our fingers as if pulling them out of a fire. Then I winked at my tutor. 'I've got an idea.' She smiled and we recommenced the seance with my addressing the entity in a friendly voice.

'Jack, why don't you step aside and allow my spirit guide, who should be standing nearby, to show you how to use the board properly? You're not making a very good job of it and you might learn something.'

The pointer gave an excited shiver.

OK

As soon as 'Jack' released his grip White Owl took immediate control of the seance. All at once the indicator whizzed around with a strength of purpose that conveyed the presence of a totally different personality. White Owl wasted no time in instructing us.

He is not 'Jack' – he lied to you. 'Test ye the spirit' – always

I asked, 'Why didn't you stop him interfering with our seance?'

He pushed his way in. We are peace-loving souls who would not forcibly remove an earthbound entity: if we did, we would be no more evolved than he. It is up to you to be sensitive to the possibility of receiving unwanted visitors at your seances. You must always use your faculties of reasoning when you receive messages from our side of life, as you did on this occasion.

Mrs Palmer and I exchanged knowing glances.

Do not be afraid to question us. Genuine communications will withstand the test of your intelligence. Please finish now, before this man becomes a nuisance and attaches himself to these surroundings to fulfil his desire for amusement. Good night.

'Good night,' we said – and the pointer immediately ceased moving, though we still had our fingers on it.

Howdy, partners

'So long, mate!' said Mrs Palmer – and we stopped at once. 'He can clear off as quick as he likes, the cheeky beggar!' And she packed the Ouija board away into its flat cardboard box. 'Never mind, Stephen, we'll try it again, some other time.' And without further ado we broke the link with 'Jack' by taking our minds off communication and settling down by the fireside.

I got up from the table and tipped some shiny black coal from the scuttle onto the roaring fire, and banked it up against the cold weather.

Mrs Palmer thanked me, stood next to the fire and riddled the ashes, then muttered something under her breath as if answering a secret voice in her mind, 'Aye. Now's as good a time as any.' Then she leaned down and took something out of a brown paper bag at the side of her comfy armchair. 'I'd like you to have this, Stephen' – and she held out a navy-blue woollen scarf.

But I made no move to take it.

'Go on,' she said, gently shaking it back and forth. 'It's a gift. It belonged to Bill, my husband. That plastic anorak of yours is so thin it'll be the death of you in this snow. Here!' – and she stretched out her hand and gave me the scarf – 'You must be freezing. It's of no use to my Bill now, God love him; and it's helping nobody, stuck upstairs in the wardrobe, gathering dust.'

My fingers closed around the soft deep wool; but I didn't know what to say. 'I . . . it's . . . very kind of you, Mrs Palmer.' And I placed it around my neck. 'It's lovely and warm.'

'I'm glad.' We sat down.

Then I glanced at the clock and thought it best to be off home, for the snow would soon harden into thick ice that would make the pavements treacherous to walk. As I stood up and put on my plastic anorak Mrs Palmer rose, tidied my new scarf, then popped a bar of chocolate into my hand, 'To keep out the cold.'

We said good night and I moved to the kitchen doorway, ready to leave.

'Oh, before you go, Stephen, there's something I'd like to tell you, about the Saturday Open Circle,' she said, sitting down in her comfy armchair again.

I was all ears.

'What with my chest playing me up, and my getting so easily tired these days, I feel in need of a bit of a rest during this cold spell . . . I'm in my mid-seventies now and I can't keep going like I used to; I haven't the strength; so, I thought I'd close the Open Circle for a few months.'

Angelic young lads in story-books would have perfectly understood and replied, 'Why that's fine, dear Mrs Palmer. What an excellent idea.' But I wasn't an angel and I was so stunned that I leaned against the stanchion of the door and rather selfishly blurted out, 'But I need to develop my mediumship. I need to work it and test it on the public.'

Poor Mrs Palmer was taken aback and I immediately felt so ashamed of my immaturity and insensitivity that I could have died – right there on the spot. I instantly regretted my youthful outburst and wished that the floor would open up and swallow me.

She must have seen my red neck and ears, but she fixed me with a kindly gaze that was filled with understanding and replied, 'God will never let you down, you know, Stephen. He is the One who opens and closes all the doors in the world; I believe that. I believe He's the only One with all the keys.'

I broke my embarrassed silence with, 'I'm sorry for speaking out of turn, Mrs Palmer . . . but' – and then I said more positively – 'if you'll let me, I'd like to help. I could run the Open Circle for the church,' I gabbled, more confidently. 'I could take the meetings.'

Her wise eyes flickered with . . . what was it? Uncertainty about my abilities? Concern about my youth and inexperience? I couldn't tell.

At length, she asked quietly, 'Are you sure you want to do this?'

'Yes!' I declared with all the enthusiasm of youth (which rarely understands what it's letting itself in for).

I could practically 'hear' her mind seeking for guidance from Higher Authorities, then she bent down and picked up her handbag from beside the hearth, placed it on her lap, opened it, and handed me a set of jingling keys.

'Very well, then. I'm the President, and as such I have the authority to let you run it. I'll inform the committee of these arrangements.' Then she explained to me the many responsibilities that the job involved.

'I'll fulfil them all,' I promised, zipping up my anorak and wrapping the navy-blue scarf tightly around my neck.

We made our way to the front door and when I opened it a blast of cold air hit me as I turned to face a dark and snowy night. I gave her a peck on the cheek, dropped the church keys into my pocket, then called out to my friend as I crunched through the thick snow along the street:

'Thank you for the scarf, Mrs Palmer! And don't worry! I won't let you down. I'll run the Open Circles properly, starting from this Saturday night.'

And I did.

7

Hauntings and Apparitions

Every week for the next six months I ran the
Saturday Open Circle at Oxford Street Church.

Whether it snowed, shone, or thundered with rain,
I bathed at five, caught the bus from home at a
quarter to six, and was the first to arrive at the
church by 6.15.

I opened the doors, arranged the chairs in a
circle, then prepared the tea-things for the public.
I distributed song books, chose the hymns, then
checked the Secretary's booking-list and made a
note of the mediums for the coming week. Then
I quickly swept round the carpets with a creaky
Ewbank carpet-sweeper.

From half past six onwards I was seated while
the public arrived in dribs and drabs until seven
o'clock when the Circle started. I usually did the
clairvoyance myself because hardly a soul lifted a
finger to help me; a few local mediums sometimes
attended but they seemed to prefer to receive
messages from me, rather than to deliver their own.

I chaired the meeting, prayed, jollied up the
singing, worked as a medium for a solid hour,
gave the announcements, delivered the Benediction,
gathered the collection, counted it out and entered it
into the Treasurer's book; then I made the tea, served

it, washed the cups, answered the public's questions, bade them all good night, tidied up the room, and reset the chairs ready for a Sunday service.

Afterwards I locked the church then walked to the Treasurer's home to deliver the meagre collection which rarely exceeded two pounds, despite the fact that sometimes fifty people had attended the Circle. There was never any claim from me for expenses; I was just happy to gain mediumistic experience.

My single-handed meetings were a novelty and I became quite popular. The congregation numbers swelled but the public saw only a smiling and youthful personality, and not the hidden frustration and stress from which he suffered.

I made weekly reports to Mrs Palmer, of course, at our evening meals and at her psychic development class, where she often said, 'As soon as you need to rest, Stephen – just give me the nod.'

'No, it's OK!' I'd reply brightly; and it took me an exhausting six months to accept her sensible advice – by which time I was dead beat.

After receiving the church keys from me she shook my hand. 'You did a grand job, love. Lots of people were helped, so don't feel bad about finishing. It's not that you weren't capable, it's just that you're young; but you've gained invaluable experience.'

I smiled, but I was relieved it was all over; I had other more pressing worries at home, where my father often vented his anger about my involvement in the Spiritualist Movement; we were forever arguing, and the summer heat just made things worse. He'd accuse me of being stupid, then I'd shout him down. Then he'd snarl, 'You're in your twenties and you're chucking your life away, boy! It's a load of bloody rubbish! When you're dead, you're dead – and that's the end of it. Nobody's ever come back!'

'But mediums give *evidence* of survival, Dad. And some of them have been tested by great scientific minds.'

By now his blood was up. 'The dead can't speak, boy!'

'Well, that's news to me,' I snapped back. 'You know I saw Mam standing at the top of the stairs, three months after she died.'

'Imagination.'

'It wasn't! Oh, what's the use of arguing?' My temper ebbed away. 'You've never been to a Spiritualist church, so how would you know what goes on inside them?'

'Because I'm smart' – and he tapped the side of his head with a thick forefinger, then he grinned and delivered one of his clever sayings. 'Everybody wants to get to heaven, but nobody wants to die.'

Full of suppressed annoyance that made me feel like a shaken-up bottle of lemonade, I stomped upstairs to my room. I was seething. My father had never understood me; since as far back as I could remember he'd always been right, and everyone else had been wrong. But I couldn't contain my bubbling rage any longer and I stormed out of my bedroom and shouted down the stairs at the top of my voice:

'I don't tell *you* what to do! This is *my* life, Dad – not yours – and I'm going to live it my own way. And I won't give up my mediumship.' Then I ran down the staircase and out of the miserable house, slamming the front door behind me.

Walking in the warm summer streets I remembered that from the moment my mother had died, my father had been hell to live with. He'd disliked me since my childhood, and now – with my mother's protection out of the way – he treated me with open disdain.

Little wonder that in her new world my Mam couldn't 'rest in peace', as they say, because she was fully aware of Dad's thoughts and still deeply concerned over my welfare. In the quiet hours of many a warm night that summer, I often sensed the warmth of her gentle spirit presence as she stood by my bedside and conveyed to me the radiant glow of spiritual healing.

She also gave me good advice. 'Take no notice of your father,' she said. 'He doesn't understand spiritual things; but please don't fight. Do your best to get along together.'

'I'll try,' I promised, grumpily.

'Stephen, you know I love you,' her spirit voice replied, 'and that's why I want to ask a favour.'

I listened intently.

'I'd like to move further away from the earth to travel up into higher spiritual planes; there's a lot of work for me to do with young children who've crossed over and who need my kind of help. Will you give me your blessing, son?'

'Of course. But you don't need my permission for anything, Mam. Why do you ask?'

Sadness flooded her voice. 'Because you're the only one in the family who *knows* I'm still alive,' she said.

Deeply stirred by her spiritual thoughts, I

answered gently, 'Mam, it's *your* life. Go.'

Then I sensed the warmth of motherlove shining in the psychic atmosphere around her, and she said, 'I'm proud of the work you're doing – and I'll come back from time to time, to see you. I promise I'll keep in touch. I'll *always* be there for you, whenever you need me.'

And then she ascended . . .

My ability to sense the auras or psychic atmospheres that surround people or objects, whether they exist in this world or in the next, steadily increased with use, and it became an invaluable asset whenever I was called upon to perform some of a medium's more unusual duties, like investigating 'haunted' houses.

I remember one hot night that summer after an Oxford Street Church service when an emergency call for help was received from two hysterical teenage girls. The blonde seventeen-year-olds galloped frantically up the stairs at refreshment time and begged that I should visit their house because it was haunted by a poltergeist, or 'troublesome spirit'. I explained that strictly speaking, the President ought to do it. 'But Mrs Palmer's not in church tonight because she's got a bad cough.'

But before I could offer the girls further help, one of them swivelled towards the black-eyed, ear-wigging Nettie and in a hysterical voice pleaded with her to, 'Please, clear our house of this evil.'

Well, that settled it for Nettie, who needed little encouragement to 'perform' at the best of times: she jumped at the opportunity and fled from the church dragging the excited teenagers behind her; in the interests of the girls' sanity, I thought it best that I join them.

During the sunny car journey I bit my lip and hoped that Nettie would behave sensibly, and wouldn't let her imagination run wild. When I tried to wipe my sticky palms, I looked down and discovered that all my fingers were crossed.

We soon arrived at the drab mid-terraced house in the poorer quarter of the town, where the two hysterical girls introduced us to their flat-mate – a sixteen-year-old male lodger. He was sprawled most ungracefully on a grubby bean-bag that had been thrown into a corner of the shabby living-room. I disliked him the moment I saw him: too thin to be believed, he sported a wispy brown goat-like beard, was smoking one of those roll-your-own 'God-alone-knows-what's-in-it-but-it-doesn't-half-smell-awful' cigarettes, and he needed a damn good wash.

I didn't sit down because the furniture was so stained and smelly.

Stupidly ill-dressed for such hot weather, Nettie swept into the room wearing her long black mackintosh which she dramatically swirled around like Dracula's cape, as if she'd just finished being a bat.

Whatever had happened in this house had already pushed its three tenants to their wits' end, and now their fear had been fanned. Through heaving sobs and tears the thinner blonde girl suddenly blurted out, 'We're haunted by a poltergeist!' Her voice trembled and stammered. 'Objects have moved b-by themselves. N-nobody touched them!'

The cadaverous Nettie, now sweating with heat

and anticipation, crouched forward like a hump-backed Igor, plonked her big bony frame onto the saggy sofa, inclined her head towards the girl, and strained her ears to catch every juicy syllable.

'What do you mean?' I asked.

'Dracula' boomed out imperiously, 'I'll handle this, Stephen.' Folding the huge coat around her spindly legs she demanded of the girl, 'What do you mean?'

'W-well, you know,' she stammered, mesmerized by the vision in black that sat in judgement before her, 'Things have been . . . flying ab-bout. And we've heard this spooky sound, like . . . like a s-spirit, weeping, in the front bedroom . . . upstairs.' She pointed a quivering finger directly up at the ceiling.

Nettie was up like a shot and a black blur whizzed past me and flew through the living-room door: she was off on a ghost hunt. The three of us crooked our necks towards the door that she'd left swinging on its creaky hinges, and listened as Nettie clumped her size tens up the stairs and stomped them noisily across the landings.

The shifty-eyed lodger put out his thin cigarette and scratched his goatee beard as a trickle of sweat ran down his forehead. 'What the hell is she doing?'

'Oh, take no notice,' I replied brightly, trying to break the tension; 'she doesn't get out very often, you see.' He cast me a strange glance.

I was glad Nettie had 'ascended' for now I could get on with my job. When I nodded to the girl to continue, she pointed a shaky finger at the lodger. 'He's had bother, too,' she said. He twizzled the thin strands of his beard, shuffled his feet, then swallowed a noseful of phlegm. 'Go on!' she cried. 'Tell him everything.'

His reply was a grumpy one. 'I'm not getting involved! Neither of you will let me sleep with you, so why should I care what happens in here? You can all rot. Leave me right out of it.'

He'd stated his position very candidly, I thought.

Meanwhile, we raised our eyes again because we heard Nettie dragging something over the landings; it sounded as though she'd put a dead body into a sack and was having trouble yanking it through a doorway. Then she suddenly called out indignantly into the air, 'Oh, you *will*, will you? Well, we'll soon see about *that*, mate!'

Pathetic glances circled the room. God alone knew what she was doing, but I wouldn't have been at all surprised to have heard her screaming out at the top of her voice, *'Be gone, you swine!'*

By now the stammering blonde girl had gathered her wits and had eased her sobbing. 'We've had t-two upstairs windows smashed. A b-bottle of his aftershave broke them. The poltergeist threw it through the bathroom w-window, from *within* the room, but there was no broken g-glass found on the p-pavement outside – it was all *inside*, on the bathroom floor. And the cabinet mirror was c-cracked.'

'Who was here when this happened?'

'Me and her was out dancing,' she said, pointing to the other silent girl. 'He was the only one in at the time.'

I cast the dubious lodger a sideways glance, and noticed he sat stony-faced with a sheepish grin on his mouth.

Suddenly the living-room door burst open and the girls jumped out of their skins with fright.

Nettie swept in, swirling her cloak, and my spirits immediately sank: I'd just managed to calm down the highly-strung girls, but now all hope of a sensible solution had shot out of the smashed window with the bottle of aftershave.

The glittering-eyed Nettie crooked her back and wagged a bony finger at her captive audience, which seemed to aggravate their fear:

'Now listen to me . . . *all* of you!' she commanded, panting in the stifling summer heat. 'I've cleansed this house of something *malicious* tonight' – and she half-whispered that word 'malicious' as though she were a guilty slimmer who had just savoured the forbidden delights of a delicious cream cake.

I closed my eyes for a few seconds, because I couldn't believe it.

'Within these walls, there is—' (and here she paused for the greatest dramatic effect) '—*evil* upstairs!'

The girls let out a strangled gasp, but the lodger and I sat dumbfounded.

Nettie unfolded her melodrama as she moved around the room with her long arms outstretched and her fingers splayed. 'There's an evil entity taking over the house, see. Don't scream out! Get a grip on yourselves. It's only a man who blew his brains out in the front bedroom. Be quiet! There's no need to sob,' she said in true Hammer horror-film style. 'He won't come down the stairs now, because I've placed a crucifix on the top step.'

I didn't know whether to laugh or cry. If someone had stepped into the room and presented Nettie with an Oscar for 'Most Promising Newcomer', I would have applauded and not been a bit surprised. She'd have won it fair and square.

But then the sweating 'medium' really went to town by dropping her voice into a hoarse whisper, and stunning the girls by commanding them to, 'Tell me the truth. Don't be afraid . . .' (I dreaded what might come out next, and rather hoped she might faint in the heat – but she didn't). 'Has any thick green slime oozed out of the walls or come up through the carpets?'

I covered my moist face with my hand and stood up. All eyes turned on me; I could no longer stay in the same room as Nettie.

'Listen – don't worry, please,' I said calmly and in a steady, measured voice as I gathered my composure. 'Everything'll be sorted out before I leave here tonight; I promise you. May I stroll around the place, and see what I can psychically sense?'

The three tenants responded well to my quiet confidence; they smiled and nodded – and I left the floor to Bette Davis.

At the top of the stairs I stepped carefully over Nettie's crucifix and wondered if the Other Side would help me to resolve this case. Then I heard White Owl say, 'You have been well trained, and can deal with this yourself.'

As I walked through each sunlit room I was aware of no malevolent forces in the vicinity; in fact, the psychic atmosphere in the house felt tranquil and calm to me.

Standing in a quiet corner of the humid bathroom where the phenomena were said to have occurred, I closed my eyes and prayed that the spirit people would bring down a blessing upon the house, that they might cleanse and purge it of any bad influences – even though I couldn't sense any there.

As my quiet thoughts went out, filtering into the room there came a fine gold-coloured mist, so vibrant and glowing – and it filled every ounce of the psychic atmosphere.

When I opened my eyes the golden mist was no longer visible to me.

Puzzled as to why Nettie had been so certain of the 'evil' that I could find no trace of, I slowly made my way back down the stairs towards the living-room. But just as I reached out for the doorknob I was startled by the sight of two ghostly apparitions, and I stopped dead in my tracks.

There, before me, standing within a grey, foggy psychic light against the wall stood a tall young woman who looked very bedraggled; her shoulder-length hair was dark, greasy and lank, and her careworn face was far too old for her years; her plain blue clothes were torn in places and they'd seen much better days. She was shrouded in a feeling of depression, and yet a kind look gleamed in her green eyes.

I immediately sensed she'd once lived in this house. When I asked her name, she didn't respond but seemed far more concerned about the little grey bundle that nestled in her arms: she nursed it as if it were the only thing she possessed in the world.

Completely failing to communicate with her, I simply prayed she might find peace for her soul; and then she floated out through the wall, and vanished from sight.

I knew I'd have to tell the tenants about her, of course, but only after Nettie had gone.

Back in the living-room Nettie had reduced the trembling girls to heaps of quivering jelly, and to finish her 'performance' she now stepped into the centre of the room – as though she were a ringmaster at the circus – and declared with bravado, 'Your house is cleansed! Never be afraid, girls! Death is nothing to fear!'

And with a swirl of her big black mackintosh, she took her leave, thank God, and the room fell deathly silent.

A sense of relief was plainly etched on the three young faces before me; and the blonde girl stammered out, rather timidly, 'I'm more f-frightened of *her*, than I am of *it*.'

'Well,' I chipped in quietly and sensibly, 'it's best to pay no attention to Nettie. Now, as to my own findings . . .' Everyone sat up straight, and I knew that if they started asking awkward questions I'd have to be on my mettle to draw from the knowledge that Mrs Palmer, my extensive reading, and my spirit friends had conveyed to me.

Taking a deep breath, I assured the tenants that, 'I psychically sensed the atmosphere in each of the rooms, and scanned them for spirit beings. The upstairs was totally clear, but downstairs in the hall I found that this house is indeed haunted – but only by two apparitions.'

The perspiring lodger came alive. 'Appa – whats?'

'Ghostly shadows – shades and images: they're just like psychic snapshots impressed in the spiritual atmosphere of the place. They're not in any way "evil", they're quite harmless,' I assured the tenants. 'Every building holds many such psychic images within it but they can't hurt you, no more than a photograph album can. Both of these apparitions once lived here, I felt; and, of course, they died here.'

'But what about the weeping we heard upstairs, and the s-smashed window?'

'I think that'll be explained shortly,' and I cast a glance at the shifty lodger, who glowered back at me.

'C-can spirits move objects then?' asked the girl, now in a much calmer frame of mind.

'Oh yes. Poltergeists do exist, of course, but they don't come "two-for-a-penny"; they're an incredibly rare phenomenon. These kinds of troubled souls draw psychic power from the atmosphere – and from the psychic energies of the people in the house – to shift objects. But most of this type of activity isn't caused by "noisy spirits" at all, but usually by youngsters in the house who are releasing vast amounts of psychic energy through being angry, frustrated, fearful or distressed.'

'And those energies can m-move something?'

'Oh yes – but it's nothing to do with the spirit people.' I smiled and silently congratulated myself on remembering Mrs Palmer's wise teachings. 'But I don't think you've got a poltergeist here; so there's no need to worry.'

The goatee beard smirked.

'No, your two apparitions were good souls, benign entities. The first is a young and lonely unmarried mother who died in childbirth, and the second is her stillborn baby that passed over with her.'

The room went ever so quiet, and three pop-eyed youngsters gazed open-mouthed at me.

'Well, I'll go to 'ell on a broomstick,' said the second girl.

But I wasn't amused because I knew that a good ticking-off was needed to put a stop to the silly nonsense about 'flying aftershave bottles'.

'To be quite frank,' I declared, 'if I were a great deal older than you, and you were my children, I'd have no hesitation in putting the three of you across my knee because you're behaving hysterically.' My voice toughened up. 'You're afraid of your own fear. And the sooner it stops, the better.'

They stared at me, vacantly.

Then I turned to the shifty-eyed goat. 'And as for you,' I said, confidently. 'Trying to scare these poor girls by breaking windows and making silly crying noises! You should be ashamed of yourself!'

His mouth gaped open in astonishment, then it closed and opened again; but he didn't defend himself.

'Right!' I declared with as much authority as I could muster. 'I'm leaving now, and the quicker you all calm down and stop acting like children and start behaving like adults, the sooner you'll forget this nonsense – and peace will return to this house. Does everybody understand?' I asked, rather masterfully, I thought.

'Yes,' chorused the girls, rather feebly, but at least they were calm and relaxed now. The lodger gave me a guilt-ridden nod.

As I made my way to the living-room door I assured them, 'I'll see myself out; please don't worry. I've asked for a spirit blessing on this house and it's been given; and from tonight I'll send out Healing Prayers and Thoughts for you all. My spirit guide has also promised me that no more phenomena will bother you.'

Giving them all a friendly smile, I added confidently, 'There'll be no more "poltergeist" activity here,' and they bade me a grateful good night.

I strode out of the room into the cool hallway on my own and made for the exit. But when I passed a small recess, there was a sudden flash of light that froze me to the spot, and I stood face to face with a grumpy old grandma-spirit who wore an old-fashioned ankle-length dress that was covered by a starched grey pinafore.

Both her hands rested on her ample hips, and a deep frown glowered on her brow. She looked very annoyed and I slunk away backwards and quickly unlatched the front door. The old harridan cackled with anger that flashed in her wizened eyes. She clenched her fists in readiness.

'That's one for you to deal with, White Owl,' I said mentally as the crone took a menacing step towards me and shook her fist in my face, and issued loud commands:

'Now get out of my house, you nosey old bugger!' she yelled. 'I don't like men, and I can't *stand* bloody aftershave!'

Startled, I slammed the door, bit my lip and tiptoed down the warm stone steps and out into the evening sunlight – and I didn't look back.

8

Healing Hands of Light

'Now then . . . just close your eyes, and relax.'

Mrs Palmer was standing behind the hard wooden chair I was sitting on, next to the cool hearth in her friendly kitchen, and she continued quietly, 'I'm going to attune my mind to the God-Force of Spirit, within me, to give you a spiritual healing treatment . . . because you need it.'

My eyes were closed, as were hers, and the summery room was very still.

Under the gentle touch of her hands that rested featherlight upon my head I felt my endless months' of tension, built up through trying to cope with my father's aggression, ebbing away, and my body started responding to the wonderfully calming influence of spiritual power.

'Try to relax your body and your mind, Stephen. Try to stop your thoughts jumping around, and to forget all your nagging troubles and anxieties, and let the power fill you with peace . . .'

And into the darkness behind my eyes there came a bright spiritual energy that lit up my mind, relaxing me, urging me to fill my lungs with air, and making me sigh deeply. All my noisy thoughts ceased, drifted away like fine dust in a hot summer breeze . . .

Tranquillity filled my soul.

After a while Mrs Palmer's hands lifted from my head and then rested lightly on my shoulders for a further ten minutes or so. 'From the Spirit of God, through the healer's spirit, and into the spirit of the patient,' was how she'd often described this healing process – and now, I could sense it.

I was aware of other things, too: the presences of many compassionate spirit friends, family members, guides and helpers from the invisible world seemed to gather around us, and each soul added his own love and power to the treatment. It was a very comforting experience.

During the healing silence, while the mantel clock gently ticked away, I thanked God that Mrs Palmer was such an excellent channel for the regenerative power of love, and realized that she possessed this ability because she herself was such a compassionate person.

Wrapped in serenity my thoughts seemed to float away from the sun-streaked room, away from the warm earth, and I couldn't hear the clock anymore . . .

In the stillness I reflected on how fortunate I was to have received Mrs Palmer's private tuition, to have been given so much of the secret knowledge that spiritually advanced souls impart only to their chosen initiates. In her nights of instruction and in her private home circle she'd revealed to me how closely the next world can influence our own; she'd taught me how to use my psychic powers and how to develop my mediumship; she'd set my feet firmly on the road towards knowledge and spiritual understanding. But above all, she'd been so kind and thoughtful. Not many people would have fed a grieving youngster, or given him books on spirit teachings; and then there was her late husband's woolly scarf 'to keep out the cold' . . . She'd been like a mother to me; and she was so sensible, so down-to-earth. Yes, I was very fortunate to have Mrs Palmer as a teacher; and I was glad she was my friend.

All at once the rhythmic ticking of the clock sounded again in my ears, and I remembered where I was.

'Now then, Stephen . . . I hope that'll help you.' Her hands lifted from my shoulders, and I felt so much better. I thanked her and she sat down in her favourite comfy armchair beside the cool hearth.

When I sat opposite her she looked at me rather thoughtfully; then she took down the clock, wound it up, and set it back on the tiled mantelpiece. She finished sipping the orange drink she'd poured, and I wondered what she'd say next.

'You've worked your mediumship too frequently, Stephen, and it's drained your physical strength,' she warned.

I replied, 'I've been very tired these last few months.'

'I'm not surprised, love. Psychic work burns up nervous energy, and we mediums have to be careful. We've got to replace it.'

Before I could ask 'How?' she anticipated my question.

'Plenty of rest, good nutritious food, and pure air and water is what you need.'

'Right,' I said, making a mental note of her prescription, then confessing, 'I've been picking at my food again, I'm afraid. And . . . it's been tough at home lately,' I said, thinking of the rows I'd had with my father.

She finished her drink and placed her empty glass on the table, then momentarily pursed her lips together as if they'd been pulled in by a draw-string.

I felt clumsy, and silly, and added, 'I miss my Mam, and . . . living with my Dad hasn't been easy. He . . . he can be so hurtful . . .'

The silence that followed seemed endless.

'Yes, I expect he can,' she said sympathetically. 'But you were born to be a medium, Stephen, and he'll just have to get used to it, you know. God-given gifts can't be ignored, they're meant to be used in service to others.'

A tight knot of tension gathered in my neck.

'You see, some parents don't seem to . . . well . . .' Her clear grey eyes shone with concern, 'Look, I'm sorry it's been difficult for you.'

That was just what my mother would have said, and a lump formed in my throat.

'Don't get too despondent, love. Just pull through as best you can, and try to cope with the strain.'

My eyes blinked and they felt hot.

'You see, in his own way, I'm sure your Dad does care about you. It's just that sometimes, well . . . when a man loses his wife . . . that kind of pain takes a long time to heal. It can hurt so much that . . . well, he might find it hard to remember . . . to tell his son, "I love you."'

The words I wanted to say seemed trapped in my neck, and when I did find the power to release them

101

they were so quiet that they barely escaped my lips. 'Thank you,' I whispered, 'You've been . . . very kind to me.' And I swallowed hard.

'Not at all, love,' and she leaned across and patted my hand so lovingly.

I felt the teardrop when it trickled from the corner of my eye, but I didn't like to wipe it away.

Mrs Palmer smiled kindly and her voice brightened considerably. 'You just look after yourself, now. And not too much mediumship, mind! And plenty of rest – and some play. We haven't come to earth just to help others, you know. We need time for ourselves, too.'

I sniffed, and drew my sleeve across my cheek.

'And as for your Dad . . . well, don't worry about him. Mark my words, love: one day, he'll understand,' she said in a compassionate voice. Then she quickly changed the subject. 'Now then: I received a message for you a few minutes ago.'

I perked up a little.

'The spirit people said they were very happy with the progress of your own spiritual healing work at the church. Isn't that nice to hear?'

'Yes,' I said, and I gradually became myself again.

'How long have you been healing at the Wednesday afternoon services now?'

'A few years,' I said, straightening my back. 'I love to do spiritual healing, more than I do my platform work.'

'And there've been some very good reports about you.'

I must have looked surprised.

'Oh, not much escapes the ears of the President!'

she exclaimed. 'If news doesn't reach me from *this* world – it comes to me from the next.'

Our laughter broke the tension in the kitchen. Mrs Palmer looked funny when she laughed: her wrinkly hand flew up to cover her mouth and she threw back her head to let out the joyful sound.

'It's good to have a laugh,' I said.

'Aye, it's good to have a laugh. Laughter's a great tonic – if someone could bottle it he'd make a fortune,' she quipped, and we chuckled again. She was such a happy person.

But when her smile subsided a look of reverence passed slowly across her face. 'I think spiritual healing is one of God's greatest gifts, don't you?'

'I do.'

'Well now—' and she slapped her thighs with the palms of her hands, 'do you want to hear the rest of the message I received?'

I leaned forward. 'Yes, please.'

Her grey eyes sparkled and she pushed her spectacles back onto the bridge of her nose. 'Well, I was told that in the future you'll work at the SAGB in London.' When I frowned, she explained, 'That's the Spiritualist Association of Great Britain. It's quite a famous place.'

'Is it?' But I wasn't impressed; I knew nothing of the SAGB.

'I was told,' she continued, with a kind of pride in her voice, 'that one day you'll be a good professional medium; you know, like Mr Gordon Higginson.'

My eyebrows rose. That name rang a bell somewhere.

'Gordon Higginson is the President of the

Spiritualists' National Union and he's a very well-known medium. Travelled all over Britain, he has. Been doing that for fifty years or more, since he was a young boy, has Mr Higginson.'

Then I remembered that months previously a spirit voice had privately told me that one day I would meet Gordon Higginson.

'But I wouldn't like to be a professional medium, Mrs Palmer. It sounds awful,' I said.

She looked surprised as more of my words spilled out. 'I wouldn't want to earn my living by working as a medium, and I certainly don't want to travel.' She seemed taken aback. 'No offence,' I said gently, 'but I'm such a home-bird and I *hate* travelling. I couldn't think of a worse possible life, Mrs Palmer.'

There was a considerable pause during which I scratched my ear. My tutor patted her chest then gave a hoarse cough, and appeared to be gathering her thoughts.

'Perhaps . . .' she said, 'maybe it's for the best that we mediums aren't always aware of our own futures. I was probably wrong to tell you.' Even though the room was summery warm she pulled her cardigan tighter around herself. 'After all, if we were absolutely certain of what experiences lay ahead of us, would we walk the road, I wonder?'

I didn't know the answer, but I smiled by way of an apology for my youthful remarks; and to break this uncomfortable talk of mediumship, money, travel, and Gordon Higginson, I referred back to the services at the church.

'Why don't you ever attend the Wednesday healing sessions, Mrs Palmer? You're an excellent healer but

I've never seen you there. If you like, I could call for you this week and we'll go along together?'

With a small wave of her hand she politely declined, and for the first time revealed to me the rampant jealousies that bubble and boil within any close-knit community, such as the Spiritualist Movement. But her voice was filled with hurt.

'I used to conduct the healing services for years. But now, some of the new healers want to oust me as President so that they'll have a free hand to run the church as they please. God forgive me if I'm wrong, but some of them seem interested only in position and power, and not in helping people at all.'

'Couldn't you still attend?'

'No, love; it wouldn't be right. You see, their dislike of me is so strong that my presence there would disturb the psychic harmony that's needed to help heal the patients; so, I can't go.'

I felt annoyed.

'Ahmed told me, when I asked him about it, "You are not popular because you are capable."'

Her spirit guide's wisdom sank deep into my mind, and I was never to forget it. But my tutor seemed a little upset.

'Oh, I still help the patients as much as I can – by sending out Absent Healing Thoughts for an hour each Wednesday afternoon. I sit here alone, and . . .' Then she shook her head. 'Oh, but that's enough of me for one night. Stephen, spiritual healing's a wonderful gift, and every week for the last few years I've sat here and sent my power out to help you with your patients.'

A wave of gratitude rose within me; what a truly kind soul she was.

'And I'll continue to so do,' she promised – and she kept her word. From then onwards, each Wednesday at the church, I sensed my tutor's healing prayers adding more power to the spirit energies that already flowed through me to the patients.

These popular healing services were always opened with a prayer by one of the six or so healers who asked the Great Spirit to bless the meeting, and to bring health and harmony to the souls and bodies of the people who attended; this was followed by the assembly praying for others who they knew were ill, after the healing-group leader had read out a long list of those who were suffering physical, mental, or spiritual pain, or who were in need of peace.

Then everyone sang the Spiritualist Healing Hymn, after which taped classical music was played quietly in the background while the healers treated their patients.

All the healers were elderly and they wore white coats; I was in my twenties, and I didn't – but we all got along well together.

'Your soul is very peaceful,' the healing-group leader often commented to me; 'and that's good because it helps the power to flow.' And on the many occasions when she asked for my help with stubborn health conditions that didn't respond to her particular kind of spiritual power, I willingly co-operated.

A wide range of patients attended regularly – from babies to the very elderly – and as a general rule their long-standing complaints were usually alleviated only after weeks or months of weekly treatment. But other visitors, whose specialists had pronounced that all hope of recovery for them had gone, were sometimes healed immediately. It was all very unpredictable; and I quickly learned that the power of God's Healing Spirit to effect a cure was in His hands, and not in ours; we simply served Him as best we could, guided by skilled Angels of Light from the next world.

Patients either sat on hard-backed wooden chairs or, if they were too weak, they lay down on a comfortably padded couch that placed them at waist-level to the healers.

During my apprenticeship I helped to treat all manner of ailments, and it's no exaggeration to say that patients had their impaired sight improved, and even deafness was cured. My psychic feelings as the healing energies passed through me were as varied as the patients' case histories.

My hands would either be warm or cold, or remain at their normal temperature. Many times I was psychically aware of no power-flow at all, yet the healing process operated, nevertheless.

But I was often fortunate enough to clairvoyantly see luminous shafts of bright light, of varying colours and intensities, that radiated either from my hands or through my aura, the psychic atmosphere that surrounded me. At other times I was fascinated to watch pencil-thin rays of light as they projected from my fingertips into the diseased areas of patients' bodies.

Occasionally I also perceived differently coloured shadows hovering in the patients' auras and these indicated that the tissues beneath them were ailing, which was why the light directly above them was shaded.

One middle-aged and painfully thin man, who'd been suffering from the after-effects of a nervous breakdown, told me he'd felt 'lit from within' and that he'd gained great peace of mind after receiving treatment, and had experienced a surprising spiritual change of thought:

'Since you've been helping me, Mr O'Brien,' he said, 'I'm a different man. A few months back I wanted to die. I felt lost, like I was walking in the dark. But now I can see things clearer, as if a light's been switched on, inside me – and I want to live!' he exclaimed joyfully.

Sometimes White Owl, or other healing guides and helpers who made up the band of spirits which had attached itself to my work, told me exactly what was wrong with a patient, or else I felt drawn to the region that required help; it was as if my hands possessed a strange kind of built-in soul-radar, and they could sense the need in a sick person, whether it be of body, mind, or spirit.

I was guided by this method to the feet of one happy and amazed patient, this time a seventy-year-old woman, who had her swollen and arthritic ankles 'miraculously' returned to normality. 'The searing pain I've suffered from for years has completely gone!' she cried, with tears standing in her eyes. To my astonishment the spirit people had effected this cure after only one treatment.

Thrilled by the results, she told me, 'Last week when you touched my feet I nearly jumped out of my skin because I felt a tingling current running right up through my body. Now, look at my ankles!' she cried, like a child who'd just opened a birthday gift. 'My feet are back to their proper size for the first time in fifteen years! And they feel great! They don't hurt any more.' All we healers were just as excited about it as she was.

People find it hard to keep such good news to themselves, of course, and word of my healing ministry soon spread beyond the confines of the church.

While browsing through some shirts in a clothes store one afternoon I heard my name called from a corner of the department, and when I turned around I was being beckoned by a mature auburn-haired assistant.

'I know you,' she said, 'and I've got something important to tell you. You've often healed me of my anxieties.'

Puzzled because I didn't recall her face, I asked where we'd met.

'Oh, we've never met,' she said in lowered tones, 'but I know you're a medium and a healer, and I've received a lot of help. Whenever I couldn't cope,' she whispered, glancing right and left to make sure we weren't being observed by her boss, 'I placed one of my fingers over your name in the local newspaper advert, and I prayed – and my needs were always met.'

Her remarks stunned and intrigued me.

'I mentally draw the healing from you, you see. I saw you once giving evidence at the church, and I liked you.' She took my hand and gently shook it.

'Many times you've given me strength, and peace,' she said gratefully, 'and I thank you.'

It seems that the power of positive healing thought had, without my conscious aid, achieved its beneficent effect in a mysterious way; and this was not an isolated instance.

Another notable case was that of a 55-year-old cancer sufferer whom I advised to undertake a programme of positive mental affirmations, and she agreed to try the daily repetition of bright thoughts such as: 'My body is cleansing itself of impurities, and healing itself – second by second, minute by minute, day by day.'

These positive affirmations, coupled with medication and spiritual healing in the form of the laying-on of hands, brought her astounding results: her specialists discovered that the growth of her malignant bowel-tumour had been stunted. The delighted lady had something to shout about.

'They couldn't believe my latest X-rays! Instead of the tumour getting bigger – it's actually *shrunk*!' she declared. 'And now they think it may be checked with chemotherapy.'

All the healers were very impressed by the power of positive thought and what it could achieve; and I realized that the mind plays a very great part in the healing processes of the body: *as we think, so we are*, and I told all those who asked for help, 'If you believe that the power of spiritual healing can help you, then your faith may make you whole. But it isn't absolutely necessary to have faith in order for the healing to work, because it's a psychic science.'

Naturally, this advice was always followed by

the caution that each patient should keep their ailments under strict medical supervision, and not throw away their tablets in a rash move to rely exclusively upon spiritual healing to treat them. After all, we were healers, not doctors.

But generally speaking our patients did hold a great belief that they would be helped – all bar one rather overweight pensioner who surprised me at one session when she whispered seriously into my ear, 'Stephen – I'm wearing my whalebone corset today. Do you think the whalebones'll stop the power getting through to heal my aching back?'

Grinning, I assured her I didn't think they would.

'Nevertheless,' she confided in hushed tones, 'I won't wear it next week. It can't be doing me any good – I can hardly breathe when it's on; and some nights, I'm bloody choking.' Then she scratched under her blouse with a tail-comb and blew out a huge sigh that would have made any harpooner cry out *'Thar she blows!'*

There were lots of happy moments like that at the healing services because they weren't miserable sessions, but joyous occasions; even when terminally ill patients passed over, we knew that the healing they'd received had helped them to make a more dignified and peaceful crossing, and we thanked God for that.

People who didn't respond too well to their treatments, and there were always some, had the opportunity to talk over their problems with the wise healers, and they eventually discovered that the illnesses they'd suffered from had brought them to the spiritual realization that the hidden

Power and the Love of God had never ceased to operate in their lives; and then they counted their blessings, instead of cursing their difficulties, which was a change of thought that always added to their sense of well-being.

And every week, month after month like clockwork, I reported my healing progress to Mrs Palmer in her friendly kitchen, where she continued to give me expert guidance on how to perfect the art of developing my mediumship and spiritual healing abilities; and she also cooked me some delicious meals.

There was always much to chat about, especially when the black-eyed Nettie had made a sudden appearance one week and had announced she wanted to be a healer. Although I felt guilty about it afterwards I'm afraid I seriously doubted her motivation, and I told Mrs Palmer so.

'I've known Nettie for years, Stephen, and many times I've tried to help her – but she still went her own sweet way. May God forgive me, but I think she just uses the platform for self-expression, rather than for service.'

'There are plenty like Nettie about,' I sadly concurred, quite unsurprised by Mrs Palmer's spot-on psychic appraisal of Nettie's character. My tutor was a gifted sensitive and she'd always been an excellent assessor of people's hidden motivation; she could see the deep feelings in a person's heart before they themselves knew that they were there.

In the four years of serving my early psychic apprenticeship under Mrs Palmer's expert eye, I'd come to trust her spiritual judgement, value her mediumistic instruction, and respect her compassionate nature. I was, indeed, very fond of Mrs Palmer, for she was not only a fine medium and a lovely lady, but she was also my valued friend.

That's why I was so upset by the letter I found on the mat behind the front door one bitterly cold January morning. Its few lines had been hurriedly penned by one of Mrs Palmer's sisters: *Flo had a nasty bout of bronchitis just after the Christmas break*, (it said) *then pneumonia set in, which brought on an angina attack and she was rushed to Morriston Hospital.* (My heart was thudding in my chest.) *We know you think a lot of her, and thought you'd like to know.*

With shaking hands I thrust the crumpled note into the anorak I was hurriedly pulling on over my jumper, and quickly wrapped around my neck the navy-blue scarf Mrs Palmer had given me 'to keep out the cold' – and my heart was beating fast in the back of my throat as I flew through the door and rushed down the street to the nearest bus-stop.

9

'O, Great White Spirit . . .'

It was such a cold January morning that my feet
hardly felt the stinging blows they received from the
hard pavements as I belted at top speed through
the bright sunshine, down the hill towards the bus-
stop. A bus was waiting and I got there as it was
pulling out – and I jumped inside just as the doors
thudded shut behind me.

My breath came in short quick gasps. 'A return to
Morriston Hospital, please.' I was panting.

The young driver smirked. 'You're going the right
way to get *admitted* there, matey boy – dashing
around like that.'

I paid no attention: Mrs Palmer was on my mind.
He took my money and I flopped down onto the
front seat. The sweat was pouring down the inside
of my plastic anorak. I was hot and sticky, and the
bumpy journey seemed endless; it was supposed to
take twenty minutes, but it felt like for ever.

My spine juddered whenever we hit a pothole in
the road and I couldn't keep my thoughts straight.
How would Mrs Palmer be feeling now? Was she
conscious? Would the nurses let me in to see her?
I shook my head and told myself I was being stupid.
Of course they would. I shouldn't be so silly.

In the cold bus I thrust my hands into my pockets

to find warmth, but instead I found the crumpled note. I took it out and scanned the scrawled lines again: . . . *a nasty bout of bronchitis . . . pneumonia set in . . . brought on an angina attack . . . rushed to Morriston Hospital*, and I shuddered. Only recently, Mrs Palmer had confided in me that her heart had been considerably weakened by a painful bout of bronchitis she'd had last year.

My thoughts were whirling and confused. I screwed the note into a ball, threw it onto the floor, and sent out a prayer to my spirit guide.

'Please be with me, White Owl,' I said, mentally. 'If we can help Mrs Palmer in any way, please let us. I'd like to give her some spiritual healing . . . I know you'll be there, White Owl; and her own guide, Ahmed, too,' I said, with absolute conviction. Then, sensing my guide's powerful spiritual presence next to me, I added, 'So I'll thank you now, for your help.'

The big bus jerked to a halt and I strode briskly through the crisp air and up the steep path and into the hospital. A nurse directed me to the correct ward but when I arrived a few members of Mrs Palmer's elderly family were gathered at her bedside, and the brief glimpses that I got of my friend revealed to me a small, tired, and depleted woman.

But her relatives were wreathed in smiles and full of beans. I didn't dream of disturbing them, so I decided to walk around the grounds and return a short while later, after they had gone.

When I next entered the hospital I noticed there were three elderly women in the quiet ward; two of them were sound asleep and the third was Mrs Palmer, who was lying peacefully in the bed nearest the bright window, and her eyes were closed.

As I slowly stepped to her bedside I was shocked by her appearance: propped up on some pillows, her frail body looked small and thin wrapped inside a loose pink nightdress; her neck was sinewed and extended because her head lay far back on the pillows. I felt indescribably sad: she looked so vulnerable, like a helpless child.

I stood silently and gazed down upon her face, while outside a hungry chaffinch whistled on the window-sill, and then flew away into the bare winter trees.

Mrs Palmer's grey hair was unwashed and it had been roughly brushed back from her eyes, and wisps of it had stuck to the glistening beads of perspiration on her forehead; her spectacles had been removed, leaving two purple indentations on either side of her pinched nose. But it was her closed eyes that drew my attention and shocked me most: the lids seemed much fuller and paler than normal and they'd sunk into two large dark blue sockets, which were circled by the fine white ridges that were her cheekbones. All trace of rosiness had left her face, and her waxen skin was as pale as moonlight. The cheeks that had once been so round and full of laughter were now hollowed out and shaded, and her shrunken lips seemed to have caved inwards.

Slowly, her dry mouth opened then closed, and she gave a little sigh. Then, as if by some inspired thought, she turned her head on the pillow until it faced me, and opened her clouded grey eyes. She tried to focus them . . . then she saw me for the first time.

In a barely audible, hoarse whisper, she said, 'Now then . . .' and my heart skipped a beat. '. . . Hello, love . . .'

'Hello, Mrs Palmer,' I replied, softly. She gave a faint smile. 'I've come to see you.'

'Sit down . . .' she whispered, and she patted the bedclothes with a tired hand that had a clear plastic tube inserted into the back of it. Noticing a nearby chair I drew it up, and sat down next to the bed. She tried to ease herself into a better sitting position but couldn't manage it; so, I fluffed up her pillows until she felt more comfortable.

'Oh . . . that's . . . better. It's lovely to see you,' she said, so very quietly; but her smiling voice was full of warmth and affection.

I reached out and gently clasped her wrinkled hand, and a glimmer of light flickered in her clouded eyes. She knew I was going to give her spiritual healing, and she closed her tired eyelids and accepted it without comment.

For several minutes words were unnecessary, and in sacred silence the Great Spirit's healing power embraced us both and we were surrounded by clouds of golden psychic light that flooded my being and my soul, and then flowed into the weary body of my ailing friend. Soundlessly, we both knew that the strength of our faith had drawn it close. It was a gift of golden light; a blessing from the world of spirit; a radiant tide of healing that brought peace in its wake.

Mrs Palmer lay back and so gratefully received the spiritual help for which I felt she'd prayed, and a contented smile flickered across her lips; there was a quiet joy in her expression that revealed her thoughts to me as clearly as if they'd been written across her brow: 'In my hour of need, my Father has not forsaken me.'

And I whispered softly, 'God will always comfort the lonely.'

It was difficult for her to form her words, but at length she replied, '. . . He will.'

While the golden light embraced us in its clouds of power, within my mind I spoke some words of comfort that seemed to travel through my spirit, as if they wished to pass silently down my arms and out through my hands and into the soul of my weary friend in the bed. *The Lord is my shepherd; I shall not want. He maketh me to lie down in green pastures: He leadeth me beside the still waters. He restoreth my soul.*

Mrs Palmer's eyes flickered softly under their lids.

Yea though I walk through the valley of the shadow of death, I will fear no evil: for Thou art with me . . .

The silence that followed was punctuated only by the distant sounds of birdsong from a flock of starlings perched in the bare trees outside in the hospital grounds.

When the gleaming psychic light subsided and Mrs Palmer opened her heavy eyelids, she gave a faint smile and whispered, weakly, 'My niece just left . . . She was crying . . . because she said to me, "Oh, you'll come, Auntie Flo." And I said, "Aye, love – so will Christmas."'

We smiled together. Despite her serious illness she hadn't lost her lovely sense of humour.

Gently, I turned my thoughts to other matters that

were strongly on my mind and I said, 'Mrs Palmer? I wanted to . . .' And I paused, unable to express myself properly. 'I . . . I'm very grateful to you.'

She slowly blinked her eyes. 'I know, love,' she whispered; then she took a deeper breath, which brought a little more strength to her voice. 'But then . . . you're a good lad. You're bright, and you'll go . . . a long way . . . and I'm glad I've been able to help you.'

I smoothed her tired hand, and gently let it go.

'I mustn't tire you,' I said. 'You know my prayers are with you; and I'll come and see you again, on Sunday. But I just wanted to . . . to thank you today.' Her eyes shone. 'Not only for the instruction but for your friendship, for the meals, and the scarf, and the books, and . . .'

She gently shook her head and pursed her dry lips. 'Shh, shh, shh . . . what are friends for?'

My throat was tight with emotion.

Then she raised a crooked finger on her right hand that was resting by her side, and slowly beckoned to me. 'I want to tell you something,' she said. 'Lean a little closer.'

I did.

And her voice, now failing, said, 'Don't worry about me . . . I'm not afraid. I know where I'm going . . . and I'll be with Bill . . . and my three children.' Her eyes glistened. '. . . My time is near—'

Silence gripped me.

'—I'm seventy-eight . . . I've had a good life.' She closed her tired eyes.

A tide of emotion rose within me, but I held it back; I mustn't cry; it wouldn't be right; I must be strong, for her sake.

Barely above a whisper she continued, 'Now then . . . I want you to remember something . . .'

She beckoned me a little nearer and said some words which, as they left her lips, seemed to indelibly brand themselves for ever upon my mind, spiritual words that I would never forget:

'Think of all those who are suffering in the world, and . . . what the Power of the Spirit can do for them, through someone like you . . . Stay the way you are, Stephen – don't change . . . Always be humble . . . and serve God's children . . . who are in spiritual need.'

Her tired voice trailed away, and she wandered into a very deep sleep. I looked at her child-like face, closed my eyes for a moment and in my mind said 'Thank you' to God, for the privilege of knowing this woman.

'I'll see you again on Sunday,' I whispered, but I don't think she heard me.

The birds had stopped singing in the trees, and I rose quietly from my seat and leaned across the bed, and lightly kissed her goodbye on the forehead. Then I left the ward.

Heavy-hearted, and lost in a cloud of happy memories that Mrs Palmer and I had shared together, I wandered out of the big hospital and into a wall of bright hard sunshine that hurt my eyes. The day was bitterly cold, and so was the bus when I sat in it and thought of all the things I should have said to her, all the words that just wouldn't come to my lips while I'd sat by her bedside. But it was too late to speak them now, this time. Maybe next time. Yes, that was it. I'd tell her how much I cared for her, next Sunday when I visited again.

Then I clearly heard the voice of Mrs Palmer's spirit guide, Ahmed, say to me, 'That is the last time you'll see her alive in your world.' I immediately hoped he was wrong. But by the following Sunday, Mrs Palmer was dead.

The next time Mrs Palmer and I were together in the same room I was seated near the front pews in Morriston Crematorium, and her frail body was resting in such a small coffin beside a pulpit that was covered with perfumed flowers.

People filled all the seats around me; her life had touched so many; she'd been well loved, and she was going to be missed.

The service was delivered in a flat, monotone voice by a weathered old clergyman that I didn't recognize, and neither had Mrs Palmer known him. Throughout it all, as I sat and wondered why the vicar seemed so intent on propounding his doctrine instead of thanking God for the life of my friend, I don't think the full impact of losing Mrs Palmer had hit me. But later, when I stood outside in the fine cold rain and watched a vast and overflowing crowd of sad and tearful mourners file out of the crematorium, the loss became more apparent.

The mass of black-coated people that moved with one accord contained many Spiritualists, two of whom were the thoughtful elderly women who, at the Saturday Open Circle four years previously, had helped the frail old soldier home in a taxi on that freezing snowy night. Solemnly, they approached me, and with quiet sincerity one of them clutched my arm.

121

'Dear me, Stephen,' she said. 'What a sad occasion. What a very sad day this is . . . Whoever would have thought it?' Her lips quivered with emotion and she began to cry while her sister tried to comfort her. 'I thought the world of Mrs Palmer, you know. She helped me a great deal when I lost my husband, God love her . . . I can't take it all in. Flo Palmer . . . Dear, dear . . . the Spiritualist Movement has said goodbye to one of its best mediums.'

'Much more than that,' I replied, sadly. 'The world has lost a sincerely kind woman.'

While the two dear pensioners consoled each other I told myself to be strong, and I fought back my tears and remained silent. When they got into their car, still weeping, and I was standing alone, I turned my head away and the world around me blurred at the edges. But no teardrops fell; instead, my eyes fixed their gaze on the vague outline of some black, frost-bitten leaves that were desperately clinging to the branch of a nearby winter tree.

Before those leaves had fallen, Oxford Street Spiritualist Church had asked me to conduct Mrs Palmer's memorial service; and on its platform, when I faced a crowd of mourners, I wondered how many times I'd stood there in the past four years. Too many to recall. It was Mrs Palmer who'd arranged my first ever public service of mediumship, and I'd taken it here, in this church which she'd served with such sincere dedication, in this place of worship that she had so dearly loved.

Honoured to pay tribute to my tutor I gazed out at the gathering before addressing them. Every seat was taken, and people were standing in the aisles and at the back of the upper room. Some of these souls were the silent and faithful regulars, and others formed part of a crowd of strangers to whom Mrs Palmer had obviously brought comfort during her years of public service. Could the number of souls she'd touched, on both sides of life, ever be counted, I wondered. And I decided that the task would be impossible.

I looked at the mourners' faces and sadly noted that absent from this farewell tribute was the ungrateful Nettie – whom Mrs Palmer had often helped – and a few other of my tutor's 'fair-weather friends'. Her family were not in the church, either. But what was it Mrs Palmer had taught me, such a long time ago, when I'd started my apprenticeship? Her wisdom echoed down the years: *It's a lonely path, and people who can't see the wonders of Spirit like we can, don't understand us. And what they don't understand, they fear. And what people are afraid of – they try to hurt.*

Was Mrs Palmer herself in the church tonight? I didn't sense her presence, but then my mind was full of the service I was to take – yet I guessed she'd be with us, listening, watching.

The atmosphere was charged with emotion as I started my tribute.

'We are gathered here this evening, in this place that has been consecrated to serve others through the Power of Love, to remember an exceptional woman: a thoughtful woman who cared; one of God's children who did her best to help people. How the trumpets must have sounded in Heaven to welcome home Flo Palmer, who was such a faithful servant of the spirit.'

Some elderly ladies in the front row took handkerchiefs out of their handbags and dabbed at their eyes. Their tears touched me, but I controlled and steadied my voice; it wouldn't be right for me to weep, like the old man was doing at the back of the church.

'She'll be sadly missed. We'll miss her cheerful words of encouragement, her wisdom and leadership, and the shining example of her mediumship with which she comforted those in need. But most of all we shall miss her kindness.' I controlled the tears that were gathering in my throat; I stopped, paused, breathed a little deeper and told myself to be strong; then I said, 'Mrs Palmer was my friend.'

Several of the mourners were now weeping and I wanted to join them, but knew I shouldn't, so I swallowed the lump in my throat and continued in a shaky voice, 'Nevertheless, our loss—is God's gain.'

From the lectern I picked up a sheet of paper. 'In memory of our church President and colleague I'd like to read the words of a prayer that was spoken by my spirit guide, White Owl, and to dedicate it to Mrs Palmer's life and work, as a tribute from us and from her many friends in the spirit world.'

Then I took a deep breath and delivered White Owl's words of comfort:

O, Great White Spirit,
we pray for strength
for those who must continue
their spiritual evolution
after suffering the pain
of losing a loved one.

124

Divine Father and Mother,
we render to Thee our thanks
for freely pouring
Thy Spirit of Love
into all hearts that are heavy-laden
with sadness or despair;
and we are ever thankful
for the knowledge that
no-one is spiritually neglected
in times of distress,
and no-one walks alone.

From the foundation of the world,
every life has been firmly held
in the palm
of Thy Powerful Hand.

And Thy Mighty Will
is done on Earth,
as it is
in Heaven.

Yet, we ask that comfort and solace
may come to those who grieve,
and that the continuous blessing
of your guidance
may inspire those who mourn
to freely draw upon our strength
and our healing peace of mind.

We thank Thee, too, for the privilege
of welcoming home
into our Realms of Light

all travellers who have transcended
the slowness of the flesh
and inherited the quickness of the spirit.

And we pray
that the veil between the worlds
of Heaven and Earth
may be lifted,
so that when sadness strikes the heart of Man
and beclouds his mind with fear,
or fills his soul with tears,
he will be able to hear us say:

Blessed
are those who mourn,
for they shall be comforted.

I looked into the faces of the sad people in the crowded room and I was moved by the sound of their weeping; and a profound silence seemed to fill the atmosphere, during which I had a sudden realization:

Mrs Palmer's physical voice had now been silenced; and from that night onwards I would have to forge ahead under my own determination and try to develop my mediumship without the benefit of her wisdom and guidance.

The only voice that would be available to me now, would be 'the still, small voice of the spirit' which resounds deep within the soul. But could I receive it? Was my sensitivity developed enough? Would I be able to hear it clearly?

All around me in the church, people were dabbing their eyes with their handkerchiefs.

Then a huge sigh rose up from the depths of my being, bringing with it a very unnerving thought:

I was now on my own.

PART TWO
The God-Power Within

Behind the body
a mind vibrates . . .

Through the mind
a soul breathes . . .

Illuminating the soul
is the light of consciousness . . .

And within the light
is the Spirit of God . . .

10

A Voice in the Wilderness

The heat of the sun beat down in waves upon my bare back, and I kicked up the sand between my toes as I strolled along Swansea Bay, thinking of days gone by.

I felt the warmth of the low sea wall when I sat on it, then filled my lungs with ozone and listened to the hypnotic ebb and flow of the tides. A salt taste was in the air and on my lips; it had been a swelteringly hot summer, and now this lovely season was coming to an end.

On the beach there were children laughing and patting their sandcastles with red plastic spades. I smiled. It was a glorious day. I was twenty-five years old, lean and fit, an ordinary young man at the height of his strength, and yet . . . I wasn't quite the same as the other youths who were sunbathing on the beach, because I could see people who had 'died'; I could talk to them, and they to me.

Closing my eyes for a moment I listened to the swishing sound of the waves . . . and they seemed to wash away the scene of the seashore in my mind, and in its place there came a succession of powerful memories from my past . . .

I saw my mother's 'dead' body lying in her bed and

I witnessed again her spirit-return, which happened three months after her funeral, when she'd appeared to me standing in a blaze of golden light at the top of our staircase; then I 'heard' my father shouting his disbelief at me when I told him, his eyes flashing with anger. The pictures shifted and I viewed again my first faltering attempts at relaying spirit messages to the public; and lastly, there came the kind face of Mrs Palmer followed by the many meals she'd cooked for me, the gifts she'd given, and the secret knowledge and psychic instruction she'd shared with me in the hope of developing my mediumship. People like Mrs Palmer were one in a million . . .

A warm summer breeze caressed my skin and I began thinking about how everything in life moves in cycles, about how special people seem to powerfully impress their love upon us, about how quickly circumstances can change, as swiftly as a butterfly can alight on a succession of summer flowers. Nothing stays the same.

Touch and Go

> Everything touches
> and everything goes
> Everything ebbs
> and everything flows

People touch
and people go
But people love us
deeply so

And when two cleave
to one another
Nothing else matters
but their lover

Then babies come
and children cry
And adults live
and adults die

And as they go
we fill with woe
Yet still we rise
to love them so

For mem'ries glint
and gleam and stream
And flow to weave
a lover's dream

In mystic magic
wonderment
Before they came
and when they went

They stole our heartlights
clean away
But they touched our lives
They found the way

Their laughter came
and their laughter went
But their laughter moved us
heaven-sent

133

For everything ebbs
and everything flows
But nothing remains
it touches and goes

> And even when mem'ries
> flash the mind
> People still cry
> because they find

Some thoughts come
to stay and grow
To kiss the soul
and never go

Seagulls squawked in the brilliant sky, and I
opened my eyes as an olive-skinned man offered
me some of his suntan lotion. 'You'll burn in this
heat with so little on, mate,' he said.

We laughed, and I accepted the glob of thick cream
and watched him walk away with his three children
dancing behind him; and I thought to myself, 'Deep
down, people are kind. It just takes time to break
through their fears and accept that everyone has
problems of one sort or another to deal with.'

I was growing up: the lad was becoming a man.

The midday sun was so hot that I immediately
rubbed the cream on my body, then closing my eyes
I sent up a silent prayer to the Great Power. 'I've
searched high and low, but can't find another teacher
as wise as Mrs Palmer. There's no-one who can equal
her depth of wisdom and knowledge; so, I need your
help because I'd like to be guided properly,' I thought.

Gulls squawked beyond the sheet of yellow light that filtered through my eyelids. 'Mrs Palmer,' I whispered out loud, 'thank you for training me.'

The tinkling chimes of an ice-cream vendor made me open my eyes and I saw a crowd of excited children jumping around beside the colourful van. Lazily, I picked up my shoes and shirt, ambled slowly up the beach, crossed over the road, and headed towards the town.

As I walked home in the bright sunshine I made the decision to soldier on with my mediumship, albeit physically alone, and I hoped that God would send me all the guidance I would need.

In the months that followed I made other decisions, too: I set my mind firmly upon studying the paranormal and I began to read more extensively and to examine the teachings of respected writers on spirituality. I also continued dissecting the work of mediums in the churches: nothing escaped my critical eye and I used my findings to improve my skills of public presentation.

I also decided to sit in silent meditation each day for about an hour, during which I learned how to still my mind. 'A medium,' I remembered Mrs Palmer saying, 'must have tremendous mental discipline: a will-power of steel. If he wants to hear the spirit world more clearly, and to develop his sensitivity, a medium must learn to quieten his jumping thoughts; he must learn to be the master of his mind, and not its slave.'

So every day at home I sat alone in the silence that I loved – and thus began my many mystical out-of-the-body experiences.

My daily routine was invariably the same: I'd close the windows, draw the curtains and lock all the doors. (Dad didn't have a telephone, but if he *had* owned one I would have unhooked it because when the inner spirit leaves the physical frame and 'astral-projects' it's important not to subject the body to sudden noises which can cause it harm. Mrs Palmer had once told me that a projectionist she'd known had haemorrhaged with shock when boys outside her house had thrown building bricks onto the tin roof above the medium's head, just when her spirit was leaving her body; so I took all the necessary precautions.)

Sitting comfortably in my father's armchair next to the fire, I relaxed and offered up a prayer for guidance and protection, then stilled my body and my mind. On one memorable occasion, after I'd sat for a long time in the shadowy room with my eyes closed, suddenly my spirit body projected out – and on this spirit-walk I saw something remarkable:

On the grassy hillock at the foot of which I stood, there appeared a rough-hewn wooden cross about fifteen feet high. As I gazed at the cross, a semi-naked man materialized upon it: he was bruised and thin, and tired and dying. Although I knew instinctively that this man was not Jesus of Nazareth, but another unfortunate victim of Roman judgement who was being punished for daring to speak about the Truth as he saw it, I was fascinated by the vision.

Then I became aware of another form standing next to me. When I turned my head I beheld, face to face, the shining features of a man whom I can only describe as a radiant Being of Light who was dressed in loose-flowing robes. Awestruck by the pure spiritual atmosphere emanating from this Wise One, I could scarcely breathe.

He extended a graceful arm towards the crucified figure suspended upon the cross. I looked at the dying man and saw his tired head lower itself until his chin rested upon his breast – and then he gave up his spirit.

Then his flesh shimmered, withered and shrank, and it fell like dust until all that was left upon the cross was a white-parched skeleton; then this, too, turned into powder and it drifted onto the hillock at the foot of the tree. Then the cross faded from sight.

These bright symbolic images held me in their powerful grip.

Then, without a word being spoken, I 'heard' the thought-voice of the Being of Light, who now stood right in front of me, say, 'They did this to the prophets of old who laid down their lives for the Truth that would set men free. Are you willing to dedicate your life to this service?'

I reached out my trembling hand to meet his own and our palms touched, and I said, 'Yes . . . I am willing.'

And upon the instant, I was wide awake again and sitting back in my father's armchair in the darkened room on earth; but my right arm was extended before me to its full length, and was clutching at the empty air . . . and I realized that a new stage in my spiritual life had been reached.

Following this unforgettable experience, the demand for my mediumship throughout the South Wales Spiritualist Movement dramatically increased and I was asked to travel widely throughout the region.

Eager church Secretaries started 'ticketing' my meetings and they were well attended. 'You're new, you're young, and you're handsome!' was how one wily old bird explained my sudden popularity. 'But what about my mediumship?' I asked. 'Oh, that'll improve, dear – eventually!' she quipped; then she booked me again!

Many churches made quite a lot of money for their funds through the ticket sales of my 'mid-week demonstrations' which enabled them to repair their buildings or install central-heating pipes and suchlike; and I also had my own image revamped, it seemed, when to many of the old ducks I became the platform's 'darling boy'.

Naturally I felt stressed: I was a healthy young man and these extra responsibilities devoured all my spare time; worst of all, they prevented me from enjoying the freedom to come and go as I liked, the joy of personal relationships, and the social activities of my life, all of which flew right out of the window.

There were further problems at home, too, with my aggressive Dad: we'd always been at loggerheads but now he treated me like a simpleton because of his friends' attitudes.

'My mates are laughing at me because of you, boy! You were advertised in the paper as a medium!' he bellowed. 'I'm a laughing-stock. I've told you before, when you're dead – you're *finished*. After that, it's just the worms.'

He softened when I didn't respond. 'What's the matter with you, boy? Why don't you pull yourself together and get a better job than working in that stupid department store? There's no money in that, and it's woman's work. And quit that church nonsense. Get married and settle down and have kids like everybody else.'

My reply was delivered quietly. 'We're all individuals, Dad – and this is me.'

But his temper flared again. 'I'm telling you for the last time: forget this stupid rubbish about life after death!'

I answered him with a penetratingly calm stare, then I stomped out of the house to clear my head in the midnight air.

Wrapped in the cold moonlight I strolled along the deserted streets. It was a cloudless night, and in the distance a dog barked as if it wanted to be released from a locked shed.

Deep in thought I leaned against a garden wall. How much longer could I cope with living in the stifling shadow of my father's petty-mindedness? My patience with him had now worn paper-thin.

Other worries surfaced, too – niggling ones about my spiritual work. I was still a young medium, still frustrated because my clairvoyance wasn't as accurate as I would have liked. But what was it Mrs Palmer had said? 'You can't buy experience: it has to be earned.' Yes, she was right; we mature through facing our challenges and tackling them.

The cold night air chilled my bones and made me shiver uncontrollably. What on earth was I doing sitting on a stranger's garden wall in the early hours of the morning? Good God, I must be mad. Then I made an important decision.

I must leave home. I must get away from my father.

My name had recently come to the top of the council housing list after a two-year wait; so tomorrow I would set the official wheels in motion to try to get myself a flat – which I did. Then I waited . . .

Meanwhile, every working day at my job in a department store bored me to distraction. I was in my mid-twenties. I was restless. My feet were itchy. I needed a change. And that's why I obeyed the inspiration that I'd battled with for several months: the spirit people had kept asking me to become a semi-professional medium, when all I'd wanted was to be left alone.

Yet the Other Side had been adamant: if I was to help more people I must buck up my ideas and remove my reservations; and to this end they reminded me that 'The labourer is worthy of his hire.'

This decision was an agonizing one to make because I'd never wanted to earn money from my spiritual work: guidance is freely received, and I believed it should be freely given to others; in the past, I hadn't even claimed travelling expenses from many of the churches I'd served.

However, in the end the Other Side won – and I dutifully wrote to some thirty or so Welsh Spiritualist churches requesting the meagre sum of £2 per meeting, which would supplement my very low part-time wages at the department store, and present me with more opportunities to serve as a medium. Then I posted them, and waited . . .

Then came the shock.

The Spiritualists completely misjudged my motivation, and they callously cast me out. They refused to pay – and many of them shut their doors in my face.

I was deeply hurt, especially when I thought of the years of service I'd given them without any thought of personal reward, and a sudden bitterness welled up inside me because I couldn't understand why they'd been so unkind.

My banishment, of course, gave gossips the opportunity to waggle their tongues, and the malicious Nettie used hers until it was numb through defaming my character.

Hurt beyond words, I made another sudden decision – I completely shunned the Spiritualist Movement and cancelled all my public engagements.

But in one of my daily meditations White Owl's voice told me, 'You leave a boy – you return a man, with power and understanding.' Cold comfort indeed, for in those days I knew what it was to be a voice in the wilderness, a prophet without honour in his own country.

Many times I walked alone up onto a mountaintop to pray, and I wondered if my guide's prediction would be fulfilled; but only time would tell.

Meanwhile I happily erased from my mind the idea of semi-professional mediumship: 'And good riddance!' I thought.

But how I longed to find a place where I would feel spiritually 'at home'. I even day-dreamed of opening up my own church, where the public could receive not only survival evidence, comfort and hope, but also the education about all things psychic and mediumistic that I felt was woefully lacking in some of the churches at that time.

If I'd had the money I would have opened up a Centre for Psychic Awareness. But then, if I'd had any money at all I'd never have asked the churches for the paltry £2 service fee, and they wouldn't have ostracized me; and so all hope of setting up my own psychic establishment floated away down the Swanee River.

But at least one of my wishes was suddenly granted when I made a lightning-fast move out of Dad's house and into a scruffy council flat that was offered to me. I didn't have so much as a stick of furniture, let alone a teaspoon to my name – but I was happy. I was alone at last, and overcome by the joy of it. No nagging, no arguing, just peace and quiet and my own sacred space – and I loved it.

Dad thought I'd be back with him in a week, but he was so wrong.

Even when my part-time job ended and I tried (but failed) to exist on government hand-outs, which were then called 'Social Security', I soldiered on and kept cheerful, despite the fact that I was stony-broke and those first few months in my flat were the toughest in my life.

Money was scarce, but two friends were especially kind to me: Jeff Rees Jones, a tall fair-haired lad who was twenty, and his mother, Marion, both of whom I'd met a few years previously at a local Spiritualist church. Thoughtful Marion often sent me big parcels of food. 'Here you are, love,' she'd say. 'I know it isn't easy to build a home for yourself.'

Poverty certainly pinched, but I survived the bruises.

Never one to be beaten by a crisis I smiled through it all and applied my mind to learning new skills. I studied counselling methods and the healing of psychological disorders with two more new friends, the Revd and Mrs Jewsbury, who also asked me to sing at their Christmas concert in the Unitarian Church; I immediately agreed (because the proceeds were to be presented to old-age pensioners in the parish, to help them meet their winter heating bills) and I gave a spirited rendition of *Raindrops Keep Fallin' On My Head*!

Reverend Jewsbury also invited me to serve his newly formed Psychic Research Society by taking 'An Evening of Clairvoyance'. 'Delighted,' I said, and the Unitarian Church hall was packed. But in the front row sat the cadaverous Nettie who glowered at me from under her thick brows, and loudly tut-tutted her disapproval throughout the meeting. It wasn't the lack of precision in my mediumship that made her behave so badly: she was just nasty. And for weeks afterwards she delighted in grumping to every Spiritualist she met: 'It was disgusting! That disgraceful young whippersnapper didn't even start with a prayer!'

She was wrong: I'd sat in the vestry for fifteen minutes before taking the platform thinking, 'Dear God, please let me meet the needs of these people.'

The seasons rolled around, and after a long and drawn out eighteen months' absence from Spiritualist church platforms, I still couldn't figure out why I'd been so cruelly ostracized; but I discovered the reason when an old lady who was a lifelong true Spiritualist from Oxford Street Church stopped me for a natter one day on the street.

'You're a young worker, dear. You're intelligent, and you're a good-looker. The public like you, and you get more "Yeses" than some of the old mediums do. They're jealous.'

So that was it.

Well, if that's why they'd been so unkind to me – I'd soon show them! This woman had made me realize there was still a tremendous demand for my kind of spiritual work, so I bit back my annoyance, and in a flash of a second my mind was firmly made up: with or without the support of the Spiritualist Movement – I was going to serve.

As fast as I could, I ran home to my flat and with characteristic determination I sat down and planned my first self-styled 'Evening of Clairvoyance', which would accomplish two objectives: firstly, it would bring the voice of the spirit world through me to the people; and secondly, its ticket sales would aid worthy charitable causes such as the National Society for the Prevention of Cruelty to Children, the Royal Society for the Prevention of Cruelty to Animals, and the People's Dispensary for Sick Animals.

I phoned the local Quaker Hall and hired it (and bang went my electricity-bill money!), designed sheets of hand-written tickets and posters, then I photocopied them and walked the town and stuck them up in as many shops as would have them. I asked Jeff Rees Jones and his lovely mum, Marion, to help at the meeting and they willingly agreed: Jeff would be a steward on the door and Marion would sell the tickets directly from her home. I was delighted, and within a week the meeting had sold out.

But Marion's phone didn't stop ringing: the public wanted more seats! 'Over a hundred people will have to cram into the hall, and the others'll have to fight for it,' said Marion, beaming.

I felt fine and dandy until the evening before the 'big' meeting took place, when I got the jitters and asked White Owl: 'Whatever you do, please don't let me down tomorrow!' Then I added, cheekily, 'Can you bring us some unusual evidence? The hall will be packed.'

And the following evening, it was. With just half an hour to go before the start I arrived and pushed my way through crowds of people without tickets, who were determined to get in.

When somebody grabbed my collar and yanked me through a gap in the blocked doorway I felt as if I was being dragged through a hedge backwards.

'Come in! Quick!' shouted the dark-haired Marion, my rescuer. 'It's the nearest thing to bedlam I've ever seen! I'm not opening those doors until the last minute. There'll be a stampede. It'll be like the Jackpot Night at the Bingo!'

I laughed.

'Right!' she boomed, handing me a mug of fragrant tea from a thermos flask, 'How do you fancy a giggle, Stephen?'

'What do you mean?'

'Well,' she said mischievously, 'two uppity Spiritualist Church Secretaries just turned up

145

without tickets and demanded to get in, if you please!'

'You're joking!'

'Nope. But I'm afraid I had to turn them away.' She winked and we smiled.

'Right!' she boomed again. 'Up-an-at-'em!' And she flung open the doors just as I disappeared into an ante-room, to get changed.

A surging mass of bodies barged in like a January Sales crowd, and they grabbed their seats; others stood, and some were politely turned away.

Then Marion poked her head around the ante-room door and announced, 'We've already made over a hundred pounds for the charities – but the natives are getting restless. It's nearly 7.30. When are you going to start?'

'Has the chairlady, and her friends from the valleys, arrived yet?'

'No. Kitty and the coach must be stuck somewhere. But I can't keep their seats much longer – the public are hammering on the doors wanting to know why they can't get in when they can see twenty empty seats through the windows.'

'Draw the curtains!' I exclaimed. 'Can't your Jeff deal with them?'

'He's running up and down the street keeping an eye out for Kitty and the bus.'

I looked heavenwards, and Marion braved the throng to shut the drapes and sell more raffle tickets for the charities.

I'd met the middle-aged Kitty, our 'late' chairlady, years previously when Mrs Palmer had taken me to a church in the Welsh valleys. I banged on a

146

window and mimed to Jeff to hold up the meeting for another ten minutes – which he did – then the fur-coated Kitty and her coach-party suddenly exploded through the doors like Christmas crackers.

'Stephen, my darling!' she gushed enthusiastically while she warmly embraced me. 'I'm moithered to death! The bus conked out, but we've arrived! Where's the platform?'

Two shakes of her powder-puff later, as the ample Kitty made a dignified entrance to the hall (with me in tow), she whispered, 'You'll be magnificent, my dear' – and we were off!

Everyone smiled when the well-endowed Kitty proclaimed to one and all: 'There is no heaven *Up There!*' – and her bejewelled forefinger swept upwards and pointed to the ceiling. Then she lowered her voice in emphatic contrast, 'And there is no hell *Down There!*' – and she aimed an outspread hand at the scuffed parquet flooring. 'Heaven and hell,' said she, opening her arms out wide, 'are purely *states of mind!* And so is the spirit world.'

She got a good clap because the audience loved it.

Then it was my turn, and surprisingly enough the messages flowed well, until one of them fell to a grumpy local medium who was in her late sixties; no-one liked her and she'd been renowned on the circuits for years for being 'a right old misery-guts'.

My heart sank when she refused to accept any advice from her frustrated 'hubby' on the Other Side. To each of his helpful suggestions she snidely retorted, 'Oh, *does* he now?' Or 'Never in a pig's eye!' Or 'Not in *this* lifetime I won't!'

For several minutes I battled valiantly on her

spirit husband's behalf until I felt we'd both been bludgeoned enough, then I cut short the message and mentally said to him, 'Don't waste your time, mate: you're much better off where you are.'

I was then astonished to hear from the spirit people that the next message was for 'Dorothy from Oz'—a huge laugh burst through the crowd when the link was accepted by an Australian Dorothy who was holidaying in Wales!

But the most peculiar link of the night came from a pernickety spirit-aunt, whom I'd clairvoyantly seen standing behind her niece in the audience. The old spirit lady wore a large-brimmed blue picture-hat, which identified her.

'I feel she was very ill before she died,' I added.

'Well, that *sounds* like my auntie,' confirmed the niece.

'And does her message about "keeping the peace at home" make any sense?'

'Oh yes, but there's one *big* problem here.' All eyes turned on my recipient. 'My elderly aunt, whom you've perfectly described, was indeed ill for a while . . . but she certainly isn't dead – *she's still alive!*'

My heart hit the floor like a bag of hammers.

All I could do was apologize. 'I'm terribly sorry for "burying her off",' I said rather sheepishly. 'But I did see her standing with you.' Then an idea occurred to me. 'May I make a suggestion?'

'Of course. I'd like this explained.'

'Could you ask your auntie what she was doing at this precise time?' The clock was consulted. 'Could you find out if you were in her thoughts tonight?'

'Certainly,' she replied firmly.

Some later research proved enlightening, for the sickly aunt had been *fast asleep* when I'd seen her standing behind her niece. I therefore concluded that the old dear had chatted away to me in her projected, out-of-the-body spirit form!

This bizarre experience reminded me that I was still serving my psychic apprenticeship.

Sensible Kitty, who was herself an experienced medium, gushed to me after my first self-organized meeting, 'You were great tonight, my darling! You know, you should set up your own church; you've got such a lot to give to the people.'

'It occurred to me, once,' I said, remembering my day-dream.

'But in the meantime, my darling,' she enthused, 'you should write a book! In fact, I think you will.' Her dark brown eyes glazed over. 'Yes, I can see it all in front of me . . . You'll stand before thousands of people to bring them the good news of life after death.'

I waited for more, but Kitty suddenly broke off her clairvoyance and took a swig of hot tea, then casually added, 'You'll be famous one day.'

Since childhood I'd always known I'd be renowned for something. Could this be it, I wondered. 'Meanwhile, Kitty' – and I sighed heavily – 'there's still a tremendous amount for me to learn.'

And not just about mediumship, either – for quite a few other surprises regarding human nature lay in store for me, just around the corner.

11

Destiny

When I was asked to serve churches outside South
Wales I groaned because I loathe travelling; I'd
never been a sight-seer, and I was a real home-bird.
But the spirit people nagged me to accept these
invitations to gain experience, and I did gain it –
in more ways than one.

One church booked me to demonstrate at their
town hall and I was accommodated by a very 'arty'
middle-aged bachelor who met me at the railway
station, swiftly bundled me into his car, then whisked
me away to his plush home.

No sooner had we arrived than he waltzed me
enthusiastically through the hall to the staircase.
'To your room!' he declared. '*Allez-oop!*' I smiled
weakly, and clumped up the stairs after him in
silence. 'Those bags look really heavy, but I'm
sure you're strong enough to manage them,' he
commented over his shoulder.

When we reached the top landing he flung open
a door with a '*Voilà*', and I was stunned by the
opulence of a red-velvety boudoir. In its centre stood
a king-size brass four-poster bed with a pink silk
duvet thrown across it.

My host revealed a mouth full of teeth and grinned.
'It's big, isn't it?'

'Yes, it is,' I replied, thinking, 'Much too big for one, in fact.'

'*This*!' he exclaimed with a flourish of his hand, 'is *my* bed!' I stared unblinking into the room. 'But you can sleep in it tonight, sir.'

He must have seen my astonishment because he added quickly, 'I'll be in the spare room across the landing, of course . . . should you need me for anything.'

I plonked down my heavy suitcases as he swept towards the marble wardrobe doors. He flung them back and there in front of me were— rows of women's clothes.

My jaw dropped.

Long sparkly dresses and frocks of all colours hung from the rails: there were ostrich feathers and flouncy frills in abundance, and hundreds of sequins glinted in the sunlight. He pushed several aside and made some room.

'You can hang your suit in here,' he said. 'Oh, I know what you're thinking! Well, don't look so worried: I'm not a transvestite. I play the part of the Dame in the church pantomime every year.'

'Oh, I see,' I said with a weak smile.

Later that evening my town hall meeting went fine, and when we got back I was so tired that I went straight to bed. Before undressing I noticed there was no lock on the door so I rammed a hard-backed Regency chair under the doorknob. But I still didn't get a wink of sleep all night because a loose central heating pipe kept knocking against the skirting-boards and I'd convinced myself it was the sound of Widow Twankey's shoes clomping along the landing.

Oh, what it is to be cursed with a vivid imagination!

Since childhood the powers of my mind have always amazed me, but never more so than on the important occasions when they've pushed themselves forward to totally change the course of my life – as they were about to do again.

As the months passed by I became aware that major turning-points were approaching, and – almost imperceptibly at first – I sensed strange spiritual impulses building up within me. Stephen O'Brien, the young physical man, was happy to be left well alone to trundle through his life, encountering as little hassle as possible; but Stephen O'Brien, the older soul that was within the man, had quite different ideas altogether: it was intent on following a programmed spiritual blueprint.

I was positive that discarnate intelligences were directing me to step into a much brighter public spotlight, and I was reluctant to do so; but 'Important decisions must be made,' these inner voices seemed to say, 'and you must make them – now.'

One of these inspired directions was that I should work at the SAGB, the Spiritualist Association of Great Britain, in London. I knew the Association required seven work-references from churches that the applicant had served, after which it was prepared to offer an audition.

An audition? 'Dear God,' I thought, 'please spare me that.'

But He didn't.

The references were easily obtained, and on the London train I realized two things: Mrs Palmer's prediction about my working at the SAGB was now being fulfilled; and the challenge of this venture had fired in me my natural determination to succeed.

For moral support I was accompanied by two friends, Jeff and John, and we had an amusing encounter with the then largely unknown medium, Doris Stokes. We were sitting in the refreshment area, opposite Doris, when she shouted across to John, 'Don't worry, lovey, we were all nervous when we had our auditions. Good luck! You'll get through it OK!'

John was gobsmacked. 'It isn't me, missus! It's *him*!' he said, pointing at me, then adding to us, 'I thought she was supposed to be psychic!'

Ten minutes later I took the platform in the Sir Oliver Lodge Hall and stood before forty people. My chairperson, Mr Jolly (who lived up to his delightful name), whispered, 'They've paid for a solid of hour of clairvoyance. Now, young man, I expect we're nervous and want to get it over as quickly as possible.'

'No,' I said, 'I feel fine.' And I got off to a good start by re-uniting an elderly man in the hall with his 'dead' housekeeper, placing the link by asking to speak to, 'A chimney sweep.'

An old man waved his hand.

'Do you understand an Uncle Bert who kept chickens – in Merthyr Tydfil?'

'Yes, boyo.'

The spirit people had found me a Welshman in the crowd!

'Sir, he mentions something about an illness. Wait a second and I'll try to hear it more clearly . . . Ah, yes

. . . He talks about "Gangrene in Blod's foot", which took her across to the Other Side.'

'I follow you, boyo.'

'And there's someone else with me, too. I get the name Daisy.'

The man's face brightened as though a spotlight had been thrown upon it. 'Thank you, *very* much,' he said, beaming with happiness. 'Daisy was my devoted companion and housekeeper.'

'Oh, good . . . but I can't get much from her – it's difficult to make out her accent.'

'That's because she's Italian.' The audience smiled at the thought of an Italian housekeeper being named 'Daisy', while I asked the spirit world to translate her speech for me, which they did.

Daisy told me she was 'not rich on earth', and reminded her gentleman that when she'd died he had placed two pennies over her eyes to keep them shut. In broken English she said, 'When I comes Over, I have twopence to spend for me!'

Afterwards Mr Jolly slapped me on the back. 'Our Council members were hidden in the audience. Congratulations, you've passed with flying colours.'

Strangely enough, I wasn't overjoyed; I just accepted it, but I worked at the SAGB for only seven days because I didn't like it at all. I took private sittings galore and realized that under this kind of intensive pressure no medium could produce his best work.

But because my name was already known in the Spiritualist Movement I agreed with Tom Johanson, the Association's Secretary, to give some 'Guest Demonstrations' of mediumship whenever I could get to London; and although I became one of the SAGB's highest-paid guests, I never made a brass farthing. I received £20 per appearance but my rail fare was £23! Furthermore, the dear old Social Security (known locally as the SS) docked this pay from my weekly allowance!

It was on one of my visits to the Association that I first saw the Spiritualists' National Union President, Mr Gordon Higginson, who was then in his sixties. When Mr Higginson entered the medium's room everyone turned to face him.

While drinking a cup of wishy-washy coffee I watched 'the old ducks' (as some of the female staff were affectionately known) greet a stockily built white-haired man of average height, dressed in a dark suit; but his most striking characteristic was undoubtedly his plummy English accent that turned 'Hello' into 'Hellair', as he shook each medium's hand.

The sensitives seemed dumbstruck by his famed reputation as a veteran medium in the Spiritualist Movement, and by his presence.

'Hellair,' and one of the old girls actually bobbed a curtsy!

The hand-shaking and cheek-pecking went on, and on. 'Hellair . . . hellair . . .'

After he'd left the building I realized that another spirit world prediction had been fulfilled: 'You will meet this man,' they'd said long ago, and I had.

That night in the shabby sleeping-quarters at the rear of the SAGB I was disturbed by some rustling sounds in the dark bedroom. Upon opening my eyes I was astonished to see a small black girl with one of her hands rifling about in my lunch bag on the table. She was after my Golden Delicious apple!

'Oi!' I called out. 'Leave it alone, missy! That's my dinner, if you don't mind.'

She instantly vanished with a giggle – and my diet was saved.

When I next saw Kitty, my fur-coated friend back in Wales, I told her about this incident and she gushed, 'Oh yes! That's one of Gordon Higginson's spirit guides. She gets everywhere, my darling. After Gordon's paid a visit she's often seen poking about in people's drawers!'

We had a good laugh, and then Kitty revealed a snippet of information that Mr Higginson, who'd been a good friend of hers for twenty-five years, had confided in her. 'Stephen, don't get big-headed, and keep this under your hat. Gordon told me you'll go right to the top as a medium.'

Innocently I asked, 'And where's "The Top", Kitty?'

She smiled good-heartedly. 'I know what you mean, my darling – there's no such place. But he knows you'll make your mark. Take things easy and don't push yourself forward, he said. Oh, and Stephen?'

'Yes?'

'Be a sensible lad – and don't cross him,' Kitty winked and I knew what she meant.

Soon afterwards it was Kitty herself who unwittingly gave me a push forward when she recommended my services to the Bookings Secretary of Mr Higginson's church in Longton, Staffordshire, and this turned out to be another turning-point in my life, another step towards my mediumship gaining country-wide recognition within the Spiritualist Movement.

Longton posted me my rail fare, and my services seemed well received. Afterwards Mr Higginson took tea with me and asked, 'Would you like to come to Stansted Hall?' This was the home of the Arthur Findlay College of Psychic Studies, a most respected teaching establishment of which Mr Higginson was the Principal. 'Would you like that?'

'Yes, but I couldn't afford the fees,' I said, 'I'm on Social Security.'

'No, I meant to *work* there as a member of the teaching staff.'

I thanked him and accepted, not knowing that another milestone had been reached in my calling as a medium.

Stansted Hall was a beautiful Jacobean mansion in Essex, set in fifteen acres of gorgeous grounds, and there I learned a great deal about the craft of mediumship by mixing with reputable sensitives who were far more experienced than me; and for this I was very grateful.

I gave private sittings and public services, and was also called upon to lecture on paranormal topics – a new challenge for me, which I met with enthusiasm: I'd been well trained by Mrs Palmer and had gained much experience and knowledge through my church work, so I found the job both enjoyable and challenging, even if a little nerve-racking at first.

'You're a natural teacher,' one seasoned tutor confided in me. 'You don't waste time by waffling on about your personal experiences, you communicate the main learning points in a precise and interesting way. Keep up the good work!'

At Stansted people told me that Mr Higginson's mediumship must have impressed and comforted many thousands of people during his many years of service to the spirit world, and that he was a well-known and charismatic personality within Spiritualism. His psychic abilities undoubtedly made people think, for as well as being a popular travelling medium, an ordained Minister of the Spiritualists' National Union, and its national President, he also conducted trance-mediumship seances where it was claimed that the very rare gift of the materialization of spirit people occurred in his presence, though I never personally witnessed these aspects of his work.

But my psychic senses buzzed when they registered the marked air of authority that Mr Higginson carried about him, and they told me that when he made decisions, he expected them to be accepted and not questioned, that when he gave orders, he expected them to be obeyed.

However, I absorbed as much knowledge as I could from his informative lectures on 'How to Master your Mediumship', and I found his clairvoyance impressive. At a workshop held one morning in the sunlit library he astonished a woman by giving the christian name of her only daughter, purely through his powers of telepathy.

'Now let me see . . .' he said in plummy English tones, as he stood beside her chair, placed a hand on her nervous shoulder, and moved his eyes from side to side as though he were searching the space above her head for details, 'yes . . . your daughter's name is quite short. It has . . . four letters in it. I'm perfectly correct, aren't I?'

She gasped. 'Yes.'

'Of course I am. I can't be wrong because I'm the best there is!' he quipped, and the students laughed. 'And, ahem . . . Ah, now I have it! She's called Dawn – and she lives in San Diego.' (But he pronounced it 'Sahn Dee-ah-goh').

The northern woman beamed like a lighthouse. 'Ee by 'eck! He's spot-on!' And the audience applauded.

Then it was my turn. When I singled out a woman near the back of the room my psychic impressions seemed rather silly to me, but they startled her.

'Suspended about nine inches above your head I can see a string of bright glass beads,' I reported. 'They're crystal beads, I think.'

The woman's mouth dropped open. 'But that's my surname!' she exclaimed. 'I am Miss Crystal!' The students clapped again and Mr Higginson gave a broad smile, but it didn't seem to touch his eyes.

Later that day, when everyone had assembled in the Hall's luxurious green-and-cream-coloured lounge, Mr Higginson organized the next teaching sessions and instructed me to take into the Sanctuary a group of twelve students, most of whom were in their middle years or elderly.

'Tell them what psychic abilities they possess,' he said, 'and assess their mediumistic potential.'

Embarrassment swept through me. 'Oh . . . I . . . I don't think I can do that,' I replied politely, my cheeks flushing red.

An icy silence gripped the air. People's backs

stiffened. Then nobody moved. Evidently the Principal's commands should never be questioned.

Mr Higginson paused, turned his head towards me and smiled widely. 'But I think you *can* do it,' he said. Then he stared directly into my eyes.

My ingenuous reply was gentle but immediate. 'But I've never done that before, because I believe we all have psychic potential within us and people should choose their own path.'

No time lapsed between this statement and the Principal's reply. 'I'm sure you'll be all right.'

Then Eric Hatton, the Vice-President of the SNU, piped up and cracked the ice. 'I'll sit in with you to help you, Stephen,' he said kindly; and this broke the tension of what some might have thought of as a clash of wills. But that had most certainly not been my intention, I'd simply spoken the truth.

I thanked Eric, but instinctively knew Mr Higginson had made a mental note that young Stephen O'Brien possessed a mind of his own – and he wasn't afraid of using it.

That first week at the College was very enjoyable and lots of students expressed the hope that I'd return next year. 'Great!' I replied. 'You're on!'

I'd learned a lot at Stansted and I liked the spiritual atmosphere of all of its rooms, bar one – the Blue Room where the mediums congregated, because it was filled with the gossip about the students and my fellow teachers. On the rare occasions that I'd sat there at teatimes, I'd noticed that people's real spiritual colours had been flown.

So I'd chosen the company of my professional colleagues very carefully; but one of these, who was a quite famous and gentle Spiritualist medium, astonished me with her frankness when she said something into my ear, on our last morning as I hugged her goodbye. Though her voice contained no malice or crude undertones in it, she whispered quietly but pointedly, 'Don't forget, people can be bastards.'

I immediately released my hold and stared into her eyes. What on earth did she mean? Why had she said that? Could she, perhaps, have tried to prepare a naïve young man to face the cynical world ahead of him? Or had these phrases been uttered without her knowledge? After all, she was a medium and this could have been a warning.

Too shocked to ask what she meant I said goodbye and left, but later realized that during my many absences from the Blue Room the mediums had discussed me and my work.

But I shrugged off these thoughts and told no-one of them when I returned to Wales. Even when I visited my father and he asked how things were going I gave him the simple answer he wanted: 'OK,' I said, but added, 'Why don't you come to my flat one night, Dad, and I'll cook you a meal? Don't pull a face. You've never set foot inside it yet. Come down.'

The old man shifted awkwardly in his armchair by the gas fire. 'I'm a poor visitor, boy,' his deep voice growled. 'No, I can't be bothered.'

After all those years he still called me 'boy'. What was the use of trying to reach him? I'd often hoped he and I could relate as a father and son should, but I was fighting a losing battle. I was certainly no angel but I'd offered my hand in friendship and felt as if it had been bitten off. I closed the door and decided to walk home through the sunlit Waun Wen Park, to cheer myself up.

Amongst the calming sound of leaves rustling in the big trees all around me I sat on a grassy bank and listened to the birds singing, and suddenly memories of Mrs Palmer floated into my mind, and my train of thought changed. For some strange reason I recalled that she hadn't believed in coincidences; and neither had I. And I still didn't, especially when I reflected on what had happened to me since her death: it seemed that each important event had been linked to the one preceding it and to the one following it; and that every memorable episode was like a thread that had been woven into a pattern, a plan.

Fate, I decided, had certainly played its part in my existence; it seemed to me that so many people had been manoeuvred by some Unseen Power into the right places, at just the right times, so that important connections could be made.

And Destiny hadn't finished with me yet, for she was about to engineer a remarkable sequence of events – five in all – and the first came within a matter of weeks, when I was once more warmly embraced by the Welsh Spiritualists and I became a well-known personality in the national Spiritualist Movement more or less overnight after *Psychic News* articles had acclaimed my mediumship. White Owl's prediction materialized: 'You leave a boy,' he had said, 'but you return a man – with power and understanding.'

I had certainly matured.

The second working of destiny followed close

behind when I befriended a very intelligent lady called Dell Round whom I met at Oxford Street, Mrs Palmer's old church. The church itself had changed in the few years since Mrs Palmer's death: it had disaffiliated from the Spiritualists' National Union and had passed into other hands, and to my mind it was not the same as when Flo Palmer and the Union had run it – which was why I rarely went there now. New brooms sweep clean, and all that.

And one of the 'new brooms' that had gained a foothold on the committee was, in fact, not a new brush at all but an old besom – the delightful Nettie!

Nettie had invited Mrs Dell Round to run the Saturday Open Circle where I met Dell and befriended her straightaway. Fair-haired Dell, a hospital matron in her early forties who was slim and bespectacled, took an instant liking to my mediumship, and over the next few months she and I worked very hard to re-establish the popularity of the Open Circle. We introduced lively question-and-answer sessions after the meetings, which were welcomed by a public that was thirsting for knowledge.

It was no surprise that the Circle attendances suddenly swelled, and that the glowering Nettie became insanely jealous of our success.

Fate's third stroke came on a frosty night when Nettie, who was bristling with anger, barged up the church stairs after an Open Circle and stood defiantly in the doorway, hands on hips, eyes glittering black. Her sharp vision took in all the people. Yes – she had an audience – and she started yelling like a virago.

'Now, *get out of this church – all of you! At once!*'
Everyone was stunned. 'I've heard that people have
been seen talking in this church until after midnight
on some Saturdays! And I won't have it! Everyone
out – this minute!'

Dell stood up. 'Calm down now; we've only
been holding discussion classes and sharing our
knowledge.'

Then a disabled man stepped forward and
challenged the white-faced Nettie with, 'Now, hang
on a minute, missis. You're not the entire committee,
so you don't have the right to throw us out.'

Nettie swung around to face him, her eyes bulging
in their sockets and her bosom heaving so much that
I thought the buttons on her black mackintosh were
going to pop right off into the man's face. Her voice
reached screaming pitch. '*Get out of this church*,
before I *kick* you down the stairs, you horrible little
man!'

He shouted back, 'I'll go, missis – but you can
jump in the bloody dock!' Then he stomped down the
stairs.

I thought to myself, 'My God, Mrs Palmer would
turn in her grave if she could see this now'; it was
such an horrendous scene that none of us knew
what to do next, except Nettie, who swept around
the room with her hands flapping before her like a
demented black bat and ushered the startled and
confused people towards the exit:

'Out! *Out!* Everyone of you – right *now*! I'm going
to lock these doors – and that's the end of it. Dell! *Give
me the church keys!*' This imperious command was

accompanied by an outstretched arm and a ferocious stare.

As the harassed public left, Nettie snatched the keys from Dell. 'There'll be no more nonsense in here!' – then she locked the doors and stalked off home, clutching at her banging headache – and little wonder.

Outside in the snowy street both Dell and I apologized profusely to the departing public.

'God, that was awful,' I said.

'I feel sorry for Tom and Roy, and Sally,' said Dell. 'The poor souls are mentally handicapped and they only come along each week because it's somewhere warm and friendly to sit, where they can have a hot cup of tea and some spiritual healing.'

I felt sick inside.

The snow began falling harder and the twelve of us that were left stranded on the pavement started to shiver; so when Fate inspired one of the people to pipe up and suggest we should all go to her home and hold a private Saturday circle there, we immediately accepted her kind invitation – and the fourth thread in the pattern wove itself into place.

We bundled into a few cars, and each Saturday night for the next twelve months I taught these twelve people the mechanics of mediumship and discussed with them every aspect of the paranormal. It became a happy weekly event, and we grew in knowledge and enjoyed sharing our experiences without realizing that our footsteps had been slowly guided towards the fifth step in some Great Plan . . .

The twelve of us had become firm friends when,

quite out of the blue, one member of our group touched upon an old day-dream of mine: she'd heard of some upstairs city premises for rent.

'This is a great opportunity, and it's fallen right into our laps,' Valerie declared to one and all. 'It'd make a first-rate place where we could set up a psychic society, an educational establishment without any of the silly jealousies and pettiness you get in some organizations. Swansea needs it,' she said. 'So how about it, boys and girls?'

Without hesitation every hand voted in favour and each voice clucked its approval, all bar one. Mine.

'Now, let's not be too hasty,' I cautioned. 'It'll be a lot of hard graft, you know, running a place like that properly.' They all stared at me in disbelief. 'I'm the only working medium amongst us, and I know how much responsibility I'd have to shoulder.'

Their silence pooh-poohed my objections, and I sighed.

'OK,' I said, 'I give in.'

And that's how the Swansea Psychic Centre was born.

12

Temple of Light

My twelve colleagues and I paid the weekly rent of
the upstairs premises of the Swansea Psychic Centre
from our own pockets, while planning permission
was being sought to register the building as fit for
public use and the society was registered with the
Local Authority as a charitable place of worship.

We painted the high ceiling in white and the
walls in peach, laid cheap beige-coloured carpets
then purchased 150 second-hand wooden chairs and
some calor-gas heaters. Bank accounts were opened
in the society's name and the legal requirements
of officers and committee were elected from among
us. Because of her maturity and experience as a
hospital matron and nurse tutor, Dell Round became
our President, and I was given the Vice-Presidency
because of my training abilities and my fast-growing
reputation as a medium.

Fears about a lack of funds started to grow among
our group, so a month before opening night I
took it into my own hands to quell these by
booking Swansea's Patti Pavilion on the sea front
for a major demonstration of mediumship. 'I've
already telephoned and secured the services of
Gordon Higginson, and Mary Duffy of Edinburgh,'
I announced.

'And *you* must represent Wales,' said Dell and the committee, 'and now the Centre will step in and meet all the costs out of ticket sales.'

I agreed, and suggested that monies raised be divided between some local charities and a Centre Fund.

They nodded – and our event was one of the biggest meetings of mediumship that South Wales had seen in many years. The venue was packed to the rafters, and Dell was breathless. 'Nearly 700 people have crammed inside!' she exclaimed, gasping. 'Every seat's been sold and they're standing at the back, sitting on radiators, and crouching in the aisles to see the mediums working!'

Welsh television and press had publicized the meeting, which was a great success; and when cheques for £750 were presented to the blind and handicapped children's societies the audience raised the roof with resounding applause.

We were sad that dozens of people had to be turned away for lack of room, but they were told of the opening of the new Swansea Psychic Centre in St Helen's Road; I was to take the first demonstration there the following week, and admission would be £1.20 per seat.

On this first big night in March 1983 the atmosphere at the Centre was charged with excitement, and long before 7.30 a queue over a hundred yards long had formed outside. Ticket or no ticket – everyone was determined to get in! Poor Dell was perplexed. 'My God, where are we going to put them all? It's not funny, Stephen. What are you chuckling at?'

'Come and see,' I said, doubling up with mirth

and beckoning her to glance through the window where I stood pointing into the street. I just about managed to wheeze out, 'There's a second queue of people lining up over the road, waiting to get into the Swansea *Cycle* Centre!' Dell and I screeched with laughter, and our tensions soon dissolved. Then we quickly pulled ourselves together and Dell straightened her back, brushed her skirt with her palms, and strode towards the exit, still giggling.

'What are you doing?'

'I'm opening the doors, good boy. Stand well back!' she shouted as I dashed into the privacy of the little medium's room next to the platform.

No sooner had she turned the key than a rush of people flooded inside and filled the place to capacity. 'Standing-room only!' someone called down the stairs to the grumbling hordes.

A worried Dell confided in me, in the medium's room, 'There's 150-odd bodies out there. I'm petrified they'll crash through those old floorboards and plummet into the baker's shop downstairs.'

Thankfully, they didn't; and in my first meeting I was carried away on a bristling tide of psychic energy that the audience generated; the messages were well received, and so was the new Centre, despite the wicked comments of some people like black-eyed Nettie who'd predicted, 'I'll give it six months and it'll be shut.' She couldn't have been more wrong; in fact, the new establishment went on to attract many hundreds of visitors from all around Britain (and from overseas, too). It went from strength to strength, and sustained its popularity for years to come.

And for the next three years my time was chock-a-block with activity and I didn't have a minute to spare.

Because I was the only working medium among the founders I became the Centre's Senior Lecturer and had to train the others' psychic abilities and formulate the students' complex educational programmes for their awareness classes. These were tough jobs but I met the challenges head-on and gained a great deal of practical teaching experience. From the outset I stated my objectives clearly: that the students should achieve excellence in all aspects of mediumship, psychic work, and the philosophy of spirituality – the organizing of which kept me and Dell, the two principal tutors, very busy indeed.

But on top of all this I also held down five other demanding offices: I was Vice-President; Assistant to the Secretary; Mediumship Tutor; Platform Presentation Co-ordinator; and Publicity Officer; and, of course, Resident Medium – and I was so busy that my feet hardly touched the ground. I vigorously used my writing skills to create complex training programmes for the aspiring mediums who enrolled in our evening classes; I wrote sheaves of educational notes and photocopied them, and this work, plus my lectures on mediumship and psychic awareness that I conducted for six long nights every week, all but exhausted me.

There was also a very active Spiritual Healing group on Wednesdays and, more often than not, I attended this and delivered whatever power I had to those who were sick, and made endless cups of tea for the patients and visitors.

To me, all our work was fulfilling desperate needs in the community; the Psychic Centre was a Temple of Light, a place of learning and of spiritual worship that shone brightly. But there were other equally important temples of light *within* its walls, and these were the radiant spirit bodies of the many aspiring mediums and healers whom I taught.

The Beginners' Class

'Your spirit body is hidden within your physical frame,' I informed the newly enrolled students in the Beginners' Classes, 'and it's an energy-vehicle which your mind uses to express itself – and it's full of psychic light.'

The forty people of all ages and backgrounds eagerly opened their notebooks and started writing.

'Within this spirit body of light there are psychic gateways that channel to you from the Great Spirit your very life-energy, and this is what gives you consciousness and life.'

Dozens of wide eyes scrutinized my coloured chart on the blackboard and marvelled at the seven main energy-gateways I'd drawn.

'These vortices of power are known as Chakras, or Psychic Centres, and it is through these that communications from the next world will reach you. As mediums you must gain control over these centres, and in this intensive twelve-week course we'll identify and explore their functions, learn the main psychic laws that govern life, and spirit-communication, and read the theory of psychic phenomena, as well as the history of Spiritualism and the paranormal.'

One or two youngsters sighed at the daunting prospect.

'We expect you to work hard and to study diligently. There's no room for ignorance in this Centre. Your true motivation for wanting to train as a medium will also be carefully examined and assessed, because if it's wrong – that is, if you're undertaking this calling for self-glorification and not for the privilege of serving others – then all kinds of spiritual and psychic problems will beset you.'

Quizzical eyebrows were raised.

'Don't forget that like attracts like, and if you want to be guided by evolved souls who are both kind and knowledgeable you must earn their co-operation and friendship by developing those characteristics yourself. If you want the best, you've got to *be* the best, and that's a Universal Law.'

Judging by the expressions on their faces, I think I'd made my point.

'Being a medium isn't easy,' I cautioned, 'there are lots of cynical people out there in the world who are ready and willing to humiliate you because they don't understand you. So your backs must be strong, and your knowledge must be sound, and you must learn to take objective criticism without being offended.'

A few nods accompanied my remarks, and a few frowns, too.

'Weekly home-work will be set, and at the end

of the three months' course, only if you pass our written examinations can you gain entry into the next group – the Intermediate Class.'

The Intermediate Class

'In these initial twelve weeks you will be taught how to use your psychic abilities *without* the need to contact the next world. We'll study the human aura and learn how to interpret the tell-tale vibrant colours in it which allow clairvoyants to know what the person inside the aura is really like. We'll try some telepathy, too. But tonight we're going to experiment with the skill of psychometry. This Greek word can be roughly translated as "A measure of the soul of things".'

The students sat attentively in their seats, fascinated.

'All seemingly inanimate objects have psychic energy-fields surrounding them, called auras, and information has been impressed into these by the minds of their owners. These "invisible" auras act like sensitive photographic plates that capture and preserve images – and once you learn to "read" them, you're a psychometrist.'

I looked around the interested group.

'May I have a volunteer?'

A brave forty-year-old woman came onto the platform and gave me the jewelled wedding ring from her finger, then I addressed the class.

'I'm now going to attune my mind to the vibrations of this ring's aura and try to "see" and "feel" the details impressed within it. It's important to speak out the thoughts that pass through your awareness when you try this kind of experiment, and the results must always be verified.'

The room went quiet. I held the ring in my hand and began relaying the immediate clairvoyant impressions that came into my mind.

'I feel you're on the verge of a new beginning,' I announced. (I'd registered that she was soon to be divorced, but didn't feel I could openly reveal this.)

'Yes,' she nodded.

Then I became aware of a great fear. 'I pick up strong thoughts from this ring about a man with a jealous nature.'

'That's acceptable.' (This was her husband.)

'I also see a sum of money that looks like £655 . . . it's been hidden . . . no, secretly banked away.'

'I'm not sure,' she said tentatively, denying the information.

'Well, I can't get it right *all* of the time,' I quipped, and everyone laughed.

(But later she privately confirmed that she'd banked £650 – I was five pounds out! – to prevent her husband stealing her savings, but she didn't want to admit this in front of her friends.)

She also refused a number of other details I gave. 'Well, either I'm wrong,' I said, 'or *you* are!' which produced loud chuckling from the students. 'But there may be another possibility. The information could have been recorded by a previous owner's mind.' The woman frowned. 'Has anyone else worn this ring?'

'It's been passed down my family line.'

'Then some research might verify what I've given,' I suggested.

She nodded and said she'd think about it.

Undaunted I continued, 'There's some kind of connection to southern France.'

'One of my great-grandparents came from there, I believe, and she owned that ring long ago.'

Then I psychically sensed a sudden rush of laughter and a tide of happiness that washed two names with it into my mind. 'Does Freda, and Sylvie, mean anything to you?'

'Yes, they're two of my sisters.' And she gave an affectionate smile.

Then all at once I felt engulfed by a great sadness. 'And who, or what, is Peppi?'

'Oh dear' – her hand went momentarily to her mouth – 'he was my dog that died. But that was twenty years ago,' she added in astonishment.

'That doesn't matter; psychic impressions linger for much longer if they've been charged with emotion,' I instructed the students.

Pens scribbled in notebooks. 'And why do I get the name Cyril quite strongly?'

'I don't know,' she said, but afterwards she told me she liked Cyril very much, and hoped he would be her new paramour.

I then concluded this demonstration of psychometry to the Intermediate Class by relaying a memory that startled my recipient; but I hadn't gleaned the image from the ring – it had come from her own mind, from within the aura that surrounded her head:

'You went scrumping (stealing) apples from the local farmer,' I declared, much to her bright red embarrassment.

'Well, I *never*! That was nearly forty years ago, when I was only a nipper,' she said, giggling.

'Yes, but the memory hasn't vanished. It's still very much alive in your subconscious thoughts. Right!' I declared loudly to the applauding students, 'everyone find a partner and then psychometrize each other!'

The Advanced Class

'In these ongoing Advanced Classes you'll receive personal tuition while you develop your mediumship. As a sensitive you must first learn to control your mind: you must become the master of it, and cease to be its slave. Only then can you purposefully direct your thoughts to communicate properly with the spirit people.'

The aspiring mediums nodded and made copious notes.

'You must learn how to "open up" your inner psychic awareness and then how to "close it down". You mustn't remain hypersensitive all the time, or your health will suffer.'

More frantic scribbling.

'Many students, and members of the public, are perplexed by one question: how can one tell whether a medium is working purely on a psychic (or telepathic) level when he's giving out "messages", or whether he's operating as a medium who is a true channel for spirit communication?'

Lots of eyebrows knitted together, but a cheeky young chap piped up, 'I've always wondered about that!'

After the laughter had died down, I continued with, 'There's a tremendous difference between psychics and mediums. Psychics don't make contact with discarnate personalities – but mediums do. Psychics forge telepathic links with people or objects in *this* world, but mediums link telepathically with people living in the *next* world. And a true spirit message always contains survival evidence that proves the presence of a discarnate communicator.'

The young chap called out again, 'So if a sensitive tells you all about yourself, all about your own thoughts and feelings, your own desires and hopes for the future, or your past traumas – that's a psychic message, and not a mediumistic one?'

'That's right.'

'But if a medium relays evidence about a "dead" person, and actually tells you what they're saying, or holds a kind of conversation with the communicator – that's mediumship?'

'Nicely put!'

The class gave him a well-earned round of applause which he acknowledged by nodding to the left and right, and he grinned all over his face.

Teaching the Advanced Class always tested and tried my patience to its utmost, and usually gave me a throbbing headache. For five solid hours a night, sometimes twice a week, I'd mentally 'tune in' to the spirit people who were desperately trying to communicate with the inexperienced students, one after another, who strained to 'hear' them and then tried to relay their messages to their fellow class-members.

I was frequently called upon to perform sustained mental gymnastics.

'When you're trying to get a contact,' I'd explain to the students, 'I must monitor four areas of consciousness at once: the spirit communicator's message which is being transmitted to you; your own thoughts as you try to receive it; the voice of White Owl, who instructs me on how to perfect your psychic gifts; and I must also register your recipient's responses.'

Studiously, they said they understood. 'The most I can do at this early stage of your development is to encourage, guide, and train you,' I told them. 'You are the only one – you alone – who must master the art of attuning your mind to the spirit people. I'll teach you special exercises that will strengthen your abilities, but you must totally dedicate yourself to do the work.'

During one class when a blind-folded young student struggled to catch the spirit world's voice, I told her that radiating around her throat, 'I see a circular green psychic light. You're developing clairaudience, the ability to hear spirit voices,' I said.

'But why would the power gather around my throat?' the student asked.

'Because the throat is sensitive to sound vibrations. It's a psychic creation- and registration-point for sound,' I explained, much to her astonishment. But my words were later proved correct when I plugged up her ears and she still heard the spirit voices – vibrating in the region of her throat.

Just as I did with all the other trainee mediums, when she couldn't clearly see or hear the messages that were being transmitted I instructed her to 'Focus your attention on the Other Side and not on the audience. Go back to your communicator and mentally get more facts from him. The only place where you should fish for information is the spirit world.'

'But I can't hear anything,' she said.

'Then try again. Ask for clarification and more evidence.'

'It's no good. I can't see anything, either.'

'Don't be so negative! You're shutting out all possibility of contact by having an attitude like that. Try again; and this time close your eyes, forget about the expectations of the audience and pay more attention to the spirit world.'

Her features tensed.

'Do your best to sense the spirit person next to you; use your mind to blend with his aura and personality. Now, describe what he's like.'

She then amazed herself by giving an accurate description of her communicator's character!

I used to get so frustrated when the students were struggling away like that. If only this young woman could have seen the people from the next world who had gathered all around her. If only she could have sensed their presences and felt the glowing radiance of the golden soul-lights they projected into her mind while they tried so desperately to link with her.

179

Figures of Light

Hands that Pray
bring love
that's just a finger-touch away

Figures of Light
aware of every plea,
swirl the thoughts of those
who see

Minds in Flight
deliver
deeper insight

Souls of Golden Light
have soundless voices
that split the night

Lips of Power
kiss a tear-stained brow,
fulfilling
a solemn vow

Hearts of Joy
ever caring; ever sharing,
all forbearing,
forever beating
through no divide at all

Our students were often give opportunities to try
their 'mediumistic wings' at special public services,
and after one such event, during which I'd also

worked with the classes from the platform, Dell had to rescue me from the clutches of a middle-aged divorcee who'd been plaguing me with her outrageous flirtations for months on end. This woman could always be seen gazing up at me with glassy-eyed adulation from the front rows of my meetings. I was so grateful to be yanked away from 'Ol' Glass-Eyes' and marched into the medium's room. 'He needs some coffee and a rest! Come along, good boy,' Dell declared, much to the woman's astonishment.

She banged the door shut. 'They never leave you alone for a minute, do they, Stephen?' she sympathized. 'Everywhere you turn the public are milling around you like flies round a honey-pot, as if you're something special.'

A heavy sigh lifted my shoulders.

'You should be more sensible. When people are desperate they tend to see only their own needs. I ought to know, as a Matron I have to deal with crisis situations all the time. But what about your needs, good boy? If you allow them, you know, the public'll bleed you dry.'

She certainly had a point.

'How on earth do you do it?' she asked. 'How do you cope with all this sickening public attention and adulation?'

'I don't,' I answered, wearily. 'To be quite frank it's getting me down. Last week "Ol' Glass-Eyes" wanted me to jump into a marriage bed with her! They're forever falling in and out of love with "the medium" but they don't care a toot about "the man". It's all so tedious.'

'It must be very annoying.'

'It is. It's taken me years to overcome my reservations about facing crowds of expectant people and trying to give them messages from the next world, and now – just when I've nearly beaten it – all this other attention's come along! I wouldn't mind, but I'm such a private person and I never mix business with pleasure.'

Dell grinned widely.

'Besides, I've no time for personal relationships; this place keeps me on the go, and when I get to bed all I'm fit for is *sleep*! Anyway, I *like* living on my own. I've chosen it.'

Dell smiled and nodded, and for a while we sat in thoughtful silence, drinking our mugs of coffee; then it was her turn to sigh.

'Well, Stephen, I know one medium who won't have to cope with the public's adulation any longer.'

'Who's that?'

'Nettie,' she said. 'She lost her battle against cancer, and she died last night.'

There was a respectful pause.

'Yes, I was on night duty at the hospital. I took her the flowers from all of us at the Centre,' said Dell, poignantly. 'But last week she was in a terrible state.'

'I'm very sorry to hear it,' I said quietly, and there was a long pause. 'But isn't it odd? Nettie always made such a song and dance about death being nothing to fear. Poor soul.'

Dell curled her fingers around the hot coffee mug and became pensive. 'She sought comfort and reassurance about the reality of the spirit world from all her Spiritualist visitors, you know.'

I looked down at the floor. 'That's awfully sad.'

'Yes. The last time I saw her she took my hand and said, "Tell me it's true, Dell. Please, tell me it's true".'

We both registered the desperation Nettie must have felt during her last moments on earth, and both knew that had she been a genuine medium her passing would have been taken much more serenely, and with greater dignity.

Dell got up quietly and went out into the hall to form the chairs into a circle ready for the questions-and-answers session that I was booked to take for the Advanced Class students; it was due to start.

In the still moments that followed I closed my eyes and sent out my good wishes to Nettie and told her that I bore no grudge over the way she'd behaved in the past, because I'd always understood her fear and insecurity. I also prayed that in her new world she'd be helped with her spiritual progress.

My silent prayer was broken by Dell's voice when she popped her head around the door. 'Come along then. Everyone's ready with their questions,' she said.

And I got up and walked out into the hall.

13

Questions and Answers

The Psychic Centre meeting was called to order and I joined the large circle of Advanced Class students, who shuffled papers on their laps, and addressed them.

Good evening, ladies and gentlemen. We haven't a great deal of time tonight for our questions and answers; so, we'll make a start. Who's first?

Last week when White Owl entranced you and gave us a lecture on spirit communication, was he inside your body?
No, he stood behind me, within my auric field. Spirit people don't 'enter' mediums' bodies; that's impossible. Not even the medium is 'inside' his own body! Mediumistic control is effected through the aura and the mind.

Can the spirit people see the future and predict it?
Some of them can because they've developed that special talent. But a great many of them can't.

What do they see? Is it a set of possibilities?
Sometimes, but the more evolved spirit beings

The medium, Mrs Palmer, and 20 year-old Stephen, her young apprentice. 'She taught me the secrets of mediumship'.

18 year-old Philip Humphries, victim of a tragic car crash, was reunited with his mother through Stephen's mediumship.

The magnificent Arthur Findlay College for Psychic Studies (Stansted Hall) in Essex (*top*) where Stephen lectured on, and taught, mediumship; and Ystalyfera Spiritualist Church, nestling in the Welsh Valleys, where Stephen conducted his first 'out-of-town' service under the ever-watchful eye of Mrs Palmer.

All part of Stephen's work: filming for television, attending photo shoots, and signing books for the public.

Jeff Rees Jones, Stephen's Manager, is kept very busy organizing the medium's nation-wide tours, travel arrangements, and media commitments.

Off on another 50-city British
tour to deliver survival
evidence, comfort and hope,
to thousands of people in
packed auditoriums...

... and a cuddle and a bouquet
for '89 years young' Nanny
Davies, one of Stephen's
faithful 'fans'.

Stephen and Professor Arthur Ellison, past President of the famed Society for Psychical Research (SPR), after a televised debate on the paranormal..

With television celebrities William Franklin, Molly Parkin and Nerys Hughes, after a radio broadcast together.

With Tim Haigh, editor of *Psychic News*, who invited Stephen to become the newspaper's Psychic Agony Uncle.

A rare moment of peace and tranquillity on the cliffs at Gower, Wales. Time spent in quiet contemplation is an essential part of Stephen's spiritual life.

Stephen's Spirit Guide, an American Indian named White Owl, is always aware of his medium's needs; like a beacon of light, he directs Stephen's spiritual work and offers his love and support in times of stress.

Stephen's favourite photograph, which has
been requested by thousands of his followers
around the world.

definitely know what will occur because they've learned to 'slip time' and perceive it.

Stephen, why do so many of us new mediums work in pictures and symbols? It's so annoying!
The spirit people will use any means to reach us, and often pictures are the easiest way because the mind is used to working with images. But as you strengthen and develop your skills, your ability to see, hear, and sense the finer worlds around you will be heightened. These things take time, and they develop through use. Remember, you're just starting out; but if you're dedicated you'll be patient and persevere.

Why are so few mediums trained these days? We seem to have a glut of questionable talents on our public platforms.
That's the fault of the people who book the services of undeveloped 'mediums'; in my opinion, they should be far more choosy. There'll always be mediums who want to learn and progress, and others who can't be bothered to make the effort – more's the pity.

Any other questions?

Yes. Do we all create thought-forms in our minds?
Certainly; the mind is a picture-making entity and when its thoughts are projected into the auras surrounding us, we can see them. That's why, in mediumship training classes, when referring to your consciousness I often use the phrase 'the mirror of the mind'.

*Why do we need to sit in silence to develop our
mediumship?*
After we've stilled the mind and quietened any
disturbing and unnecessary thoughts, a great peace
is discovered; and it's in this calm state of mind
that we have a better chance of registering the
quicker, more subtle sights and sounds that are
communicated to our Higher Selves from the world
of spirit.

Our turbulent thoughts can so easily sweep away
our awareness of our spirit friends.

*How do the spirit people operate the Ouija board,
or move objects in our world?*
By blending their life-force with those people on
earth who are in the vicinity and then directing
these energies through the power of their will.
The Ouija board pointer, or glass, is moved by
a mental direction that's partly effected through
the mediums' subconscious minds which produce
a physical 'push', and partly by the thoughts and
desires of the communicators.

But in the best instances of this phenomenon the
pointer is dominated by the discarnates' energies,
and the mediums know nothing of what will be
spelled out.

Do our guides and spirit family protect us?
From what?
Evil entities, bad or malevolent forces.
You are your own protection. You can only link up
with the spirit influences that you've drawn to
yourself through the universal law of attraction;

so, the only person you need protection from is yourself.

But when specific communication is to take place our guides do try to repel influences that would be detrimental to the seance.

Spirit family members and friends do gather around us, of course, because they love us. And sometimes they're able to send us advice or even a warning.

Is it right to diagnose medical conditions as a spiritual healer? I've tried, but I can't do it.
You don't need to. Under British law no-one is allowed to diagnose an illness unless he is a qualified doctor. The spirit people have experts on their side of life who can see exactly what's wrong with the patient by looking into his aura; and they can make the diagnosis and deliver the corrective treatment through you.

As a responsible spiritual healing medium you are just a channel that enables the power to work its effect; you're not a doctor.

Can we prevent someone we love from dying? Could we keep them here on earth for a little longer? For a few more years, perhaps?
Opinion is divided on this, but not as far as I'm concerned. When your time's up you must cross over, and nothing will prevent that transition taking place.

But some people who were close to death have been saved and their lives have been prolonged by transplant surgery, or transfusions and suchlike.

It's all a matter of personal choice, of course, whether or not to take the kind of treatments you've mentioned. But there's a time to be born and a time to die, and if terminally ill patients make a seemingly miraculous recovery, then their moment to 'die' obviously hadn't arrived.

Are there any other questions?

Why can't I astral-project out of my body and have some of the wonderful experiences you've told us about?

You can, but some people need a great deal of practice before they can achieve it; and don't forget that there are a number of dangers involved in consciously projecting out: your body can be damaged by sudden noises, for example.

Never dabble with things you don't fully understand.

Interestingly enough, I've heard it said that mediums have 'a loose etheric (or spirit) body', that is to say a spirit body that can easily slip in and out of its physical frame. That's a rather unusual idea but I think there's a lot of truth in it.

Stephen, why do you think the Spiritualist religion hasn't made a more powerful impact on today's world?

Because it's placed too much emphasis on developing psychic powers and trying to prove survival, instead of concentrating on teaching the spiritual ethics that would satisfy the deep yearning in man's soul for the truths that will set him free from ignorance, give him

188

a fuller understanding of Life and its meaning, and help him to progress spiritually.

As to offering proof of the afterworld's existence, I've said this so many times before: mediums can't *prove* survival; they can only offer *evidence* of it, and there's a world of difference between these two claims.

A medium's job is to serve.

Is there some advice you can give us sensitives that would make our spiritual work more comforting and more fruitful?

Yes. Mother Teresa of Calcutta has said: 'Let's do something beautiful for God.'

Surely, the ultimate purpose of mediumship is to help man to realize more fully the presence of his Creator in everything? If you can hold that thought as your objective, then I think your work will move along more fruitful lines because your motivation will be to serve a greater power than yourself.

Why do you teach that the earth-world is 'the shadow-world'?

Because Spirit is the Reality, and Matter is just an Illusion.

I believe that Life here resembles a shadow-dance that is cast by the Great Light of God through a slow-vibrating veil of matter, known as the physical world.

Why do people seek a soul mate, someone to whom they feel spiritually attracted?

Human beings have positive and negative psychic

189

energies within them and people search for a partner who will 'harmonize' or 'complete' the picture of their sexuality.

Males seek females: females seek males.

But a gentle man may desire as a companion a more masculine male; and a masculine female might seek the friendship of a more feminine woman; each soul is attracted to its partner in an effort to balance its esoteric, or hidden, spiritual energies.

But if people searched more deeply within *themselves* they'd find all the qualities they needed to balance their soul energies, and they might not then require an outside stimulus.

Can you tell us, Stephen, how can we be happier people?
Happiness is different things to different people. But to experience true happiness I think man must undergo a spiritual change, an inner re-birth. A much better word for 'happiness' is 'contentment', and contentment is purely a state of mind.

No matter who we are or what we've got, or whatever we want, if we can cultivate an attitude of contentment as we stand within the ever-changing circumstances of our lives, then we're more likely to feel peace within ourselves.

And to me, happiness is peace.

Should we only pray for the well-being of others?
In praying exclusively for ourselves we're obviously selfish; but we're human beings and we often need personal guidance, refreshment for the soul, and a sense of being unconditionally cared for by some

Greater Power – and we can achieve all of these things by 'touching base' so to speak.

Our prayers for others are undoubtedly helpful, but I think it's good to seek peace and progress for your own soul, too.

But I find it hard to pray. How should I pray?
God's Spirit is *within* you, so you already have an intimate relationship with your Creator.

Try this: quieten your mind and relax your body, then speak either mentally or vocally, directing your thoughts inward towards, perhaps, a vivid image. You might visualize a religious icon; or maybe a candle flame; or a colourful flower; or perhaps a peaceful countryside scene, bathed in sunshine.

On the other hand you may feel more comfortable imagining God as a Great Light whose rays flood your entire being. Or perhaps He shines like a bright flame in the centre of your heart, which is where many mystics claim that God's Spirit is located in man.

Some people find it easier to talk to God as though He were an old friend; while others mentally write a letter to Him and then imagine launching it into infinity.

There's no 'right' or 'wrong' way to pray because whatever method you use to connect with the Inner Power that created you, your prayer will be heard.

Do you think that God has a personality?
Yes, I do.

Billions of people have accepted that God is Love alone, but others believe that He expresses

Himself through the three mighty powers of Creation, Preservation and Destruction. These philosophers see Him as a Living Spirit whose personality is evident in Nature, where life-forms are continuously 'created' then 'destroyed' (by sometimes cataclysmic forces) only to be later re-formed into other creations. For example, the dust-clouds and star debris from an exploding supernova are propelled into space where they join with other material then suddenly collapse inwards towards their centre of gravity, and thus a new star is 'born'.

Our Universe is a living entity which is in a state of constant change; it's forever evolving, just as we are, and just as I believe The Great Spirit is.

To discover the personality of God we must carefully examine the Pageant of Life and Consciousness around us, and within us, for it is there that His nature will be revealed.

So is God 'Our Father', or 'Our Mother', or both?
Both – God is all things.

I see The Great Spirit as an androgynous Power that contains both the masculine and feminine aspects within it, and this is why I believe that we, who have a spark of the Divine within us, are also androgynous in essence.

Do you think that man's free will can overpower, and thereby negate, the Will of God?
No, I don't.

In my opinion God's Will continuously presses through the minds of all the life-forms He has created.

There is only one authority: the omnipotent, omniscient, omnipresent God; the all-powerful, all-knowing, present-in-all-places-at-the-same-time Creative Spirit of Consciousness-Being, and none can overpower His Almighty Will.

Then Dell piped up, 'Well, I'm afraid the clock's beaten us again, ladies and gentlemen. Thank you all very much.'

14

Whisperings Within

After its first two years of service to the public, the Swansea Psychic Centre was being hailed by one and all as an undoubted and ongoing success.

Spiritually, we'd helped thousands of souls to gain knowledge of the afterlife; we'd organized several teach-in seminars and had trained students from different countries, at the meagre charge of £15 per person for the full weekend course; our awareness classes had produced a number of new platform mediums, some of whom went back to their regions and formed satellite study groups based on the knowledge they'd gained from us; even the Spiritualist churches, who'd originally condemned the idea of our organization, now began to book the mediums we'd so diligently trained.

The national Spiritualist newspaper, *Psychic News*, carried reports of our large publicity meetings that were regularly held in Swansea's world-famous Brangwyn Hall, where I was privileged to share the concert stage with some of the country's leading mediums.

As news of our success spread further afield, our hall became chock-a-block with visitors, and I received more offers to work at Stansted, though I declined them because of an undercurrent of bad feeling that seemed to ripple through some of the mediums at the College whenever my name was mentioned there.

The Psychic Centre was a financial success, too: our voluntary work had realized £3,000 for it in its first year through ticket sales. Of this, £2,000 was donated to national and regional charities, and the other £1,000 paid the rent and kept our charitable organization running.

Everyone was bristling with life and laughter, but I was completely knackered.

Then White Owl stepped in and made a prediction. 'Within ten months you will move to Newcastle upon Tyne in England,' he said, 'to continue your work.' And, after a nine months' and twenty-seven days' wait, he was proved perfectly correct when a council flat came up for exchange in Gateshead, Tyne and Wear.

I was thirty years old, strong, and determined to listen to the voice of the spirit, which is why I really looked forward to moving the 400 miles north and to making a new life for myself. Dad, however, warned me, 'It's a big mistake, boy!' But when he realized I was serious he wished me well.

My friends at the Psychic Centre, which was now up-and-running because I'd trained six mediums to serve in it, gave me a huge send-off and I said goodbye to Wales and set out on a bumpy eight-and-a-half-hour journey north, hunched up on the floor in the back of a rented three-ton truck, surrounded by my meagre possessions.

There was plenty of time on the long smelly trip in the van for me to remember what White Owl had told me years previously. 'Just go where we send you,' he'd said, 'for there's much work to do. We are about our Father's business.'

And here I was, obeying this call which eventually landed me in one of the filthiest areas I'd ever seen. Full of rough people who'd made it a debtors' paradise and a watering-hole for blood-thirsty adolescents, the council estate I lived in was destined to frazzle my nerves very quickly.

It was a good job the Social Security paid my rent because, if they hadn't, the bailiffs wouldn't have got a brass farthing out of me! However, I made the best of it, and tried to settle in.

Never one to wallow in self-pity, I kept myself very active and got on with 'my Father's business', and my time was fully occupied; everything was so new and thrilling that I was carried along on a high wave of enthusiasm.

Most evenings I helped new northern psychics to find their mediumistic feet; I also lectured or demonstrated in churches and taught people the most successful ways to unfold their sensitivity; and I conducted informative question-and-answer sessions. I also ran two private psychic awareness classes each week and, accompanied by some of my new friends, attended countless Open Circles in the north-eastern churches, where I gave survival evidence to the public.

These church visits provided me with excellent opportunities to make fresh studies of other mediums and their work, and I discovered that, just as in other parts of Britain at that time, there were only a handful whose survival evidence really impressed me.

But one easily frightened old medium was always a joy to watch! My friends and I used to chuckle when his neck suddenly sank into his chest every time he received a stinging refusal from a recipient. This made him adopt the infuriating habit of playing safe with his facts and he would then frequently make plaintive statements to buxom battle-axes like:

'Now, pet, I'd be wrong to give you Canada, wouldn't I?'

'Yes, *you would*!'

'Aye, I thought so.' And in went his retractable neck!

Although I lived alone in the north, on the dreadful estate, I didn't feel lonely because I'd consolidated a few old friendships that I'd founded in my earlier travelling days, and I'd made some new ones, too.

One of these was kindly Sheila who was in her forties and who was Secretary of Jarrow Spiritualist Church. She was a very spiritual lady who became not only my good friend and confidante but also my telephone bookings secretary – a thankless, voluntary task, if ever there was one.

Black-haired Sheila and I laughed a great deal, and because she'd attended a Catholic school when young and had been taught by nuns she was ably fitted to be my personal 'Mother-Confessor'. On many chilly evenings when we sat by her gas fire, sipping her first-rate cups of tea, I'd comically beg her to:

'Forgive me, Mother, for I have sinned.'

Her mischievous eyes twinkled and she reverently steepled her fingers. 'And what is your sin, my child?'

'Well, as you know I'm a vegetarian, Mother, but

yesterday I couldn't get proper food and I downed a bit of fish!'

She smiled and announced wickedly, 'In that case – you must take next week's Sunday service, my son!' And we both chuckled because Jarrow church got quite a few bookings out of me like that.

Whenever I travelled in the region to take my meetings, kindly Sheila looked after my newest friend: a lovely grey and black, but mostly white tabby cat called Sooty, who'd been rescued from an animal sanctuary along with another beautiful tortoise-shell called Bess. They were as close as sisters, but poor Bess developed sudden meningitis and, sadly, her life ended.

After dear Sooty and I had got over the inevitable grief that followed, we loved each other all the more. Always a mischievous bundle of fun and fur, Sooty was a lively moggy and a very special little person and she and I became the best of inseparable friends and companions. She'd mew up at me whenever I went out:

Oi! Claire Voyant! Take me with you!

And she was definitely psychic because when I got back in she'd be standing on the hallway mat waiting for me, with a haughty expression on her face:

And tell me, prithee, where hast thou been this fair eve, sire? – Fancy leaving me here on my own. Bloody cheek!

(She was a bit common, but she liked Shakespeare.)

I'd sweep her up into my arms, flip her over on her back and lovingly kiss her belly until she squeaked with delight!

Do it again, sire! I like it!

Many's the night when I couldn't get into my slippers in the hallway because she'd made little nests of sticks and dried leaves in them while she'd waited for me.

'That's a sign of love,' the wise Sheila informed me; she knew because she was ruled by felines of her own.

But love, of course, couldn't buy me the money I needed to rise out of the poverty trap I found myself in. Times were certainly hard but, despite this lack of funds, my life up north was quite exciting; and it was made all the more so when the spirit people asked me to write my autobiography (and if I could get this placed with a publisher, I reasoned, it would also earn me an honest bob or two).

'You'll write a book one day, Stephen,' my fur-coated friend Kitty had often gushed to me when I'd lived in Wales. In fact, I'd lost count of how many other mediums had said exactly the same thing. So, obeying my spirit voices, I blotted out the dreadful depression pressing down on me in the estate, and threw myself into this massive task, and wrote the manuscript in the early hours of each morning.

With my portable Brother DeLuxe typewriter across my knees I typed away with three fingers of each hand for a few months, and wrestled with my mind, soul, and vocabulary until I'd completed *Visions of Another World*; great sections of the text had flowed into my mind, as if they'd been inspired. Then I photocopied the 300-page manuscript that was weighed-down with white *Tipp-Ex* correction-fluid and posted it (at a phenomenal cost) to one of the largest publishing houses in Britain.

Included with the package was the return postage and details about me and my work, and of the few regional television, radio, and newspaper interviews I'd given over the years.

The book's merits were then considered for an agonizing, nail-biting month, after which it winged its merry way back with a polite rejection slip that praised my story and my writing skills but stated that the book was 'not suitable for our lists'.

So off it went again to another publisher, all 300 pages of it.

And back it came again, and again! But several editors said they felt certain that my autobiography would indeed be published – though not by them.

So into the post it went again, and when a letter arrived a few days later I naturally thought it would be another rejection slip – but it wasn't . . .

It was an invitation from the Spiritualists' National Union to demonstrate alongside its President, Gordon Higginson, at two major meetings of clairvoyance in Winchester and Swansea, as part of his forthcoming nationwide tour that was being organized for the SNU by a London man called Derek Robinson.

But why had they chosen my name from hundreds in the country? I'd never been a member of the SNU; I liked being a free spirit, a free agent. Before replying, I carefully considered my position, knowing that my name had been suggested because of a certain amount of box-office attraction it might have down south; and I hadn't forgotten that Mr Higginson and I had clashed in the past. If I accepted, these would be my first appearances for the Union in their large publicity meetings.

Then, when a female official involved in the southern branches of the Union quite seriously informed me that, 'I suppose, Mr O'Brien, we're looking for guest mediums to be "also-rans", to support Mr Higginson's "starring roles" in these meetings,' my hackles rose.

She laughed; but I didn't. Some of the country's leading demonstrators had been chosen and I felt they deserved better treatment. Little bells started tinkling in the back of my mind: I'd encountered this sort of thing before; so, I made a firm stand on behalf of myself and my colleagues when I politely replied:

'Yes, I'll be happy to come to Winchester and Swansea – provided certain conditions are met.'

'Oh? And what would they be?'

'Well, I'd like one hour on the platform in which to give my demonstration because I'll be travelling such a long way. And I think anyone appearing should be named on the posters and in the press adverts—'

'Ahemmm—'

'I don't want any payment, but if you could give me a crossed cheque for £50 for the NSPCC, as a charity fee, that'll be grand.'

There was a long pause. She wasn't sure. She'd see. Could I write it all down for official consideration?

'Certainly,' I said. And no-one was more surprised than I to learn that these terms were acceptable.

So about a month later, Sooty was left at Auntie Sheila's 'on holiday' and I made a gruelling nine-hour journey by train down-country to Winchester Guildhall, in southern Britain.

'Hellair,' said a plummy voice behind me in the theatre wings. 'How are you?'

I turned, shook Mr Higginson's hand, and returned his kind greeting; but he seemed unusually quiet and he walked away from me.

Instead of sitting down calmly and directing my thoughts to the next world as I always did, I found myself pacing up and down behind the curtain, alongside the apprehensive organizer, Derek Robinson.

Beyond the drapes the crowd was busy talking, and I felt very uneasy. How would the meeting go? Would I hear the spirit voices clearly enough? I was to go first but would the audience speak up? An unresponsive audience can kill a demonstration. It was such an auspicious occasion for me and I did so want to succeed and give comfort to the people. This was my first big meeting for the SNU and I was anxious because there was still so much I needed to learn about handling large crowds.

Moments later my name was announced and I wiped my palms on my suit trouser-legs, strode onto the stage and began with a ten-minute talk on the spiritual aspects of communication and how it worked. The audience warmed to me, I thought, and I now had fifty minutes in which to deliver my clairvoyance.

I started with an unusual message to a grey-haired spinster in the auditorium who responded when I asked if anyone knew the name 'Mary Millington' that had been whispered into my mind.

'Yes, I do,' she said, waving her ticket in the air.

'Then I must relay to you this phrase, word for

word: "God, first; others, next; and self, last". Does that mean anything to you, please?'

Through the radio-microphone the cultured lady said with great dignity, 'That is the golden rule by which I've endeavoured to live my life for the last sixty years.'

The audience applauded.

I then launched into another reasonably successful link but didn't get the chance to get into my stride and finish it properly because the chairman, who was a Union official, called out curtly from behind me, 'Time, Mr O'Brien.'

Momentarily startled, I stopped speaking at once. No more than twenty minutes could have passed while I'd been on the platform, but I would never cause a public fuss – so I smiled at the audience, thanked them for their kind attention, wished them well in their investigations into Spiritualism, and then sat down.

Their warm applause couldn't counteract the cold disappointment that swept through me in waves. Why on earth had I been stopped?

Mr Higginson immediately took the microphone and delivered some sparkling survival evidence for the next hour and forty minutes, but I missed a great deal of it because I kept thinking of my dear friend Mrs Palmer and what her guide Ahmed had told her many years previously, 'You are not popular because you are capable.'

I dismissed these thoughts from my mind; but later that night, when tucked up in my plush hotel bed, I shivered at the prospect of the following evening's repeat appearance in Swansea, my home town, and dreaded the thought that the same thing might happen again . . .

Swansea's Patti Pavilion was full of people and I pushed my way through the waiting crowds to get in to the green-room, and entered it just as Mr Higginson was leaving it through another exit. He looked terribly upset.

My good friend Dell Round, the Psychic Centre's President, got up from a sofa and warmly embraced me. 'Lovely to see you, good boy,' she said; and I returned her kindness. 'And guess what? I'm your chairperson for tonight.'

I smiled and heaved a sigh of relief, then glanced across at the door through which the President had gone. 'What's wrong with Gordon, Dell?'

'Oh,' she said flatly, 'he's not happy. He is not a happy man.'

'Why?'

Fair-haired Dell plonked herself down on the sofa again. 'Well, he asked to speak to me privately, then glided in and said, "You know, of course, that Mr O'Brien can't possibly have one hour on the platform. He must take twenty minutes, and I must have one hour and forty minutes in which to demonstrate."'

Slumping onto the sofa next to her, startled, I asked, 'What did you say?'

She was quite matter-of-fact. 'Well, you know me, Stephen – I told him straight. "I'm sorry, Mr Higginson," I said, "but that's not the way we do things here in Wales. You both have one hour each in which to work with the audience, as previously agreed." I think he was stunned.'

I bit my lip.

'Then I reminded him about the coach parties that had booked and the importance of running the meeting to time, and suggested that if he'd like an extra fifteen minutes on top of his hour, he'd have to work the interval.'

'Aren't there any refreshments tonight?'

'Of course. I told him a lot of ladies had prepared loads of food and they didn't want to see it wasted.'

'Oh dear,' I said, sipping a glass of water from the coffee table.

But Dell simply shrugged her shoulders. 'Don't you worry, good boy – it's not your problem. It's tough enough for youngsters to make a name for themselves in this field as it is, without all this extra aggravation. You know what a stickler I am for fair play – always have been. I've no time for all that silly nonsense,' she added, rising and slapping me on the back. 'Well, you're here to demonstrate, good boy, and I'm sure you'll do Wales proud. You look very smart. Now, come on. It's time to start.'

As we left the green-room and climbed the stairs to the stage she muttered to herself, 'I hope Mr Higginson's waiting for us in the wings.'

He was.

'Hellair, Stephen. How are you?'

'Fine thanks. And you?'

'Oh, so so.'

The three of us made an entrance to loud applause and after a few preliminaries I relaxed and felt so much more at ease knowing that Dell was controlling the meeting; and I hoped I'd do well.

I began my demonstration by re-uniting a young spirit boy with a group of women seated right at the back of the hall, and pinpointed this link by asking for a response to the names of 'Trevor' and 'Llewellyn'.

'Back here! It's us you want!' shouted one of the ladies.

'This young lad's voice is just a faint whisper in my mind,' I went on, 'but I think he wants . . . Yes, that's it. "My mother should be with you," he says. "But she was delayed by an emergency phone call and couldn't come". Is that correct?'

'It is!' shouted another group member.

'And he's mentioning "Baglan" here.'

'He used to live there.'

'But why is he singing "Happy Birthday To You"? Hold on – don't answer that! *He's* supposed to tell me, not you!' The audience laughed. 'Whose do you mean, son?' I asked the lad out loud. And he said to me:

'My Mam's.'

'Yes – very soon.'

'He mentions August the thirteenth.'

'That's her birthday.'

The audience applauded and I thanked the boy out loud for communicating so clearly; then helped him to end his connection by asking the group who'd claimed him to give his mother a lovely message:

'He says he'd be so grateful if you'd tell his Mam that he loves her and that, to him, she'll always be a very special lady.'

'She'll be over the moon!' was the happy reply.

One link followed another – some of them were clear and fully accepted, others contained details that needed to be researched – and before I realized it my full hour had run its course and I sat down, relieved that my contribution was over, and pleased that it had gone well.

I was looking forward to getting out of the public eye and relaxing. Earlier on, I'd been so tense that I'd drunk several glasses of water to stop my mouth from drying out, and what I needed right now was a loo – but I was most surprised when the interval didn't materialize.

In a twinkling of an eye, Mr Higginson rose from his seat, stepped to the microphone and launched into his demonstration which contained some of his recipients' full names: one was 'Eva James', and another 'Carole Delwyn Bowen', and their messages were understood.

Time went on, and on, and I was desperate to visit the loo, but I crossed my legs, smiled, and remained seated – and *Ooww*! my chair was rock-hard and my bum had gone to sleep.

Mr Higginson worked for an hour and forty minutes and then, after several attempts by Dell to politely call him to time, he concluded the meeting.

Waving to the crowd, I walked calmly off the stage – then belted through the wings and into the nearest Gents!

Afterwards, on my way out to the stage door, I made a decision: from that night onwards I vowed to steer clear of Gordon Higginson's influence. I'd never walked in anyone's shadow, and didn't intend to start now. (Although in later years Mr Higginson and I were to share the same platform on several auspicious occasions, this was never of my doing.)

In the street, Jeff, who'd been in the audience, met

me. 'Your work was accurate tonight. How's it going up north, then?'

'Well, you know . . .'

'Any news on that book you've been scribbling?'

'Oh yes,' I said, 'there's been a miracle. It's sprouted a pair of wings and it keeps flying back!'

He chuckled. 'Do you know, I've never been to Newcastle in my life. Could you put up with a visitor for a weekend, next month?'

'Of course,' I replied, 'if the visitor can tolerate the grubby estate where I live.'

He smiled, opened my taxi door, and bundled me and my suitcase inside. Then he and a few friends waved me off, and I was driven at breakneck speed to High Street railway station.

By the time the train pulled out I was dog-tired, but thankfully there were very few passengers travelling; the last thing I wanted was a conversation with strangers.

Oh my God, how I loathed train journeys . . .

Clickety-click, clickety-clack. Clickety-click, clickety-clack.

For hours on end the carriage hypnotically rocked and rattled, and the air was parched with dry heat. I was so tired. My eyes felt like sandpaper . . . Outside, the night sky was inky-black. Occasionally a blur of distant lights flickered past the dark windows. How I'd always hated travelling . . .

I yawned and shut my eyes against the heat . . . my body lolled and swayed in the big seat . . . I'd spent an exhausting few days. But had it all been worth it? Of course it had. I told myself not to be silly. It hadn't been easy, but I'd gained invaluable experience, and

I felt I'd struck a little blow for democracy. I'd learned a bit more about human nature, too. Dell had always told me I was naïve . . .

Clickety-click, clickety-clack . . .

The Inter-City Express shuddered and hummed as it rolled over endless miles of cold steel. I was so sleepy . . . Another yawn . . . and I dimly wondered if my flying manuscript had made another crash-landing on the doormat . . .

I frowned.

Clickety-click,   clickety-clack.   Clickety-click, clickety-clack.

How I dreaded going back to that shabby flat in Tyne and Wear with all its thugs and vandals, and its intolerable noise . . . But then I smiled because I couldn't wait to see my lovely Sooty again . . .

15

Visions of Another World

The busy cafe at British Rail Newcastle was full of bustling passengers, queueing for drinks to stave off their thirst in the hot weather. Jeff bought two cans of chilled *Diet Pepsi* and I walked him to his train.

'If I were you, I'd get out of that hell-hole of an estate,' he said.

'Sooty and I have been in Gateshead for nearly two years now, so I tried to get a council exchange up here, but no joy.'

'Pity.' We opened our cans and quenched our thirsts.

'To tell you the truth,' I said, 'I miss Wales: I'm homesick. White Owl told me I'll go back soon; but when is soon?'

'Quite. Spirit people rarely give a time limit with their wonderful predictions.'

We laughed, and he got on the train and waved through the open window as it pulled away. 'Give me a call,' he shouted. 'I'll keep an eye open for you down in Swansea, in case any flats become empty.'

The next day, acting on Jeff's sensible advice, I set all the right wheels in motion at the Housing Department and requested a Welsh property; but weeks passed with no offers, despite my being placed on their priority list because my father's doctor had written to them and recommended that I ought to be near my Dad, who had a disability.

More weeks passed and there was still no news, except that my spirit grandfather, Grancha Price, assured me through a local medium that Wales would soon welcome me home. But when?

I felt very despondent and down in the mouth: I was stony-broke, out of work, and stuck in a region whose unemployment figures were phenomenally high. With no work prospects on the horizon, how on earth could my living standards rise above the poverty line? And what were the spirit people playing at?

Months back, when I'd slogged away at writing my kamikaze manuscript, the Other Side had promised me all kinds of things. They'd engendered within me an overwhelming urge to try to follow in the footsteps of the successful medium Doris Stokes, who'd just 'died' in May 1987. Doris had generated immense media interest in mediumship, and it was through this opened door, my inspirers had told me, that I was to continue to broadcast the reality of Everlasting Life to a public now thirsting for spiritual knowledge.

So why wasn't that happening? What was going on?

Why was I penniless, and stuck in abysmal living conditions that made me homesick? And why, in the last year, had my thirteen attempts to place my life-story failed? The book had been my final effort to justify my existence, and it had come to nothing.

If the spirit people had spoken the truth, why was I surrounded by so much inaction? Their promises didn't make sense. I couldn't solve these puzzles – but I did know what I was going to do; I'd been thinking about it for a long, long time. Years, in fact. And now I was going to do it.

I made a start by stuffing *Visions of Another World* into a large cardboard box and officially shelving the project. Then I telephoned a Buddhist monastery and asked to join it.

They would ring me back to tell me the time of my appointment with their leader, whom I thought of as their Abbot.

I wasn't a Buddhist, but then I wasn't a Spiritualist, either; as far as I was concerned these were just labels people attached to themselves to gain a sense of identity, and I didn't need that. I knew who I was.

The monastery interested me because it was a closed order where the rushing world was locked firmly outside its stout walls. From my earliest recollections as a child I'd never felt that I 'belonged' on earth, and it would have caused me no pain to forsake it. I would have welcomed the joy of withdrawing from today's crazy 'civilization'.

There'd be no sorrow in my saying goodbye to its noisy television and radio sets, and I wouldn't have missed for a second the blaring newspaper headlines that are composed to shock our senses. As for the world of finance, I'd never wanted anything to do with all the false values it's engendered in the human mind over the centuries. People were slaves to money. How easily I could have thrown twentieth-century living aside and entered the blissful silence of a permanent retreat.

White Owl was silent at this time, but then I knew that when important spiritual experiences enter a medium's life, his inspirers often step back to allow him to grow from the challenges he must face.

Within the monastery's sacred walls I would till the soil and live close to nature, for I had never been afraid of hard work; and I would take a strict vow of silence. In seclusion I would shun all relationships except the most important one of all – that of seeking and finding a closer union with the Spirit of the Living God within me.

Fully prepared to forsake the physical world, I was now ready to dedicate myself to any spiritual pathway into which the Great Spirit saw fit to guide me.

My mind was made up, but my close friends were quite concerned . . . 'Stephen, are you absolutely sure this is what you want?' I replied calmly, 'Don't worry about me. I live alone – and I'm not afraid of silence.' They said they understood; and I knew that Sheila would give Sooty a loving home if I couldn't take my little friend with me to the monastery.

For many nights after making this decision, my soul silently cried out for further Guidance and Light. But no response filled the dark bedroom . . . except once, when I felt the familiar presence of an old friend standing close by.

I was so pleased to welcome my mother – Mam – who then gave me spiritual healing, comforted me, and rekindled within me that love I'd felt when as a child I'd been cradled in her arms. Obviously having sensed my distress, she had kept her promise and helped me when I needed it most.

Peacefully, I drifted off to sleep in the full knowledge that all I was waiting for now, was a phone call from the Abbot . . .

But the very next morning there was a letter on the hall mat from the Swansea Housing Department offering me a council flat in Swansea near to Dad, and right next door to Jeff!

In the face of this startling realization of the spirit world's promise to return me to my homeland, I bowed to my Fate and put on hold all thoughts of the monastery – and, at thirty-two years of age, I went back home to Wales.

It took no time at all to re-establish contact with all my Welsh friends; it was as though I'd never been away, and one dear soul I was happy to cuddle again was Phyllis, a psychic friend of mine in her sixties, who lived in a small pensioner's bungalow. Phyl handed me a steaming mug of hot chocolate and announced, with a faraway look in her eyes:

'That book of yours *will* be accepted, Steve.'

My disbelief was obvious. 'Oh yes? And when will that be? After my death?'

She chortled. 'No, soon. But not by a London publisher, it'll be a firm outside London.'

I was impressed. 'Well, it's funny you should say that, you spooky old thing, because this week I got the manuscript out, made a brief synopsis of it and parcelled up three chapters with it, then posted off six of these packages to some publishers this very morning! One of those firms is outside London.'

'Well, you'll hear,' she said with a smile.

And I did. *Visions of Another World* was snapped

up by the Aquarian Press, a division of Thorsons Publishers, based then in Wellingborough, Northamptonshire, and they invited me to their offices to discuss the project and the book contract. An appointment for a business lunch was made, and the ball quickly started rolling towards my possible self-employment as an author.

I drove to my publishers in the 'new' second-hand banger of a Ford car that I'd bought very reasonably (and in which I'd passed my test first time!), and at the Aquarian Press the senior editor and his publicity chief told me they were very excited about the prospect of publishing my autobiography, and that they felt it would do very well, following on from the success of Doris Stokes.

When the editor asked me how successful I thought *Visions of Another World* would be, an immediate answer was given to me by the next world: a spirit hand that was resting on his shoulder suddenly came into my vision, and to me this was a clear indication that the book would do well because the unseen world had guided him to publish it.

He wanted me to sign a contract immediately, but this I cautiously refused, asking that their offer be sent by post, so that I could consider it more carefully. They agreed, and I left with a mind full of whirling thoughts and a stunning disbelief that it had all happened so swiftly.

But another surprise confirmation awaited me when I was astonished to see the street sign 'London Road' just outside their offices: several months previously when the Manchester medium Mavis Pittilla had given me in a spirit message 'an important connection with a London Road' I'd denied all knowledge of it, but now it was staring me in the face.

The spirit people had been secretly active all along. While I had been impatient – they had been waiting.

As a new author with no agent to steer me through the frightening jungle of literary and legal jargon contained in publishing contracts, I wanted to know exactly what I'd be agreeing to; so, I read some weighty tomes such as *The Writers' and Artists' Yearbook* from the local library and discovered 'The Minimum Terms Agreement' which the Society of Authors recommended that non-agented writers should pursue to secure a fair deal. But I was confident now that my invisible friends had everything in hand, and a reasonable contract arrived that week in the post. After some haggling and a few fine adjustments, I signed up and the book went straight into the production line, which meant it would be released as a paperback original in about one year's time.

My biggest problem then, as always, was the spectre of money – it was a spectre because I didn't have any! To tour Great Britain giving evenings of clairvoyance as Doris Stokes had done would cost a small fortune and, until publication day, I'd still be drawing Social Security.

When she heard this news, thoughtful Dell Round came to my rescue. 'You deserve success, Stephen,' she said, 'and you shall have it. I don't own a penny-piece, but I've got a mortgage and I'm quite happy to put my house up as collateral for you to get a bank loan. Don't look so stunned. Your work's very important and you'll need £20,000 to stage your tour.'

I was dumbstruck at first, but then dimly heard myself saying, 'Thank you, Dell. But . . . what if the venture isn't successful . . . ?'

She laughed out loud. 'The bank'll take my house, and you'll have to put a camp bed up in your spare room, good boy!'

We chuckled and I gave her an enormous hug, and my promise that I'd try to find professional promoters first, rather than jeopardize her home. That's when it occurred to me to contact Derek Robinson – the man who'd arranged Gordon Higginson's nationwide tour that I'd been involved in at Winchester and Swansea. Derek had experience in promotional work and had toured with Doris Stokes in her earlier years.

When I rang him he expressed a keen interest in the prospect of his newly-formed organization ISP (International Spiritualist Promotions) arranging my tour; so, I travelled along another London Road – he lived in Wimbledon – and met him and his business partner for talks. Our discussions were fruitful and we signed contracts which bound me to give evenings of clairvoyance in approximately twenty cities across the UK, which would be exclusively funded by ISP. At the end of the contract period of some two months or so, the profits were to be equally divided between myself and ISP.

I returned to Swansea feeling that I'd made great strides forward, but I also had a strange sense of foreboding, though I didn't know why. I shook my shoulders and dismissed these thoughts, then informed Dell that her mortgage was safe. And at the same time I made a clean break with my past, and turned bravely towards my future.

When ISP and I held more discussions with the Aquarian Press publicity chief to settle final business preparations, she offered us a caution and some realistic advice.

'Don't get too excited, gentlemen,' she said, casting a glance at an enthusiastic Derek and his business associate; 'this is only Stephen's first book, you know. It'll take time to build up a public reputation and a huge following, and to create a demand for Stephen's work in the market-place.'

Derek quickly countered this by reminding us of Doris Stokes's phenomenal success, but the experienced PR chief had a ready answer. 'Yes, but media interest in Mrs Stokes had been built up over several years. Stephen O'Brien's just starting out. And don't forget that Doris received some tough media criticism. Public opinion fluctuates, gentlemen, and the press might be cynical about the claims of mediums.'

'You're right,' I agreed. 'Although I'm known to some of the population, to millions of other Britons I'm "undiscovered country".'

The PR chief smiled. 'As to your book – we think it'll get good reviews. But it all depends on what other titles land on the editor's desk on that morning. If yours catches his eye and sparks his attention, that helps.'

There was an awkward pause.

'Let's keep our spirits up,' she went on. 'We're quite excited about *Visions of Another World* and the author tour. There's everything to look forward to, gentlemen – so let's go for it!'

And on that, we all parted and went our separate ways.

Derek immediately started booking up halls in the carefully targeted cities across Britain, but a major setback occurred when his wife, Hazel, suddenly had to receive major heart-bypass surgery, which understandably caused a great deal of concern to her family, and all our business schedules were disrupted. We prayed for Hazel's recovery, of course, and hoped our healing thoughts would comfort and sustain her through her ordeal, which I'm sure they did.

My attention then had to be quickly turned back to my nationwide tour: I'd signed two contracts; my autobiography was due out in a few months' time; and theatres and halls had to be confirmed for my public appearances. The work was lagging way behind and, in short, I started to panic.

Derek readily accepted my suggestion that I should undertake the administration from Swansea, which I did; but there was so much to do. It was a paperwork nightmare of red tape, but with determination I ploughed through it as best as I could.

Then I worried a little.

Then I booked more halls across Britain.

And then I worried a lot.

In a hot-under-the-collar paddy, I turned to my next-door neighbour for help, and Jeff was very supportive. Neither of us had any previous experience of promotional management but he knuckled down and helped me to complete all the complicated arrangements, and the invoices were sent to ISP in London for payment.

The Aquarian Press were informed of my tour schedules so that their sales team could 'sell in' *Visions* to bookstores across the UK; then I travelled to their headquarters in January 1989 and sat for an hour-long photo session, one picture from which was chosen to appear on the book's front cover.

Their vast public relations engine was all geared up and revving away on the spot, ready to catapult me into the public's awareness as Britain's next successful medium. *Psychic News* announced my expected launch into wider acclaim and my stomach flipped over, then settled down, then did another flip every time I thought about what had happened to me, and how quickly it had all come about.

I walked around in a constant daze – but I was thrilled, of course, about my book: it was no mean feat to get a major work published at any time, but I'd managed it.

The thought that my message of hope and comfort would now be broadcast to millions of souls both pleased me and frightened me at one and the same time.

My days were fully occupied now, filled with long-distance telephone calls to promoters, publishers, theatre administrators, and press advertisement departments – I was lost in a whirlwind of activity; and my nights were robbed of sleep by anxious thoughts.

How would the public and the media receive me? I was just an ordinary lad from Swansea who'd grown up with something to say about eternity – but would they want to listen to me?

With just a few weeks to go before publication day I

was fraught with tension when, one sleepless night, White Owl's powerful spiritual presence drew near and his deep voice delivered a fatherly warning. 'In the years that lie ahead, my friend, you must be strong of mind and will,' he said, 'for to remain faithful to us you will need great courage and determination.'

I didn't answer him, but remained still in the bed and listened.

'To fulfil your spiritual mission you will need to draw deeply upon the God-Power within you, for great personal sacrifices will be involved.'

The warm darkness of the bedroom embraced me. I waited. But he spoke no more than this. His voice had faded away, and all I could hear now was the distant hum of city night traffic.

My spirit guide seemed to know exactly what my future would hold for me. I suspected, too, that the real me – my inner soul – was also fully aware of it; but Stephen O'Brien the physical man was not. I could only guess at it. If only I could have tapped into this soul-knowledge I'd have felt much more confident about becoming a touring author and a professional medium.

A professional medium. Dear God, it was going to happen. But the sound of those words still dealt me a stinging blow. I definitely didn't like the idea; I never had. Mrs Palmer had been right about my livelihood after all.

Life was certainly strange, and my spirit was so restless, so anxious, that it took me ages to drift into a fitful sleep, still thinking, and not at all at peace.

Then I had a frightening nightmare . . .

First I saw myself sitting in claustrophobic trains, and cars, then in planes that skimmed the seas . . . Then I stood inside a terrifying mass of flickering blurred images: my white-knuckled hands were clutching to my heart a copy of my book, while nightmare pictures spun round and around in my mind.

Breathless with tension I suddenly 'appeared' inside packed-out theatres – dozens of them simultaneously: there were so many people – people everywhere; crowds, seas of strange faces craning their necks, expectant, all leaning forward in their seats, waiting, hoping, demanding, praying for help – from me; and I feared I wouldn't be able to give it . . .

Then I stood frighteningly alone in a bright spotlight on an empty stage in front of a microphone, peering into scores of auditoriums at once; I listened, strained my ears to catch faint spirit voices – but they didn't come – they wouldn't come – and the public were restless, fidgeting, impatient. Where were my voices? – and why were the people's eyes so large and white and staring?

Then everything vanished and I was floating in a pitch-black vacuum when another set of faces flickered into view: hundreds of journalists, television researchers and radio presenters sat opposite thousands of distorted television images of me – and they questioned – disbelieved – sneered at me with cynical grins on their faces.

Suddenly a black cloud swirled down and covered me in darkness again. I fell to my knees under an invisible dead-weight that pressed me to the floor, and I knew it was the force of the demands being made upon my time and abilities.

Then a vast thunderstorm burst overhead and forked-lightning lit up my mind and I looked up into the whirling cyclone that was drawing my body into its centre. Frantically I clutched at the loose earth but it slipped through my fingers. I stood up unsteadily, fighting with the storm as I rose into it, nearer and nearer to the cyclone's eye, and I couldn't breathe – I couldn't think – I was gasping – choking – opening my mouth – gaping – crying out, but unable to make a sound – there was so much pressure in my head – throbbing – pounding – ready to burst like a balloon. Then I snapped my neck and jolted myself wide awake—

I was sitting up in bed, sweating profusely; my heart was beating fast against my ribs, and drumbeat pulses were throbbing in my neck. Sweat was pouring down my back. I was exhausted and I had a migraine headache.

It was three o'clock in the morning.

In the dim bedroom, as I wiped my glistening skin on the sheets, from somewhere deep down within me I felt a tide of tears rising, lifting, until they gathered tight in my throat. Strange sobbing noises filled the room and shattered the peace of the night—

The noises were coming from me.

My shoulders began to shake – then suddenly a floodgate opened in my soul which released a torrent of built-up emotion that swept through me and shook my spirit.

My hands flew up and covered my face; my form bent over in the bed and I was astonished by the sounds coming from the heart of it. Like a child, I cried and cried . . .

I cried for times past and for lost opportunities: for the pain my mother had suffered while she lay dying of cancer; for my father's anger over her death, and the bitterness that still tormented him; I wept for the memory of my friend, Mrs Palmer, and for the grief she must have felt when she lost her three babies. Mrs Palmer had been so kind to me, just like a surrogate mother.

I cried, too, because I was frightened by the massive responsibilities that would fall onto my shoulders when I attempted to reach millions of people with the spiritual message I'd promised to deliver; and strangely, I felt I'd have to face that challenge alone because, just then, the spirit world seemed so very far away from me . . .

My tears flowed until my strength was spent, until every ounce of hidden emotion that had been buried deep inside me for the last thirty years had risen to the surface and expressed itself.

Then, totally exhausted, I fell back onto the bed.

In the stunning silence that followed, broken only by the sound of my deep breathing, I realized the importance of my work, and I prayed I'd be given the strength to complete it.

For a long time, I remained calm, deep in thought, staring at the ceiling . . .

Since a child, I'd never felt I'd belonged on earth and I'd often tried to reject its materialism, yet now I was about to spring-board right into the thick of it: I'd have to co-operate with its banks, its money, its newspapers and its media – all the things I'd wanted to forsake by joining the monastery. But now . . . there'd be no seclusion for me within silent, holy walls, for I knew that ahead of me lay many soul-testing times, and a great deal of hard work.

Silently, I turned over in the darkness, covered my head, and then I slept.

PART THREE
Bright Shining Lights

A Voice in the Night

The Children of the Darkness
    fear the Children of the Light,
        for the Light
            reveals their shadowed hearts . . .

Go then into the Darkness
    all you Children of the Light,
        and bring to life the hearts of men . . .

16

'Is There Anybody There?'

Just before the publication of *Visions of Another World* I was groomed for 'stardom'. A few friends and I sat down and agreed that my stage costume would be a black jacket and trousers with a white shirt and dark red tie, and I got these items quite cheaply – the jacket was bought from Jeff for five pounds! I also got a new hairstyle, a pair of smart black boots, and then started vigorous aerobics and multigym workouts to get my weight down: if I so much as *look* at a bar of chocolate I might as well glue it to my belly or my bum.

Through careful dieting and exercise I lost eight pounds, flattened my stomach, and trimmed my bodyline in readiness for the television cameras and public scrutiny; but, despite the fact that i'd be brightly lit by spotlights on stage, I decided no make-up would be worn; what the audience would see, would be exactly what it would get.

Each meeting would be introduced by a mature chairlady and would be given in two halves. In part one I would give the audience a spiritual talk for about fifteen minutes, and explain to them how important it is for them to respond to the messages as they come through; then I would deliver three quarters of an hour of clairvoyance which would be followed by an interval of fifteen minutes. Part two would start with fifteen minutes of questions and answers followed by another hour of message-relaying to finish.

ISP were responsible for selling my autobiography which I'd autograph for people at the end of each night. The promoters had also been contracted to give nineteen Children's Hospitals some money from the tickets that were priced at £4.50 each.

Much quicker than I imagined, publication day in September 1989 was heralded by the arrival of a four-figure advance royalties cheque from Aquarian Press and I immediately signed off Social Security and became self-employed. I was now a new author and a professional medium. Everything was poised for take-off: I was thirty-three and ready to face the world; or at least, I thought I was.

Thousands of copies of *Visions* had been sold into bookstores throughout Britain and had been instantly sold out. The book went immediately into reprint. North of London, repeat orders couldn't be met and some people would have to wait weeks before they could read it. I was disgruntled, to say the least, especially as I'd warned my cautious publishers there'd be a 'hidden' demand for my life-story from the Spiritualist Movement. But I just had to bite my lip, take a few deep breaths, and get to work.

After a book-signing session on the afternoon of publication day I was chauffeured to London to do a three-hour 'live' national chat show for Channel Four TV.

The next day, filled with hope and apprehension, I set out on my first UK tour – which turned out to be one long series of chaos and disasters, right from the start.

After taking just two or three poorly attended meetings we quickly realized what was coming – but what could we do about it? Ruefully I commented, 'It seems that one book does not a famous person make.' We were terribly downhearted, but had committed ourselves to the schedule and we had to get on with it.

With firm resolve I knuckled down to the hard work, but was soon so stressed and addled, mainly through trudging all over Britain to find the halls in strange cities, that I became dispirited and often lost my way. And I hated staying in cold and unwelcoming guest-houses; ISP had booked no accommodation for me, I'd done it myself and had saved all my travel receipts for later reimbursement.

All the signs of impending disaster were there: we were working to the cheapest possible budget and I was a new 'personality' with a low public profile – a lethal combination that failed to attract people to spend a night out at the theatre. The big halls I worked in seemed so vast and cavernously empty that they crippled my morale. But at each meeting, I had to stand in the wings, smile and then go on, regardless of how I felt, or of how many – or how few – people were in the audience.

Promoter Derek Robinson got worried and kept saying things like, 'There's not many punters in tonight,' just before I was to make my entrances, and this narked me terribly: numbers didn't interest me just then, I was desperately trying to link with the spirit world.

Weeks of unbearable tension and hard graft flew by in a blur and I whizzed in and out of newspaper offices and radio stations so fast, and kicked up so much dust, that I resembled the twisting cyclone in *The Wizard of Oz*. I gave so many interviews that, in the end, the answers to the most awkward questions fell from my lips without hesitation.

The media took a huge interest in me, no doubt sparked off by four hundred free review copies of *Visions* that the publishers had sent them. So many flash-bulbs popped around me that I felt as if I had a continuous migraine headache; I was photographed and interviewed to death (and I dislike both ordeals).

But it went on, and on – and on.

I travelled the length and breadth of the country, entirely alone, and I felt so vulnerable, and very disillusioned; anyone could have mugged me and left me for dead at some deserted railway station in the dead of night for all the world cared. It wasn't easy to rationalize that the medium who was treated like a glittering celebrity was also the man who wanted to be back home in front of a warm fire and out of the public gaze. My need and desire for privacy battled with the New Public Image right throughout the tour, and the whole distressing issue of being 'an unusual personality' got me down.

Amazingly, despite all this stress, some of the spirit messages that came through at the meetings were evidential and comforting, and sometimes amusing.

At one venue, a message from a reformed 'miser' of a stepfather made us smile. He identified himself by giving me the surname of Pickering and the place name of Babbacombe; but when I described his appearance, at first he was only reluctantly accepted by his adopted son in the audience, until I added, 'He's talking about Terry.'

'I'm Terry!' cried the surprised young man, 'and you've got my step-Dad there, and a proper skinflint he was, too. He wouldn't give you the dirt from under his nails!'

The audience laughed. 'Well, he wants to tell you something,' I said. '"The money's up in the attic, in the big wooden chest."'

People gasped, but the young man beamed one of the biggest smiles I'd seen for many years. 'Well, I never! We wondered where the old goat had stuffed it!' he shouted back. 'I'll be up there *tonight!*'

Everyone chuckled except the spirit stepfather, who then spoke sadly of having to stay close to the earth immediately after his death because his relatives had squabbled over his money and sentimental possessions.

'I nearly tore my hair out!' he grumbled to the lad. 'I was powerless, you know – powerless to stop them! I had to stand by and watch my goodies being carted off by the baddies! I screamed at them, but it was no use. They couldn't hear me. Afterwards, I had a bloody good laugh about it, but at the time of the Big Fight,' he added more quietly and poignantly, 'I think I knew what it must feel like to experience a living Hell.' Then he chortled away to himself.

At the same meeting, another poignant contact was delivered concerning a beautifully kept alsatian dog who'd been 'put to sleep' by his devoted but nearly blind, elderly mistress who was seated in the crowd. The woman had never married, and had loved and tended the dog as though it were her child. The message began with my receiving two unusual names.

'Who are Archie and Cynthia?'

'I'm Cynthia,' called back the gentle spinster, who wore thick spectacles, 'and my alsatian was called Archie.'

'Well then, I think you should recognize the gentleman who's brought this lovely old dog here, and who's sending this message to you tonight. I receive a name that sounds like Lawrence, and' – I frowned, and concentrated to hear his voice more clearly – 'is there some kind of connection with the Air Force?'

'Yes, he was a pilot. Lawrence was . . . killed in the war. We were lovers.'

You could have heard a pin drop in the auditorium. 'You've been faithful to his memory, he tells me.'

'I never married after his death.'

'Well, he wants me to say, "I have Archie with me; I'll take care of him for you; so, don't cry"' – but the blind woman's teardrops were already falling – '"and I promise you two things: one day, we'll all be together again – and you will see us clearly."'

She whispered emotionally, 'Thank you . . .'

But he hadn't finished his link yet, and further delighted his sweetheart by stating, 'It's your kindness and your love that keep me and the dog right beside you.' Then he concluded with some comforting advice: 'Just call on our names, and we'll be with you in spirit.'

As I watched the woman's face, the haunting look

of loneliness in it seemed to evaporate, and a psychic light of joy took its place.

I witnessed much the same kind of transformation at a different venue when I delivered another touching message involving animals; it began by my asking the audience if anyone knew 'Auntie Polly', who'd brought with her a spirit cat. A young lad of no more than ten years, called out from the crowd: 'That's Fluffy!'

Everyone smiled, and the boy's cheeks flushed pink.

'Auntie Polly's brought six kittens with her,' I relayed, 'and I think they died during birth. You've been missing them.' The lad was understandably quiet. 'Does that sound right?' I asked him, gently.

His grandma, next to him, nudged his elbow and gave him permission to speak up. 'Yes,' he said, with a brave smile.

'Well, they're all safe on the Other Side,' I assured him. 'But why does Polly shout out "Scat"?'

He giggled as only young lads can. 'My name's *Scott!*'

We were all amused. 'Oh, my apologies! I don't always hear the messages correctly. Well, Scott,' I said, much more carefully, 'Aunt Polly says she'll keep the pussy-cats for you, so don't fret.' Then I added from myself, 'You haven't lost your little friends; they're being well cared for.'

The boy's eyes shone like stars. He was sitting near the front and I could see the bright metal calliper supporting one of his legs, and I made a note to send out healing prayers for him, later on. But his spirit aunt went on to mention some bullies at his school who were giving him a tough time. She didn't want them to upset him. 'Sticks and stones may break your bones, but names will never hurt you,' she said.

Scott thanked her.

'And tell me – why is she talking about a spider?'

'Spider's the biggest bully,' he confided. 'He's fat and 'airy!'

Scott's Aunt Polly smiled, then further comforted him with news of a spiritual law. 'Every night you walk in a perfect spirit body Over Here, my love, while your physical body's asleep,' she said. 'And one day – oh many, many years from now, when you're a very old man indeed, and very grey – you'll come across to us for ever – and you'll have two strong legs to stand on. There's no disability in the spirit body, my love,' she explained, which very much pleased him and his relatives.

To bring such happiness to people is an important part of a medium's job and I tried to rekindle hope in any troubled souls I met. Of course, not all of those early meetings were great successes. 'I'm only a human being,' I explained to the people, 'I'm not a computer, and mediums always make mistakes; not one of us is perfect.'

Some of the spirit messages went unaccepted by startled recipients, some were confusing, others contained information that needed to be checked, and a number weren't received by me as clearly as I would have liked. Mind-to-mind communication between the two worlds is never easy to accomplish, and the psychological pressures from which I suffered in that first UK tour made my task all the more difficult for me. I didn't work to my full potential, not by a long chalk, and I was still inexperienced in demonstrating at these big venues, but I did the best I could.

When it all got too much for me, one night, from a damp guest-house in some drab and remote coastal town, I telephoned Jeff – to ask how Sooty was – but what I really needed was a sympathetic ear.

'The halls are so huge, and the audience numbers are low,' I lamented. 'In some places there's just 120 people or so and it feels so embarrassing, for all of us.'

Jeff said he felt sorry for me and spent the next twenty minutes offering sensible words of encouragement.

But the days ticked over and I still couldn't settle into a happy relationship with my promoters; it was a pure clash of personalities and ideas. I wanted chairpersons to preside over the meetings, as we'd agreed in the contract – but ISP did not, because their expenses added to the costs. I wanted to work entirely alone, as agreed by contract – but ISP kept trying to persuade me to have other mediums on in the first half to 'warm up the audience' and give me 'a build-up'. I refused: 'Other demonstrators might bore the audiences and kill them stone dead, which would make it more difficult for me to work with them,' I said.

I took my job very seriously, but ISP kept suggesting a more light-hearted approach to it, to make it a more entertaining evening. 'But I'm a medium,' I kept saying, 'not a comedian.'

They meant well, as I'm sure they thought I did,

but I got terribly disheartened; and during one tense drive to a venue, while the two promoters shouted angrily at each other in the front of the Land-Rover, I sat spiritually numbed at the back. It was one of the few occasions that I clearly sensed White Owl's powerful presence and heard his voice. 'Keep calm, and do the best you can, my friend,' he advised. 'No-one could ask any more of you.'

At such an important period in my life my spirit friends must have been close to me, of course, but they couldn't be blamed: after all, hadn't they already warned how difficult my pathway would be?

I shall never forget the utter sense of panic that swept through me in the town hall of one of Britain's major cities. As soon as I stepped onto the premises, I was thrown into a whirlwind of chaos. The meeting was just three quarters of an hour away, and my London promoters, who were to arrange the platform, front-of-house bookstall, microphones, and lights, hadn't arrived. The minutes ticked away, and they were nowhere to be seen. The meeting loomed up. Something had to be done, so I made a snap decision: I would do everything myself.

In a frenzy of activity I dashed around the building to find technicians, then, thoroughly irritated, I set up the complicated light and sound levels with them. Sweating now, I dragged tables and chairs up onto the stage and arranged them as best I could. Then I rushed into a dressing-room to heave on my black jacket and trousers. The clock kept ticking away towards doors-opening time – and still no sign of ISP.

As I flew back to the platform, beads of perspiration broke out on my brow and my heart pounded

238

when I remembered that my publisher's Head of National Book Sales, plus her guest, was to be among the audience. She'd be reporting her thoughts on the meeting back to the Aquarian Press. What a frightening thought: how could I possibly work well under all this stress?

The clock was against me, and with less than fifteen minutes to go I frantically gabbled through a rehearsal of the apology I'd give to the audience because there would be no books on sale; then I practised introducing myself, then I set my mind firmly on taking the meeting. I dreaded the tremendous challenge, but I was going to walk onto that stage tonight, no matter what.

Adding to this anxiety, as if by magic, the venue administrators suddenly appeared and gathered at my heels like a pack of angry, baying hounds. 'This event cannot proceed,' one of them imperiously barked at me, his finger stabbing at the clipboard he held, 'unless the balance on the booking fee is immediately paid.'

'But I'm only the medium,' I gabbled, my feet shifting nervously. 'I don't know anything about it. My promoters deal with all the finances – but I don't know where they are. They must have been delayed, or something. I don't know. But I hope they'll be here soon.'

I felt so helpless but he obviously didn't believe me. 'That is not acceptable. It isn't good enough. I'm sorry, Mr O'Brien, but the doors will stay locked until we have the £500 owed to us' – he stabbed at the board again – 'and you have ten minutes to produce it. No money – no show.'

I got suddenly grumpy and blurted back, 'It isn't a show!' – I was now at my wits' end – 'It's a public meeting.'

The administrator's eyes blazed like fire. 'No *money* – no *meeting*, then!' he repeated. 'The doors will stay locked until we're paid.'

'But I . . . I'm just the—'

'That is all,' he said, marching briskly away, swinging the clipboard as he went.

As I watched him leave the auditorium, my hands started to shake. What on earth could I do? What about the public? And my publisher's representatives? I felt instantly powerless and vulnerable.

Someone hammered on the front doors, and I glanced up at the big clock when, just as its hands touched seven, two flustered promoters scurried into the hall as though their trousers were on fire. Derek was bright red. 'We were coming down the motorway in the Land-Rover, and the bloody caravan that was hitched to the back of it broke loose – and overtook us!'

Instead of smiling, my lips frantically gushed forth what had happened. ISP were obviously as flustered and concerned as I was about the whole fiasco, but my problems were by far the greater: I still had a two-and-a-half-hour meeting to take – and there was no way I could rest during it.

Derek's business associate eventually handed a cheque for £500 to the impatient administrator, while I stood and shivered. The doors were flung open and the public gathered in the auditorium; they'd paid to see my work, and I couldn't let them down; so, at precisely 7.30 I was announced and, feeling sick with tension, I smiled then walked out onto the big platform . . .

The evening's mediumship remains a blur to me, but the event felt like walking through treacle from beginning to end.

Little wonder.

By some miracle, the evidence was mostly accepted and, though my efforts were appreciated by the small audience of about a hundred and forty people, I wondered what my publisher's Head of National Book Sales and her guest had thought of it all. But I needn't have worried. 'We came in sceptical, but we're going out convinced,' she said afterwards. I managed a weak but relieved smile, and warmly shook their hands.

Later, as I signed books for the audience, a jittery woman upset me further by remarking, 'This meeting wasn't advertised enough. I've lots of friends who'd love to have seen you, Stephen, if only they'd known. I could have got a coachload together.'

Outwardly I smiled, but inwardly I groaned.

Immediately after the meeting was over, as the promoters drove a very disconsolate medium to a caravan site where we were all to spend the night, it dawned on me that over the last three tense months prior to publication, and now when working on this tour, my health had been badly affected; I didn't broadcast this, but I now had a very sore throat and a high temperature. I was tense and thoroughly depleted and I had to speak to someone – anyone. So that night, from a public call-box, I telephoned Jeff.

'How's Sooty?'

'Oh, she's settling down here, fine. How's the tour going?'

I paused. 'Oh not bad. I'm glad . . . is she . . . How . . .' My words trailed away.

'What's wrong, Steve?'

'I'm . . . I feel terrible,' I said; and when Jeff didn't respond, the sound of panic in my voice astonished me. 'I feel as though I'm locked inside a living nightmare, and I can't wake up. I wish I could get out of it, but I can't.'

For the next half-hour he listened sympathetically while I gabbled on about my misfortunes and, by the time my last 50p piece ran out, I felt emotionally washed-out, but cleansed enough to announce with vigour, 'Knackered I may be – but beaten, I am not!' Then I plonked down the receiver, stuck out my chin and strode out onto the moonlit gravel pathway, once more determined to work for the spirit world.

But that night I couldn't sleep and gain any healing rest because I found myself ensconced with two promoters in 'Spooky', their rather cold caravan which had earlier acted like an awkward supermarket trolley that had displayed a mind of its own on the motorway.

Curled up in the only 'private' tiny bedroom, with my winter coat thrown over the blankets and my black woolly hat pulled down firmly over my ears, I thought to myself, 'God almighty, if the public could only see me now. They must think my life is so glamorous, but if they only knew . . .'

Autumn dawn crept across the pale sky and I braved the blustery winds and tramped over wet grasses to reach the communal toilet blocks. They

242

smelled so bad that I refused to use them, and simply splashed my hands and face with ice-cold water.

After such a disastrous sequence of events, it's hardly surprising that during another difficult demonstration of clairvoyance, where the small audience were quite unresponsive, my patience had stretched so wafer-thin, I committed an unforgivable offence.

I'd asked the crowd if anyone could accept the details of a spirit message and there had been no answer; so I asked again, a little more forcefully.

Not a sound from the audience.

After my third attempt I suddenly stopped pacing back and forth and announced tetchily through the microphone, 'Well, if you aren't going to claim your messages – I might as well leave the stage.'

As my words echoed away, they left a wall of silence that stung my ears and filled the vast auditorium. My embarrassment was immediate when I saw a sea of eyes that stared blankly into mid-space . . .

My face flushed with shame: in a bout of irritability, I'd blamed the public for my own mediumistic incompetence.

I stuttered an awkward apology to the audience, but my dreadfully impolite remarks had made it clear to me that Stephen O'Brien was definitely not his normal self.

There would never have been any likelihood of my striding off the platform, of course, but how could those poor souls have known that?

Something positive, however, did arise from this distressing episode, when I realized that if I was to survive the taking of demonstrations in these large venues I'd have to master new presentation techniques; I'd learned the hard way that there was a world of difference between serving sympathetic Spiritualist congregations and trying to meet the far more demanding expectations of a theatre-paying public.

Spiritualists were sympathetic when the messages weren't clearly received, but the public were restless and impatient, and they expected precise, factual information every time. Unlike the Spiritualists, the public's span of attention was very short indeed, and sometimes the whole new experience of taking part in a 'mass seance' made them either nervous and reserved, or stunned and silent.

But I discovered that humour helped them to relax, and warm to me, so I had to learn to introduce it in the right places, but never at the expense of the communicators or their relatives in the crowd.

There were so many things to remember: I had to be polite and charming, to keep calm, and to smile; I had to learn how to grasp and maintain the interest of *everyone* in the theatre for two and a half hours, while relaying as many evidential facts from the next world as I could get.

'It's not easy to take large public meetings; and if anyone doesn't believe me,' I was to tell aspiring mediums in later years, 'then let him try it.'

Fortunately, the rigours of my first gruelling nationwide tour didn't completely swamp my spiritual resolve to serve. And it wasn't hard work all the time: there were a number of memorable lighter moments, like the one that happened before curtain-up one night in my dressing-room.

I'd just stripped off and was near-naked when suddenly the door burst open and in clumped a wrinkled charlady in curlers, who clanked her bucket and mop down on the hard tiles. She was bent forward slightly – and then she saw my feet. She slowly straightened her back and took in my rippling form – then she gasped and let out a blood-curdling scream: *'Aaarrgghh!'* as she fled from the room and disappeared down a set of corridors.

I grinned wickedly, closed the door, had a shower and donned my platform rig-out, thinking that was the end of it, or the end of her! But just before curtain-up, into my room stepped an immaculately dressed theatre manager with a poker-straight back. Rocking back and forth on his heels he said politely, 'Sorry to disturb you, Mr O'Brien . . . it's that little matter of the cleaning-lady . . .' and he coughed.

'Oh,' I said – but he raised a flat palm, smirked and declared solemnly, 'Do not apologize. I've come to thank you, for tonight you've made an old woman very happy!'

We both burst out laughing and the meeting went well after that. But now and again during the clairvoyance I caught sight of a smiling charlady, half-concealed behind a curtain at the back of the hall. She played peek-a-boo with me and gave me some lovely smiles and knowing little winks!

I was so relieved when my contract with ISP had run its course. The tour had finished and it was all over, thank God, and we wished each other well and shook hands, but ISP didn't reimburse me for my £500 travelling expenses, despite my having carefully filed and kept all my receipts; they claimed the tour had made a great financial loss. Our contract had stipulated that I was to see the breakdown sales sheets of each meeting, from which I could verify these claims, but I was never sent them.

So I was not only out of pocket, but also penniless because I'd received no wages. Then I faced a possible eviction from my council flat for non-payment of rent, which had been used to help with my travelling expenses. But thankfully I won my case and kept a roof over my head.

I was so glad to wash my hands of the whole depressing business, and I marked it all down to experience, then firmly put it out of my mind – but it had exhausted me so much that I slept for fourteen catatonic hours each night.

It was several weeks later when I found the time to sit down and read the first press reactions to my work as they came in, and I was pleased to discover they'd been quite favourable: some had reported me as 'a mystical prophet', and others had hailed me as 'the natural successor to Doris Stokes'; but, of course, you wouldn't have found two people more different than me and Doris: she had been an elderly and chatty grandmotherly figure, while I was a fit young man and more akin to 'the boy next door'.

On the whole I was well received. There were a few inevitable wise-cracks, of course, from reporters who'd put their tongues firmly in their cheeks, but that was to be expected. However, no-one was left in any doubt that media interest had awakened to me and my work.

I sat back in my chair and tried to relax a little, but

urgent thoughts started whizzing through my mind: I was self-employed now. I was an author. I was a public medium. I had to support myself financially.

'Nothing stands still, Stephen. Life must go on,' I murmured, thoughtfully.

A few days later, sitting in Swansea's Littlewoods' cafe, Jeff sipped a mug of instant hot chocolate while I casually ate my digestive biscuit, then spoke above the noise of busy shoppers:

'You'll never guess what.'

Jeff looked bored. 'What?'

'The Other Side has asked me to write a second book.'

Disinterest paled across his face; it was evident he'd already had enough of this tour business, thank you.

'I've even got the title,' I continued, snapping my biscuit in half. '*Voices from Heaven*, and I've started plotting it . . .'

A look of 'Spare me this' flicked over his eyes, followed by one of those 'I wouldn't if I were you' stares. He knew what was coming next.

'You see, Jeff . . . I've been thinking. You're only working part-time at the moment, and you said you don't like your job anyway . . .'

'So?' It was a defensive bark.

'Well . . . I'll have to tour again with *Voices from Heaven*, and I'd feel so much happier if you were helping with the organization, and—'

If looks could kill, I would have died right then.

'—so, how about turning self-employed, and becoming my manager?'

In utter silence, he picked up his biscuit, dipped it

247

into his chocolate drink, then took far too long to eat it. I didn't need to be psychic to see just how wary he was of the responsibilities involved.

After a while he said quietly, 'You must be bloody joking.'

Jeff had always been a cautious person who would never be pushed into anything.

'Well? . . . Will you be my manager?'

He looked me in the eye and said casually, 'I'll have to think about that, O'Brien.'

17

Voices from the Spirit World

The moment Jeff agreed to be my professional manager we booked a 'test' meeting at Stroud in Gloucestershire, and it was the financial success of this which led us to create a new business partnership called Voices Promotions (its name was given to me by the spirit world).

In the light of my experience with ISP, we knew that to form our own promotional organization in the midst of a gathering economic recession in Britain would be more than a tremendous gamble – it could fail much more easily than it could succeed. But Jeff and I were willing to give it our best shot, and to start the ball rolling we needed substantial financial backing to the tune of thousands of pounds, to book halls and pre-pay advertisements and tour accommodation; and then there were printing costs for posters and headed notepaper, etc.

Full of hope and armed with enthusiasm we visited a bank, clutching the detailed cash-flow business plan that we'd hammered out between us. But the bank refused to lend us capital until we'd proved Voices Promotions to be a viable concern, which meant forging ahead until we showed a working profit.

Now we were in a quandary. We needed money

to kick-start the venture, but we learned that the government business-aid programmes wouldn't fund organizations that dealt with clairvoyance. They were quite prepared to give applicants £40 a week to set up a restaurant that could serve food to clairvoyants, but the practising mediums themselves were denied their support.

'Don't worry,' I said confidently to Jeff, 'it'll come from somewhere.' And it did. When three kind friends from England heard of Voices they posted me a cheque for £500 – and we were off.

Jeff hurriedly booked the first few meetings of a new tour and suddenly we were ankle-deep in printed matter: posters, tickets, and publicity presspacks that were to be sent out to the media. A Post Office Box Number (PO Box 8, Swansea) was also established, which relieved my publisher of the hundreds of letters sent to me, and accepted mail orders for books from across the world; Jeff dealt with these and had to learn how to become a proficient PR man.

Following the success of a few more meetings we built up our finances to keep the business running, but there wasn't enough money for us to draw wages for the first month or so. Eventually we were able to take £40 per week each, but after tax and stoppages had been deducted I found I was earning less than I'd received on Social Security!

Then theatres rang from across Britain to ask what the major tour's ticket prices would be. 'There are so many unemployed people and one-parent families,' I commented to Jeff, 'that I think we should fix the lowest possible admission price.' He agreed. 'And could we open up the galleries, free of charge to those who can't afford a seat, so that they can hear the voice of the spirit?' I asked.

'Don't be so naïve, Stephen!'

'Well, at least give it a try before shooting me down. I know what it feels like to live below the poverty line.'

He did try, but ashen-faced theatre administrators wouldn't hear of it. *'Free seats?'* one boomed. 'You must be joking! We'd have a bloody riot on our hands!'

So our tickets were priced at £3.50 each.

The first round of the tour went well, and travelling to distant cities seemed less gruelling with Jeff's company in my second-hand Ford car. I was also accompanied by my new 'image'. A few close friends and I had re-vamped my appearance and I was now in my 'blue period': a succession of smart, well-cut light-blue suits with squared shoulders. My face was different, too, for now it looked quite normal under brilliant theatre arc-lights because of the specially purchased light-reflective make-up on it, whereas before it resembled that of a walking corpse – something that didn't inspire confidence in my audiences!

At venues I also spent a few hours with technicians to get the light and sound levels set just right. Much to their annoyance I was a perfectionist, and I'd attended Drama College for two years in my teens, so I knew all about the theatre.

I insisted on white light only, with several key-lamps carefully positioned at just the right angles so that my face would be properly lit. Most electricians were happy to comply but grumpy ones needed reminding that 'People need to see me, and to hear me.'

When sound-checks dragged on, some technicians would loudly protest, 'The mikes have been pre-set, sunshine!'

'But not for my voice,' I'd reply.

Then Jeff would step in. 'Please . . . Mr O'Brien knows *exactly* what he wants. If you meet his requests, it'll be over so much quicker for all of us!' That usually did the trick.

Because we ran a very tight budget, we had to stay at cheaply-priced, and sometimes unwelcoming, guest-houses, where we were often put in garret rooms at the top of mountainous flights of stairs up which we had to carry my books, because no-one would insure the stock, or myself.

'You see, if anything were stolen, Mr O'Brien,' the underwriters had curtly stated, 'or if for some reason you could not appear on stage, the financial risk to us would be too high.' So I wasn't insured, and the two of us had to lug the heavy boxes about.

Despite good attendances at the meetings, we certainly weren't rich. After one southern tour I returned home to find my electricity supply had been cut off! Jeff and I had a good belly-laugh about it and he ran a power cable through to me from his flat next door, until the re-connection charge could be paid.

But I wasn't daunted, for my faith in this venture was soon rewarded. *Visions of Another World* was reprinted four times in its first year and was declared 'a psychic best-seller', and vast amounts of fan mail poured through my letterbox and I was hit sideways by the public demand for my services. I answered every letter.

'Nothing succeeds like success,' said Aquarian Press, and they bought the world rights to publish my second volume of autobiography, *Voices from Heaven*, to be released in the following year, in 1991, which meant more national tours had to be booked up, with hall deposit costs paid out twelve months in advance, and this tied up nearly all of our capital. But the business managed to fork out a thousand pounds to buy me a word processor and printer, and I mastered its use at a local technical college, where I passed my Royal Society of Arts Grade One Word Processing with a distinction; after that I wrote the second volume of my life-story on floppy disks and a TV screen.

Although I felt happy to have broken what I'd always thought of as the crippling 9–5 workaday routine, I soon discovered that being a self-employed writer and business man involved putting in back-breakingly long and often unsociable hours, and there were no holidays, either; after both Jeff and I had struggled valiantly to get the business established, there were often weeks when we couldn't even draw wages – because the money wasn't there. When stability did finally arrive, we each received only £80 per week, at a time when the national average wage for a British man was well over £200.

We paid back the £500 cheque that had started us off, and as soon as Voices Promotions had at last been officially declared a viable business concern – guess what? The bank was now more than happy to back our future plans!

My media profile also started to establish itself more firmly, and invitations to work in several different countries were sent to me by post. One of these came from the Spiritualists' National Union, which again called upon me to demonstrate, but this time at two of its Centenary Celebration meetings to be held at the vast Wembley Conference Centre, London, and at Cardiff City Hall, Wales.

Before officially accepting, I heard from a reliable source that the SNU President, Gordon Higginson, had tried to veto both these invitations. I wasn't surprised, but remained quite philosophical and, with conviction, told my close friends, 'If I'm meant to be there, then that's where I'll be.'

Mr Higginson's objections were voted down and I attended, but he gave me a wide berth on both days; I think the most I got from him was a pleasant 'Hellair'.

In London, I took the stage with world-famous psychic artist, Coral Polge, before a warm and responsive audience of over 2,000 people. Coral drew the communicators' images which were projected onto an overhead screen, and I supplied their evidence; and afterwards I stood for a few hours to sign hundreds of copies of *Visions of Another World*.

The book continued to sell well, and in readiness for my second UK tour which would coincide with the release of my next literary venture, *Voices from Heaven*, I drove myself, Sooty and Jeff, 400 miles up north to stay with kindly Sheila in Tyne and Wear. Sheila had offered to keep Sooty 'on holiday' in her upstairs flat in Jarrow, while Voices Promotions set off to work in several northern cities.

When I placed poor Sooty in Sheila's arms, I felt like an anxious father leaving his child in boarding-school. Sooty wasn't amused, either – in fact, she wore a pained mask of high tragedy.

Forsake me not!

'Now you won't forget to give her a cuddle from me every night, will you, Sheila?'

'Of course not; but she'll miss you, Stephen.'

Parting is such sweet sorrow.

Sheila tickled Sooty's belly, and Sooty bit her. 'Ouch! She's usually OK for the first few days, then she sits on top of the stairs and gazes down forlornly at the front door, sighing.'

Indigestion.

I ruffled Sooty's headdress, kissed her goodbye, then drove off to tackle my first round of northern meetings.

Hurry back! The old witch pinches me as soon as you've gone!

Because I was now becoming better known, it was not unusual for me to face several hundred people at each gathering, which really thrilled me, for the message I'd been charged to deliver had been intended for the masses, and not just for the few. And my Other-world communicators always did their best to impress these audiences, and their loved ones, with some unusual survival evidence. In many instances, they succeeded because my ability to hear spirit voices more clearly had strengthened and developed through use.

At one venue, a touching link came through from a blonde girl who'd 'died' in a coma at the age of seven.

When she gave me the surname of Tinsley, a young woman in the crowd waved her hand.

'I know this,' she said. Jeff ran a radio-microphone to her, and I gave the message.

'This young girl was placed on a life-support system.'

'Yes . . .'

'And she talks about Sally.'

'I'm Sally. She's my daughter,' she replied, softly.

Then I gave a very comforting message on her child's behalf. 'Don't feel guilty about disconnecting the breathing apparatus,' I said. 'You've been plagued by the idea of whether or not your little girl was, in fact, "brain-stem dead".'

Sally nodded gently.

'But your daughter wants to reassure you: "You didn't hurt me, Mum. I was already in the spirit world before the doctors turned off the machine."'

The young mother held a white handkerchief to her mouth, and tried to stem her emotion, but she couldn't. Then, overcome with a great sense of relief, she smiled with joy when her daughter supplied her own christian name:

'"Vivienne loves you", your little girl says.'

'Tell my darling Vivienne . . . that I'll always love *her*,' was the poignant response.

I then thanked the lady and sensed that a different message was starting because I heard a much older, coarser voice calling out to me the name of 'Cassie Jenkins'.

'This lady's quite a cantankerous grandmother,' I volunteered to the amused audience. 'She was about eighty-nine years old when she dozed off in her armchair, while knitting baby bootees . . . for a relative. "I snuffed it in the chair," she tells me. I think she means that's how she died!'

During the laughter that followed, a young woman waved her flowery summer hat at me through the rays of powerful spotlights in the theatre circle.

'Me! Here! It's my Nana,' she said. 'That's just what she'd say about herself!'

'And are the details and age correct?'

'Yes!' she shouted, plonking the hat back on top of her rich auburn curls.

'And was she knitting when she passed over?' I asked, checking that I'd given the contact to the right person.

'Yeah. She was making bootees for her great-grandson. I'm a Jenkins, too.'

'Very well,' I continued, 'and Cassie's accepted your voice – you're the one we want. Now . . . ahem, oh . . . she says you've sensed her presence near to you. Is that right?'

'Well, I've sensed *something*.' Giggles rippled through the crowd.

'Cassie says, "You get shivers up and down your spine when I'm haunting you."'

People grinned nervously, and even more so when the elderly communicator described to her granddaughter an item of naughty underwear! 'I was with you last week when you bought a peach-coloured French-style negligee,' she revealed.

The girl was obviously startled. '*Was* she?'

'Yes, and she says, "But it'll never keep your best bits warm, will it? It's not so much a negligee – more of a negli*gent*!"' Everyone laughed and the nosy grandmother further delighted us by supplying the price paid: 'It was £11.99 – and you was robbed, gel!'

The granddaughter clutched her belly and laughed so much that I thought she was going to slide right out of her seat. 'She's still the same old gran, I see!' she exclaimed between wheezes – but I could only see the brim of her hat.

'Certainly! And I think she's going to comment on your personal life now, I'm afraid. Who is Leo?'

My recipient's hat nearly vanished from view with shock. 'That's my boyfriend!' Then she sat bolt upright in her seat.

'Do you want to know what she's telling me, or not?'

'Oowww, not half! 'Course I do! I want to hear it *all*!'

'Well, Mrs Jenkins's words are: "I don't like him, chick. You know what I always say: never trust a man whose eyebrows meet in the middle. But *his* eyes are too close together. He's a bad egg."'

Her granddaughter took it quite well. 'Righto, Nan! You're still an interfering old fuss-bag, then!' she shouted out, and we chuckled good-heartedly.

Similar belly-laughter, which is always welcomed by me when working with larger audiences because it breaks the tension in the auditorium, broke out in another crowd when I located a woman who, a bright spirit voice had told me, was called 'Doreen, from Bridgwater'. Doreen's crotchety great-grandmother, Elspeth, reminded her of a missing family heirloom:

'Me rabbit's foot brooch was *pinched* before I'd gone cold!' she declared; then added darkly, 'But I saw the miserable old grasper what stole it! And she'd better watch out, 'cos when she dies – *I'll be waiting*!'

Doreen's face turned the colour of a beetroot; she said she recognized the information, then laughed out loud!

But not all my spirit messages were so readily accepted, of course; and some were never claimed publicly by those to whom they belonged. At one Somerset venue, when no-one wanted 'Great-aunt Gemima', I didn't know what to do, until I glimpsed a small sparkling-blue spirit-light, about the size of a golf-ball, hovering above a woman's head. But when I gave 'Great-aunt Gemima' to her, she snapped back in a thick Devon accent:

'Never heard of 'er, m'dear.'

'Well, perhaps you could research your family tree?'

'P'rhaps, m'dear,' was the rather terse reply. But when I announced that Gemima mentioned a name that sounded like 'Fordyce', 'I am Harriet Fordyce,' said the woman.

Gemima then showed me a pet bird she'd brought with her from the Other Side: he was a magnificent green and blue parrot with huge feet. 'And he keeps squawking out "Cheeky Charlie!"' I reported.

'Aye, aye! I knows that parrot all right!' replied the woman, rather more warmly.

The spirit bird then swore like a trooper, his gravelled voice screeching out privately to me, 'Get your knickers off!' I raised my eyebrows. 'Oh, he's making rude suggestions here,' I announced.

'Oh aye – 'e was good at that, m'dear!' smiled the lady.

Next came, 'Kiss the postman's bum!' followed by 'Nellie's got big knockers!' My eyes nearly popped out of my head, but I bravely ventured to ask the woman if she knew who Nellie was.

'Oh aye. She was my sister-in-law! Charlie used to make remarks about 'er chest!'

'Well, he hasn't changed a bit!' I replied, much to the delight of the audience. 'I can't possibly repeat this in public. But he knew a number of interesting expletives!'

She called out, 'He used to shout at 'er husband, "George is a bugger!" And 'e *was*!' revealed the lady.

'Well,' I returned, smiling, 'Cheeky Charlie's lived up to his name tonight, and he's extended his repertoire on the Other Side!' And nearby, I sensed White Owl laughing along with the rest of the audience.

But I think it was always the more emotional, poignant connections that touched my spirit the most; such as the one involving an alcoholic husband who turned out to be called 'Freddie Patterson'. He'd died after swallowing his own vomit while drunk, and returned to beg his wife in the audience to forgive him for his errant ways.

I found Freddie's wife by repeating the spirit-supplied name of 'Minnie-Anne'. She claimed the message, but the moment I saw the fierce expression on her thin face, I feared her husband's presence might not be welcomed. She was Minnie-Anne, she said, but she looked as if a great bitterness had withered her features, and tightened her thin-lipped mouth.

'Your husband has a confession to make: he says,

"I was a no-good waster to you and the kids,"' I relayed. '"I spent half my wages on booze every week, and I betted on the nags. I'm really sorry for what I did, love," he says.'

A quick glance at his wife revealed that her lips were pressed tight together, and she was working them back and forth. She was very uneasy. But, faithfully, I continued his message:

'I know you can't forget the pain I caused, Min – but I need some peace of mind, real bad. Please, Min . . . will you forgive me?'

His wife sat motionless, rigid and as silent as a statue.

'"Please, Min . . . will you forgive me?"' he asked of her again.

Then she frowned hard, but softened her tight mouth, just a little. 'Well . . . tell him . . .'

I could practically feel the people in the audience holding their breath and waiting.

'Tell him . . . I'll think about it.'

A tide of tension released itself as a great sigh in the crowd.

The poor man. I felt so very sorry for him, and more especially for his wife, for it was obviously news that she didn't want to hear.

But then, we all receive bad news at one time or another, don't we? I'm not an avid television watcher – as a matter of fact, for most of the year my TV has a tablecloth thrown over it – but one night, when the cloth was in the washer, and Sooty was sleeping on my lap in my Welsh flat, I heard the BBC reporting the miserable news that Britain was 'starting to feel the tighter pinch of an economic recession'.

For a moment, my stomach fluttered, but then I yawned, put Sooty on a comfy cushion and switched off the set. There was a knock at the door, and in came Jeff.

'Did you just see the news, Steve?'

'Yes, but it won't affect us. The theatres are well attended, and the public are clamouring for more meetings. We've worked very hard to get our business established, without any help at all from the government; there's no reason to think it'll fold on us now.'

Jeff shrugged his shoulders. 'Mmm . . . I suppose you're right,' he said. 'I just made a pot of tea next door. Want a cup?'

I did, and we thought no more about television. But as the months rolled by, I made many more appearances on 'the box' and my public profile grew: people bought more books and read them, saw my telly interviews, or listened to some of the radio broadcasts I'd done. Generally speaking, the media were very kind to me; granted, there had been one or two snide attacks on my character, but what's the point of life without a few challenges?

I'm a great respecter of any man's religious beliefs and would never in a million years accuse someone of being on the wrong path regarding his faith. I've always maintained that people are intelligent and they can find their own way to the Truth. So, it was understandable that at one radio station when my motives were seriously questioned by a few clergymen in the studio, who had already labelled me 'a devil's disciple', live on air, I wondered what was up.

262

When the youngest priest, a furious born-again Christian Fundamentalist, vigorously poked one of his narrow fingers practically into my eye, and accused me of being 'a servant of evil darkness', I thought it was time to call it a day.

Vehemently he demanded, 'Stephen O'Brien, have you got the devil up there on the platforms with you?'

'I've no idea,' I relied calmly. 'What does he look like?'

The man was stunned by his own silence.

He'd walked right into it; and serve him right.

Psychic News then threw light on this tiresome subject of 'mediums versus the clergy' when it informed its readers that the British television and radio stations were advised by their governing bodies, in those days, to treat the subject of clairvoyance lightly, sceptically, or as pure entertainment.

This interesting revelation prompted me to put the record straight and to inform the listeners to my next big radio appearance that 'My work is about love, and service; it's not a side-show entertainment.'

But I wasn't unduly worried, for Doris Stokes's manager had told me in London one time, 'Once you start being publicly insulted – you know you've made your mark, Stephen.' Now here was wisdom, indeed!

Even my Dad responded to the mark I'd made on the public mind, or more specifically, on their television sets. Dad's opinion of me had changed virtually overnight and he'd made a completely out-of-character U-turn: he was now quite impressed by my growing celebrity status, but mainly because he could boast about it to his mates in the pub.

Because they'd seen me on telly, everyone thought I was stinking rich. It's funny, that. People see your face on the screen and they think, 'I bet he got a couple of thousand quid for that.'

Wrong.

Jeff insisted on my being paid adequate appearance fees, of course, but although most of the trappings of success had now sprung suddenly into my life, that certainly didn't mean that I was 'rolling in it'.

Far from it. It was only after a great deal of hard slog that Jeff and I were able to draw £120 each per week from Voices Promotions, an amount that was under half of the weekly pay of the average British man, who earned £250. Our wages were then frozen for a few years.

But we'd done it! Purely under our own steam we'd achieved self-sufficiency and, against all odds, Voices Promotions had proved itself to be a resounding success.

At last, I caught a glimpse of light at the end of the financial tunnel and our living standards went up. And that wasn't the only thing that rose: as my popularity snowballed and audience numbers swelled and packed out some of Britain's most prestigious venues to witness my mediumship, I was invited to do more TV and radio interviews. Press articles about me were syndicated to foreign countries, and offers of work from all around the world poured in.

Much to my regret, I was then often recognized in public places.

And the phone didn't stop ringing.

18

Starlight

'Certainly . . . Stephen will be happy to appear on your programme, but I do hope his item will be taken seriously and not treated too light-heartedly. A great many people look to him for sympathy and support and . . . Yes, oh good . . . That's fine . . . If you'd like to fax through the travel and accommodation details, and send on the appearance fee . . . Right . . . Thank you. Goodbye.'

Jeff replaced the receiver and turned in his chair to face me. I was sifting through a large boxful of fan mail.

'Another show?' I asked.

'Yep. National television, prime-time slot.' He jotted it down in his diary and I didn't even raise an eyebrow; I wasn't becoming blasé, it was just that I'd been interviewed on the telly and by journalists so many times by then.

Jeff had arranged many guest TV appearances on most of the major chat shows, among them *Wogan, This Morning, Pebble Mill, Gloria Live*, GMTV, Channel Four and others on some regional channels too. I'd also been filmed for documentaries and appeared in some of the top-selling magazines of the day, and the whole public relations exercise had now become just another aspect of my work.

However, it had taken me quite a while to get used to being interviewed.

Contrary to popular belief, I've never sat on the edge of my seat, glaring at the phone, ready to jump at the chance of media coverage. I'm not that kind of a man. Producers and researchers approach my manager with an idea; he thinks it over carefully; then he puts the proposition to me, and I accept if I feel it'll be done with a reasonable amount of dignity, and not purely for a lark. Each appearance was considered on its individual merit, and quite a number of top programmes received outright refusals from me.

It was the famous astrologer and television celebrity Russell Grant who offered me sound advice in this direction.

'If you know the interviewer's work, Stephen,' he said at a restaurant table one afternoon before we filmed an item for Granada TV, 'and you feel they'll be too cynical or a bit tongue-in-cheek about your work . . .'

'Yes?'

'Perhaps you shouldn't do it,' he advised pointedly. 'Do you know what I mean?'

I certainly did; I'd had my fingers burned by the media on a number of previous occasions, so I knew he was perfectly right.

After lunch we went on to record me giving Russell a spirit message. The camera was running and we sat at opposite ends of a smart sofa, but the voices I heard on that day were very faint, and I made a lot of silly mistakes and quite a bit of my information got 'fogged up', which meant I gave it incorrectly. But

266

Russell was the epitome of patience and kindness.

Then suddenly a powerful voice and vision arrested my attention, and this was the part of his message that was later screened.

'I can see a Being of Light standing just behind you,' I relayed. 'On earth he was an American Indian – and he's just thrown down a lance here, and said "Accept the challenge!"'

Russell's eyes lit up. 'Did you say he was from the States?'

'Yes, he was a North American Indian.'

'Well, I can understand that perfectly,' he said, 'because I've just signed a contract to go to America to work for Fox Television; and that will be a challenge indeed!'

I knew exactly what he meant.

For someone like me, who was born into a poor Welsh family, it took a long time to get used to being watched and judged by squillions of strangers peering into their television sets.

I often wondered what viewers thought when I suddenly appeared in their living-rooms. Once, when sitting in a motorway services restaurant and watching the telly with a couple of elderly folk, a very serious-looking woman who was standing for a high political office in Britain came onto the news. I thought her arguments made a great deal of sense, but the bored old dear sitting next to me turned to her hubby and said, 'Hasn't she got a stupid-looking face?'

What on earth would she have thought of me, I wondered, especially if she'd seen how stylishly the stations had got me to their studios: I was either flown to cities, or driven in chauffeured limousines, and then ensconced in plush hotels, all expenses paid. Sumptuous vegan meals were spread before me and all I had to do was sign on the dotted line and the TV station paid the bill. What a way to live! The hotel carpets I walked on were worth more than the entire contents of my council flat, and I was treated like a king; here I was able to get the non-dairy-produce food I wanted, whereas at many eating-places on the road with Voices, I had to be vegetarian because waitresses thought a vegan was a distant relative of Mr Spock from *Star Trek*.

After devouring one delicious tossed salad with peaches and avocado pears, I made my way to a television studio and was stopped in the rabbit-warren of corridors by a pretty but anxious researcher who nervously asked:

'Stephen? Was, ahem . . . was the hotel comfortable?'

'Yes, very, thank you.'

'Oh good!' and she blew out a huge puff of air with relief. 'Because last week, a famous actress from an American soap opera stayed there and she said it was "Too hot and tacky – and full of trash!"'

'Unlike me, she was obviously a megastar and was used to Bel-Air!' I quipped.

But I did experience my own sobering moments of mind-boggling fame, too; not many, I grant you, but enough to make me quiver whenever I think of them. I shall never forget the experience of appearing at the NBC Super Channel studios in London, when the televised radio show 'On the Air' gave me the opportunity to speak simultaneously to 56 million people in 32 countries around the globe. It certainly was a staggering thought, and without doubt the largest single audience I'd ever worked with.

For two hours I took live phonecalls and tried to give people a spirit message or some helpful psychic guidance.

Clive Pearse, the show's cheery host, had escorted me into the studio with a quick, 'Mind that step! It's lethal! The singer Lulu tripped up on it when she came in here the other day, and nearly knocked herself unconscious!'

I grinned, stepped gingerly forward, and we were on the air.

'Good morning, Europe!' said a chirpy Clive. 'And welcome to our 56 million people, wherever you are in the world. Today we're discussing psychics and the spirit world, and taking your calls on the show is medium and author, Stephen O'Brien.'

The switchboards instantly jammed with calls that came in from as far afield as Russia, Denmark, Spain, Greece, Poland, Austria and other remote countries.

Boldly going where I had never gone before, I told Philip from Frankfurt in Germany that I felt his spirit father was helping him with his new business venture: 'Do it off your own back, son,' was his parent's advice, and Philip was grateful for it.

Then Beverly from Basle in Switzerland, who was a jolly and laughing caller, was linked with her spirit auntie who revealed to her, 'You can meet me in your dreams.' Beverly fully accepted this and confirmed to the millions listening that she'd already psychically spoken to her auntie on the Other Side.

When Audrey from Heemstede in Holland asked about Reincarnation, I confirmed my belief in it but stated that we should always keep an open mind about all paranormal topics. 'People have an inherent fear of the unknown,' I commented, 'and the best way to remove this is to make the unknown, the known.'

Audrey agreed.

When the next caller named Pat rang from London, I got an immediate spirit link from her mother, and delivered it live, on the air:

'You're in grief. Don't say anything to me at all, Pat. I've got a contact for you here: it's a lady saying she's very grateful for everything you did for her before she died, and she wishes she could have had more time to see everything settled before she went. Can you understand that?'

'Yes; it's all true.'

'She's mentioning some family names here: Jean, Kate, William and Albert on the Other Side. Do you know these people?'

'Yes.'

'This lady,' I went on, 'who could well be your Mum, is saying, "Don't worry about me, love."'

(Pat was heard to sob down the phone-line.)

'And she wants to know where her ring has gone.'

'I've got it.'

'Yes, but didn't you lose that at one time?'

'Yes.'

'And she's talking about "Cancer".'

(Pat gave a drawn-in gasp.)

'And she's saying, "There's no pain here. Now get three meals a day down you!" Do you understand that?'

'Yes; I'm not eating.'

'"And why are you getting up at half past two in the morning to make yourself a cup of tea?" Is that you?'

'Yes,' and Pat gasped again.

Her Mum spoke for several minutes in the same vein, and ended by sending her daughter all of her love.

'Thank you very much,' said Pat to me, 'and God bless you.'

Clive Pearse described the show as 'a revolutionary first for the NBC Super Channel'. It was certainly a huge success, because mail for me poured in from all around Europe.

It took a long time for the idea that I might be famous (or infamous!) to dawn on me, but I was left in no doubt when, while driving through London, I got lost and Jeff asked two workmen at the roadside if they could give us directions to find the M4. They switched off their blaring transistor radio, and obliged.

Then one of them pushed his cheeky head through the open window, smiled and said, 'What're you asking *us* for? Why didn't you get him to ask his voices?'

I pulled away as fast as possible!

Radio sets of all descriptions played a significant part in my work reaching the masses. I used to underestimate this powerful medium, but I don't now; hundreds of thousands of people listen to it each day and night, and I learned to welcome the opportunity of using it to present the message of life after death, and to sometimes add my own little pieces of philosophy. When asked if I had a personal message for the listeners I'd say, 'Yes. Be kind to each other,' or 'Make peace with yourself and everyone else around you.'

Just simple phrases, I know; but what a wonderful world this would be if we lived our lives by them.

Most of my interviews on the airwaves went without a hitch, but a few weird goings-on did occur. Probably one of the oddest happened at Greater London Radio, when, after my contributions, a snapshot was taken of me with Rick Parfitt and Francis Rossi of the pop-group *Status Quo*, all standing behind the famed DJ, Johnnie Walker.

'That'll look like The Zombie's Night Out, boys!' I quipped. But when it was developed I was surprised at how reasonably good we all looked on it – considering our ages, and the early time of the morning. However, our images were accompanied by some ghostly red string-like shapes that had psychically superimposed themselves onto the snapshot! There was nothing wrong with the camera or the film, which made me think their appearance might have had something to do with the open-minded Mr Parfitt who had said he'd be more inclined to accept the existence of the paranormal if there was sufficient evidence of it.

Those psychic energies on that photo took me completely by surprise, but more surprises were in store. While waiting to be interviewed at BBC Radio Manchester I gawped when the smiling film star Liza Minnelli walked straight past me and into the lift.

Inside the studio, my disappointed young lady presenter confided that Liza had made it quite clear she was here to promote her new album, and she didn't want to be questioned about drinking habits, drug-taking, men, or her mother!

'Well, she's a big Hollywood star,' I said, pulling on my headphones.

'Yes, I suppose so,' she said with a sigh; then she brightened up. 'Now, what do *you* want to talk about today?'

'Oh, I'll leave it to you,' I replied, happy with her pleasant attitude.

Then we went live – and she transformed before my very eyes into the Wicked Witch of the West (from Liza's mother's classic film), and gave me a thorough ear-bashing! Perhaps I should have taken a leaf out of Liza's book.

Lamentably, the media seemed to revel in challenging their guests, especially if they were famous in an unusual field, and they frequently gave the impression that the orthodox Church deplored the role of mediums in society. Maybe that was the official line, but it certainly didn't hold good among the rank and file of the clergy, and I speak here from experience. Lots of clergymen wrote to thank me for the work I did, and to encourage me to continue with it. They 'loved' reading my books, they said, and some of them even admitted to sneaking in to my meetings *incognito*!

When I appeared in Dublin, several Catholic priests in full vestments sat among the crowd, and they later said they'd enjoyed themselves immensely. 'The good word spreads in ones and twos,' one surprised young Father informed me, 'but in your case it seems to have reached epidemic proportions.'

Of course, not all orthodox thinkers have perceived me in such a favourable light, and being a 'psychic celeb' who's been well advertised as appearing in the region means that I've sometimes attracted their criticism and unwanted attention. At a Plymouth Guildhall meeting, the building was virtually surrounded by seventy-five Fundamentalists who were playing guitars and tambourines, singing and, I regret to report, trying to prevent the public access to the meeting.

Afterwards, two kind ladies from the audience made me an offer I couldn't refuse: 'You and your manager can borrow our Rugby-forward husbands as bodyguards, if you like, to brave the picket-lines outside.' We willingly accepted this help from their six-footer brutes and, thus flanked on either side, we went out into a fine rain that had soaked the fray.

The Christian objectors were amazed to see our protection but they still wouldn't let my car pull away from the building; in fact, they surrounded it.

Flustered, I got out and yelled, 'Who's in charge here?'

'Jesus is in charge,' said a thin young man.

'Yes. But who's in charge of this protest?'

Not one of them had the courage to own up and face me; then one of the Rugby wives shouted at the crowd, 'You'll never see Spiritualists picketing *your* events! Get those kiddies in out of the wet, and go home! You should be ashamed of yourselves!'

But even when I left, the objectors still hadn't dispersed.

Some people's lack of common decency astonished me, especially when it was voiced through heckling.

Regrettably one or two hecklers have interrupted my meetings over the years, though thankfully very rarely; they seemed to get excited most at Question Time when they seized microphones and took great pleasure in venting their spleens. When one fiery amazon screamed a barrage of insulting remarks at me from a theatre gallery, I was rather upset, until I later learned that she'd been sitting there all through the first half, smoking and drinking bottles of lager.

However, I wasn't the only one to suffer such unwanted attention – even Jeff had his moments. At one seaside town in high summer when he went walking along the prom, he encountered a fancy-dress treasure-hunt competition that had been arranged for all the kiddies on the beach. The place was packed with sunburned holiday-makers, some of whom were adults roaming about in fancy-dress costumes, haunting the sands as decaying mummies, vampires, buxom milkmaids, and even cheeky monkeys.

Kids were charging everywhere around the bays and stopping the fancy-dressers, touching them, then getting points marked down on their treasure maps when they'd found each celebrity character.

A small group of chatty nippers stopped Jeff as he sauntered along with that 'come-day, go-day' walk of his; he was dressed in his usual loose black jacket and baggy trousers that he'd purchased from Oxfam charity shops.

'Hey Mister! Which one are you?' they wanted to know.

'Pardon?'

'Are you Barnacle?' said a red-faced little boy, panting for breath after running the length of the beach to reach him.

'No, I'm *not*,' he replied, holding back a smile, and he left the kids puzzled and dumbfounded.

'It must be him,' they whispered in a circle, 'look at his clothes.'

Jeff ambled to the nearest cliff path and had just turned a sharp bend and started to climb when suddenly, from around the corner, there came a high-pitched shout of, 'It *is* him! It's Barnacle! *Charge!*' And a hundred screaming children chased him up the cliff! He only just managed to take a bluff turn and send them in the wrong direction.

Watching from the cliff-top I was doubled up with laughter; Jeff's usually so laid back that I can never get him to move fast enough with the audience radio-mikes at my meetings – but he shot off like a rocket when those kids were on his trail! It was one of the best laughs I'd ever had on tour.

This sudden burst of unwanted fame, however, didn't dissuade him from buying his Charity-shop rig-outs, or put an end to his lackadaisical nature. At half past eleven that same night, he packed up the books and stowed away the cash-box, which contained a thousand pounds of merchandise money, into the boot of the car. As we drove from my meeting towards the hotel through a brightly lit city centre, I got quite paranoic – for every hundred yards or so people kept whizzing past us, yelling and honking their horns and hanging out of their car windows and screaming out what sounded like blurred obscenities.

Thinking my infamy had reached ridiculous proportions, I shortened my neck and tried to hide my face; after all, it had been postered throughout the city, and had appeared in all the newspapers for weeks.

'This is getting on my wick!' I complained, looking like the alien creature from the film *ET*.

'Just grin and bear it!' laughed Jeff.

Two more cars loudly honked their horns and their passengers laughed like drains.

'What are they pointing at Jeff?'

'I dunno.'

'Do something! They're shouting at us; perhaps we've got a flat tyre.'

As soon as he wound down his window, three young builders in a truck called out, 'Coooeee! It's on the top, Guv!'

Then they skidded away, their tyres screeching. I pulled over and we got out – and there sitting on the roof of the car, like a broody hen on the nest, was our red cash-box!

Jeff gasped in horror, 'My God, there's a thousand quid in that!'

He'd popped it up there while he'd loaded up the books, two miles back, and had forgotten all about it!

'It's a good job your head's screwed onto the top of your neck,' I blurted out, annoyed, 'otherwise you'd come out without it!'

But that's just the way he is; and I've had to get used to it.

He picked up the cash-box and clutched it to him as though his life depended upon it after that. (And he could well have been right!) The large amount of money in it had been gathered through the sales of my autobiographies, tapes and cards at several of my meetings.

Widespread sales of my books led to wider acclaim, of course, and meant that my postbag now filled to overflowing: people wrote to me asking if I would officiate at their weddings, or conduct their relatives' funeral services, or name their babies; they wanted me to bless their houses, or exorcize their flats – and once I was even requested to make a special trip to Scotland to cut a pink ribbon and to declare a Glasgow woman's new kitchen extension officially open!

Needless to say, I turned down dozens of these written requests, because I can't be everywhere at once. But other members of the public managed to startle me in person, at my meetings; such as the two ladies who said, 'We've flown hundreds of miles especially to see your work tonight.'

'I've come from Germany,' said one.

'And I'm from France,' added the other, who presented me with a delightful bouquet of flowers, and I was speechless. It was so kind of people to give me gifts; single red roses, heaps of greeting cards, and little 'thank you' notes often waited at stage doors for me, and I found it all very moving.

Strangers from all walks of life expressed their gratitude to me in simple, friendly ways; and one of my greatest fans, dear old 'Nanny Davies', as she's known, never failed to deliver the ultimate accolade: she was always to be found seated in the front row of as many of my Welsh meetings as her 89-year-old legs would allow her to attend. Forever cheerfully smiling and sending up so much love to me, Nanny Davies was a real tonic. The poor soul rarely got a message, but it was always grand to see her.

To thank Nanny for her loyalty and support, one night I presented her with a special bouquet of flowers 'for the lady who's eighty-nine years young.' Someone took a happy snapshot of us grabbing hold of each other in passionate embrace, and I'm told she kept this snapshot on her bedside table.

'Owww!' she said, cuddling the life out of me, 'if I were forty years younger, you'd have to look out, young man!'

'And if I were forty years older, so would you!' I said.

It's been a great privilege for me to meet so many lovely souls through my work, and I shall never forget their kindnesses. But even though the public and the media treated me as a psychic celebrity, I never allowed this to affect my sense of priorities, and always found time on tour to ring my telephone answer machine which played my pre-recorded message for little Sooty to hear. The sound of my voice brought her comfort, I know, when each night it told her how much I missed her, how sorry I was to have left her on her own, and that I'd soon be home.

There's no peace for the wicked!

Whenever I got back to Wales, the first thing I did was to cuddle Sooty, and then I immediately resumed the Battle of the Bulge – rigorous exercises, a careful vegan diet, and vitamin supplements became the order of the day, and I did everything I could to keep myself healthy and fighting-fit. If the public's written compliments about my bodily particles were anything to go by, my efforts had certainly been appreciated. Their demand for my mediumship also escalated and, to meet this, a third volume of my autobiography, *In Touch with Eternity*, was written and published – but this time by Bantam Books, a division of Transworld Publishers.

The Aquarian Press, my original publisher, had been bought up by William Collins, who then merged with Harper and Rowe to become HarperCollins – and this meant that a new editor would work with me. But she and I couldn't agree from the start, and we haggled over her proposed HarperCollins book contract, which would have removed my control over what actually appeared in the text – and this I could not allow. 'It's only fair that the author should have the final approval of the manuscript before printing,' I pointed out to her. 'This clause was granted with Aquarian, because my books should contain *my* voice, and not someone else's.'

But she refused to agree – so I left; and Bantam Books were happy to contract the third instalment of my life-story – and I was happy to join them – and the book was hurriedly rushed into their production line. I signed on the dotted line, but didn't put away my pen because it was kept extremely busy, agreeing to write eighteen commissioned articles for *Psychic News* and other contributions to *Two Worlds* and *Psychic World* magazines.

While I started planning my fourth volume of autobiography, Jeff rang to tell me that the publishers Reed International had selected me to appear in their new book called *The Best of British Men*, and PO Box 8 in Swansea overflowed again: sackloads of letters were posted from across the globe; and Sooty got her own mail, too!

Open that parcel! It might be for me!

Whenever I could find a few minutes to spare, I sat down at my desk, took a huge breath, grabbed a handful of letters from a big cardboard box, and answered them . . .

19

'Dear Stephen . . .'

I spread out a selection of envelopes on my desk
and picked up my pen in readiness. The public's
letters often lifted my spirits and cheered me up
whenever I was on one of my 'down' days – and not
just the cheeky ones, either, but even those wanting
helpful information or guidance. In many ways,
answering my mail became almost a therapeutic
exercise for me.

The first letter that I opened had been sent by a
priest in whose parish I'd taken one of my Evenings
of Clairvoyance.

Dear Stephen O'Brien,

This is just a quick note to say thank you for
your work and efforts in trying to make people
more aware of the spiritual dimension in our lives.

I recently attended one of your meetings (in, I have
to say, a somewhat sceptical frame of mind) but I
was impressed and moved by the obvious pastoral
concern and care that you had for your 'audience'.

Far from taking advantage of, or manipulating,
the people there (some of whom I knew to be
bereaved or concerned about departed loved ones)
I was struck by your ability to help folk come to
terms with their loss. In that respect, much of the

work that you are engaged in is identical to mine as a parish priest.

I hope you are able to continue with this essential work of helping people to understand that there is far more to our world than at first meets the eye.

Yours sincerely,
Father D.
Wales

Dear Stephen,

I'm an Australian medium whose washing machine has broken down. Please send me £380 for a new washing machine.

Yours faithfully,
(name and address supplied)

Dear Stephen,

I'm glad I managed to speak to you live on the BBC Radio station. I am the caller who was once a Magistrate and I mentioned how my wife gave me survival evidence by coming back within thirty-six hours of her passing to tell me not to forget the Christmas presents for the grandchildren, which she said were in the top cupboard in the living-room, which is where I found them.

All good wishes and success in your work to publicize the truth.

Mr E.
Devon

Dear Stephen,

I felt I must write and let you know how very accurate you were in the message that you gave me last week in Edinburgh.

I was so overwhelmed, especially with the microphone stuck in my face, that I wasn't as helpful as I could have been to you. I just sat there and smiled and smiled!!

You brought my Dad through, and when you said he was blind and gave a very detailed description of him we all looked at one another in our line. Then when you said he has 'a big konk', we knew it was our Dad! That's the way he used to describe his nose!

You then gave the following information which was all incredibly correct:

1   His original appearance before he died; his clothes and how his eyes appeared due to the glaucoma. (True)

2   How he would walk on the outside of the pavement when he was with a lady friend, so that he could spit up if he needed to, into the gutter! (He had a bad chest and would do this on occasions.) (True)

3   All the family will come together later this year. True, we are all going on holiday together.

4   How I'd been in the kitchen and felt a tickle on my leg, and he said it was him, and not a flea! So true to his character.

5   But he gave you three big lumps of coal, but you had difficulty in getting his meaning. Well –

Later that night in bed, my father came to me and, quite categorically *told* me that the three pieces of coal were to be given, one each, to me and my sisters.

It's a custom here in Scotland and it's meant to bring good luck!

God bless you, Stephen, for giving so much comfort to so many.

Your sincerely,

Mrs McF.

Scotland

Hi Stevie baby!

You got lovely eyes and a sexy voice. I wish you was mine!

Love ya!

XXXXXXX

(unsigned)

PS – Will you go out with me? (sae enc)

Dear Mr O'Brien,

I can't begin to tell you how much you have helped me.

Life had finished for me when my dear husband passed away two years ago.

You have opened a whole new world to me. Life is worth living again.

After reading your books, I have been given strength to go on.

From the bottom of my heart I thank you for what you have given to myself and my children.

Please could you send me a list of items available on mail order.

Wishing you peace and happiness,

God bless you, Stephen,

C.B.

Essex

Dear Chaps,

Please could you enclose in the sae a list of your publications?

I really don't want to bother Stephen personally, but, if he needs cheering up, please show him the enclosed two letters I have received from my patients (I am a GP) to whom I gave copies of his books. This was following his appearance in Liverpool last year, when I was completely bowled over.

Thanking you for your help, and wishing you every good wish for your further endeavours.

Yours sincerely,

Dr M. C.

Merseyside

Dear Steven,

At your Leeds show you asked if anyone knew of a man who had died by car-fumes and I spoke up. You asked if the person had left a note *on the seat of the car*, I said there was a note but it was left on the table in the house.

You asked me to check.

May I just take this opportunity to tell you that I have spoken with the 'dead' person's mother and I can now confirm that there was a note left on the passenger seat.

Will you please give him all of our love and tell him we often think about him, and those who have passed over with him?

Best wishes for the future,

Mrs S.

Yorkshire

Dear Stephen,

I think you are a brilliant medium and I admire you very much. Can I have a signed photo please?

Thank you, Stephen,

Yours faithfully,

Christopher

Cambridgeshire

My Son Lives

Then I opened a letter postmarked Exeter in Devon; it was signed by a Mrs Jackie Humphries who'd written to thank me for bringing messages through from her son, Philip, who'd been tragically killed in a car crash when he was just eighteen years old.

As I scanned the lines, at first the message seemed rather confusing, but then it dawned on me just how clever her son had been in choosing to return at a much younger age than when he had died; in doing this, he was able to identify himself clearly to his Mum by eliminating any possibility of confusing him with the other two teenage boys who had passed over in the same car accident.

(Some spirit people have learned how to use their power of thought to alter their appearance, and they can present themselves to mediums or relatives at any age they choose.)

Dear Stephen,

Ten weeks after my wonderful son, Philip, was killed in a car crash involving himself and three friends in Cornwall, you gave to me evidence that proved without a shadow of a doubt that Phil still lived.

Let me 'set the stage' a bit.

On the way to your meeting, there was a song on my car radio called *A Bang on the Ear* by the Waterboys, and in it are the words 'married up in Fife, ended up in tears'. This struck me as an unusual coincidence, because my parents were married in Fife, and then they divorced after 40 years together!

I also must admit that on the journey to see you working at the hall I shouted some very rude bad language (involving an F, and other words!) at a car driver who nearly cut me up in the wrong lane on the road!

Later, inside the hall:

Never having seen you before, I couldn't believe the wonderful feeling of love that was in there. I felt privileged to be a part of it.

I didn't expect to get a message I was just so happy to be a part of all that love and joy. Then at 9.50 p.m., just before the end, you said, 'I have a connection with Fife.' I didn't think it could be for me in a hall full of 500 people, but I put up my hand, just in case.

You said, 'Good – hold that connection.' And then you went on to give a person sitting next to me a message about a family called Braithwaite. Then you were back with me.

You said, 'When you spoke up to me, a little blond-haired boy, about three years old, came in – and this boy belongs to you. He's clutching a toy that looks like a small blue rabbit.'

Well, Phil was very fond of that toy, which was, in fact, a little blue teddy, but I can understand why you thought it looked like a rabbit! Even at eighteen years of age, Phil kept his teddy on the bed. And the memory of this toy linked my son as an eighteen-year-old man, with my son as he was when he was a young boy.

Then you said the lad was telling you about my swearing. You started laughing and told me, 'You can use some choice words, can't you?' you said.

I started to go red, it was so startling. 'It's no good going red,' you added, 'even when you think it, they know what you're thinking!'

You then asked if I suffered with bad circulation, and I said I had cold feet. And you laughed and said, 'Well, they know where you put your cold feet at night!' And I suddenly had a picture of my husband Paul and I in bed, and I'll leave it to your imagination to know where I put my feet!

'Each night,' you said, 'when you're nearly asleep your son comes and kisses you, and it makes him laugh because you try to brush it off your cheek, like a spider cleaning himself!'

To other people this message wouldn't mean much, but I knew my son, Phil, was there because his humour was coming through, and the message of love that you sent me from him for all the family was overwhelming.

You also explained to me why Philip had come through as a three-year-old: because he passed at 18 years with three others, two of whom were teenage boys, and when he returned as a toddler with his special memories and toy, he wanted to be

289

recognized *without doubt* as the boy who belonged
to me.

Stephen, what can I say? Words just aren't
enough. I can't thank you enough for that evening.
It helped to make sense of my life.

God Bless you,

Mrs Jackie Humphries

I sent a reply, of course, as I do to all of my letters,
even though sometimes correspondents have to wait
a long time to hear from me because I have to plough
through huge mounds of mail.

Shortly after these events, I noticed Mrs Humphries
appearing at many of my major public meetings
where she'd step forward, introduce herself, and
shake my hand, time and again. She also attended
teaching courses that I took. 'You've helped me more
than ever you'll know,' she said.

It came as no surprise, then, to receive another
letter from her asking if I'd go to Exeter to take a
large publicity demonstration of mediumship in aid
of the charity she and her husband, Paul, had set up
in their son's name: The Philip Humphries Trust for
Young People.

I readily agreed and the hall was packed out,
the meeting having been advertised as 'Christmas
Carols and Clairvoyance' with yours truly. The
feeling of kindness in the audience was absolutely
wonderful; and I'd had some songsheets printed and
had made a tape of some of my favourite Christmas
pieces. The crowd was in full voice and they sang
their hearts out, and we all thoroughly enjoyed
ourselves.

Between the songs I gave out Christmas messages from loved ones and, all in all, we raised £1,600 to support homeless youngsters in Exeter; the Trust wanted to establish some kind of drop-in coffee-and-chat centre for the kids who were sleeping rough in the wintertime, 'And there are plenty of them, too, Stephen,' Jackie informed the audience, with great sadness in her voice.

'Despite the fact that governments deny it,' added Paul, her thoughtful husband.

But the most touching moment of the whole evening, I thought, occurred at the very end of the meeting when Jackie, Paul and I were all on stage and Jackie announced that this event had taken place on her son's birthday. Emotionally, she told the audience that, 'If Philip had still been living here with us, instead of being now in his new world, he would have been twenty-one today. I told him he was special to us, and that there'd be a special celebration on his coming-of-age birthday, and there has been. It's been truly wonderful. From my son, Philip, and my husband, Paul, and the Philip Humphries Trust for Young People, and myself – I thank you all from the bottom of my heart.'

The audience heartily applauded, and Jackie's eyes shone with tears.

Later, at their family home, Paul and Jackie introduced me to their three lovely dogs, all of whom they'd somehow or other rescued from being homeless or loveless. All three were beautiful souls, but the one that stole my heart was little Jessie, a small brown-and-white King Charles Cavalier spaniel.

Yet I sensed that Jessie wasn't well.

'That's right,' confirmed Jackie.

'But she's a lovely old girl,' said Paul, 'aren't you?' And when he ruffled her coat, her big saucer-shaped eyes gazed up lovingly at him.

'Come over here and see me, Jessie,' I said; and she sauntered over and immediately lay flat at my feet.

'Ow, you're lucky!' Jackie cried. 'She's normally very fussy about strangers, because we think she was treated badly before. She's awfully timid, and she won't go to everybody.'

'Ah, well! She knows I'm going to give her some spiritual healing, don't you my lovely?' I cooed at her.

Jessie looked up at me with those big brown sad eyes. She was a beautiful soul.

I placed my hands gently on her little back while we all talked about the evening's events, and I noticed she moved her body along the floor until her pitter-pattering heart lay directly beneath the palm of my right hand.

'She's got a heart murmur,' I said.

Paul said, 'Yes, the vet told us recently.'

'Well,' I added in a quiet voice, while smoothing Jessie's silky coat, 'I'm afraid she thinks she's going to die, and she's terribly afraid of dying, aren't you my lovely?' I said sympathetically.

'How do you know?' asked Paul.

'Because it's in her mind.' Then I addressed the little dog. 'There's nothing to be afraid of, my darling. It's just like a nice big sleep after a huge doggy-dinner, and then you'll wake up somewhere else, in the spirit world.'

I'm certain Jessie understood; it was written in her eyes. But before I drove home to Wales, I urged Paul and Jackie to counsel Jessie about the passing over so that her fear of death would be removed, and her anxious mind would be calmed, and they promised that they would.

A few days later, the Humphries family wrote to tell me that directly after my visit little Jessie had taken to sleeping in the airing cupboard at night, where, one morning, they had found her little body curled up in the warmth.

She'd died peacefully in her sleep.

20

A Few Days in Paradise

After a short illness with cancer, bravely borne, my father 'died' peacefully in a coma at Morriston Hospital – the same place where Mrs Palmer had died all those years ago in the 1970s. Thankfully, Dad and I had come to respect each other much more in his later years, and this, I believe, had pleased him as much as it did me.

On the way to his cremation service, I commented to my only brother, John, 'I hope the press aren't coming today.'

'You're not serious, are you?'

'Oh yes, it'd be just like them to turn up and take a few pictures.' But they didn't come, and for that I was grateful.

Immediately after Dad's service, I had to rush home, change and then dash out to attend a two-hour photo-shoot for the cover of my third book, *In Touch with Eternity*, which probably explains the tired expression in my eyes on the photo.

The book was published in 1992, and the wheels of life spun around as normal: there were more tours, more publicity interviews, a great deal of hard work, and very little time to rest.

But when I discovered that Dad had saved several thousands of pounds and had left me half of this in his will, I sent my thanks to him and felt that better, more restful times lay ahead. And I was right, because the sum he bequeathed me, coupled with my savings and the fact that business finances had finally stabilized, allowed me to get out of the noisy and depressing flats I was living in and to mortgage the first real home of my own: a little secluded country cottage that I named Willowtrees.

Before I moved in, between tours, the dreaded builders were called in to install a damp-proof course, and in the process they flooded my lounge and ruined my new carpet! After I'd told the miserable cowboys to holster their guns, saddle up their horses and 'Git out o' town!', Jeff called round to help me redecorate the place from top to bottom.

For the first time ever, I used a professional removals firm, and then I took immediate steps to veil my whereabouts with secrecy. Past experience had taught me that grieving or curious people would move heaven and earth to find me if they were in a desperate state. I remembered the time when one anxious woman had continually rung up Jeff for weeks, demanding that she be given a private appointment with me, but she refused to take his 'No' for an answer. 'Let me talk to him,' she'd commanded in a loud voice. *'Now!'*

I'd already fully sympathized with this woman's grief and told her so in the letter I'd written to her, in which I'd recommended the services of reliable mediums in her own area, who I knew could help her. I'd also advised her to contact her doctor for the local addresses of Bereavement Counsellors, and done my best to explain gently that there's only one of me, but millions of people in need, and it'd be impossible for me to grant every request.

She ignored my suggestions and remained highly-strung and furiously angry. She wasn't listening, either; and neither would she let up. She continued to ring, time and again. But the last straw came when a private detective hammered on Jeff's front door and popped a card through his letterbox. He was not admitted.

Then I received a letter, through PO Box 8, from an English detective agency stating, 'There is a friend who needs to call on you urgently, but we cannot locate your whereabouts, Mr O'Brien. You have proved very difficult to trace' – and thank God for that, I thought – 'Please ring these offices.'

I did – but they wished I hadn't.

Ever since certain people had wrongly assumed that I was now public property such infringements upon my privacy had become far too frequent for my liking: one Indian gentleman even rang a Spiritualist organization demanding that I meet him – anywhere in the world. 'I have a private plane,' he told them imperiously, 'and I will fly to the country of his choice. If he prefers, I can land in his garden.' I presume he owned a Harrier Jump-jet; or else thought I was an earl with a vast estate.

Willowtrees was only a little cottage, but it was my home, my own place of peace and quietness, and I wasn't prepared to have that violated; so, I laid careful plans to protect my privacy.

I journeyed quickly in and out of the area, usually under the cover of darkness; all household services were procured under assumed names; I never shopped at stores within several miles' radius of the cottage, and I had no intention of mixing with the natives after the years of suffering I'd experienced with previous troublesome neighbours; and a thirty-digit security telephone number was installed. Other arrangements were made, too, but these remain confidential.

All in all, I'd made an impressive job of 'laying-low' – until that fateful day when I thought my secret cover had been blown to smithereens. If I live to be a hundred, I shall never forget it. I alone was to blame: I never buy newspapers and rarely watch television so I hadn't a clue that a Royal visit had been planned in my locality.

That morning, in blissful ignorance, I set out for the city in the car and had hardly reached top gear when sudden horror struck – as I turned a sharp corner I was greeted by colourful crowds of people lining either side of the road. I immediately froze rigid in the driver's seat. Hordes of cheering children and adults were waving their British flags, and craning their necks to get a glimpse of the scruffy man in the battered old car. My immediate thought was to take cover, but the long road was completely deserted of other vehicles – and there was nowhere to hide.

Mortified, I pressed the accelerator to try to run the gauntlet as fast as possible, but from out of nowhere a huge police motorbike appeared in front of me, complete with a leather-bedecked outrider – the kind reserved for VIP convoys.

'Please God, let me die,' my voice quivered. A lump as big as an apple formed in my throat and I felt such a twit: I'd gone to all that trouble to hide myself away and now I'd inadvertently made a right spectacle of myself! And I was trapped: I couldn't overtake the slow-moving police bike or do an illegal U-turn in the road behind him. I couldn't even lose myself amongst chauffeured limousines and pass myself off as a flunkey because Her Majesty was nowhere to be seen! So I had to chunter along behind my outrider at a law-abiding speed – but I clenched my teeth so hard I thought I'd break my jaw. Rigidly facing front, I stiffened my back and gripped the steering wheel until my knuckles went white while, without so much as a glance to the left or right, I sailed like Royalty along two bloody miles of never-ending road at a geriatric snail's pace.

The happy crowds cheered and shook their bright flags at the waving policeman and at the funny man in the banger behind. They clapped and gawped, and peered and stared, and laughed and jeered and booed as if they were being paid for it – and I'll never forget the pain. Then someone shouted out, 'He's too ugly for a Royal!' (Bloody cheek!)

If ever there was a time in my life that I'd wished the ground would open up and swallow me whole, believe me – that was it!

I didn't go back to Willowtrees until after midnight, when I was more than happy to drive through the deserted streets that were shrouded in darkness. When I slipped into bed, with Sooty purring in the crook of my knees, I was so grateful for the blessing of that moonless night, and I slept soundly . . .

But when the sunny morning arrived, I felt that something strange had happened to the world outside my bedroom window, and couldn't understand why I'd woken to such an eerie silence. After yawning and rubbing the sleep from my eyes, I listened more intently, and only then did I hear the gentle rustling of cool breezes through the woods nearby.

A bright shaft of sunshine fell across the bed, and outside the windowpanes its light warmed the giant trees and quiet gardens surrounding the secluded cottage.

I threw back the duvet, bounced to my knees on the mattress, and flung open the windows – and instantly into the room there came gusts of fresh air that were filled with the rich smell of earth and newborn leaves.

Spring had arrived.

Greedily, I drank in the perfume of wild flowers that had been brought to me over miles of country fields, then I leapt from the bed, rushed downstairs and ran out into the gardens to be embraced by the clean breezes of my first air-bath of spring.

In an effort to touch the brilliant blue sky I stood on tiptoe and stretched my body to its full height, then deeply inhaled Nature's psychic energies to re-invigorate my spirit.

It felt great to be alive, and a part of the clear morning light. I stooped down to examine the tips of new green shoots that were pushing up through the earth, while meadow larks sang and darted in and out of the trees above me.

All along the banks of the stream at the side of the cottage, I saw tiny furred creatures scuttling in the warmth, or poking their heads out of their burrows to catch the morning light. New families of pygmy shrews busied themselves and foraged for food while I watched. Dozens of blue tits pecked for insects in the waters and then flew away with them to feed their hungry nestlings.

The sunshine glittered on the stream and the sound of the waters refreshed my soul. As swift as a young pony, I sprang from the river's edge and dashed into the tool-shed. For several hours I then weeded and planted, and dug and hoed the garden, and pruned the shrubbery while I got an all-over suntan!

Just a month earlier, I'd fed the roots of the old and gnarled majestic oak, and had promised to lop off its dead branches for it in the Spring – and this I now did. Cutting away at the rough and seemingly lifeless wood, I heard the tree psychically 'purring' back its thanks for a promise kept.

Then I mowed the grasses, and a robin flew down and landed daintily on the stone bird-bath, from which she studied me while I worked. Her inquisitive eyes glinted in the sunshine like bright black diamonds.

Then she hopped nearer and nearer to me, chirruping away, whenever I rested to wipe great beads of sweat from my brow.

'Hello, my lovely,' I said, silencing the noisy lawnmower. 'It's a hot one today, isn't it?'

She perked up her fine head and stared right into my face.

Peep peep!

Between us, we struck up a soul-to-soul conversation, then in an explosion of feathers she

flew back up into a conifer tree for a few minutes'
rest, after which she swooped down to within an
inch of my bare feet, sat on the grass and fixed her
bright black eyes on my toes, as though they were
two juicy worms worthy of a peck.

Bobbing her tiny head from side to side, she took
a very close look at Man, then she rose into the
air above my shoulders – and fluttered down to
alight on my outstretched hand.

But not for long – Sooty scampered into the garden,
and off flew the robin. Sooty revelled in her new
country surroundings for prior to Willowtrees she'd
been a 'flat-cat', and now she thought it was her
birthday! Since arriving in the country, she'd moved
from her Shakespearean phase into her Big White
Huntress role:

These damn flies, Carruthers!

Any poor thing that flew or scuttered about didn't
stand a chance, especially the frisky pygmy shrews,
those grey furry mice-like creatures with black,
pin-head eyes. But word of her appetite soon got
out and the shrews started training for the 100-
metre dash. I lost count of the times Sooty had
come scooting through the kitchen, flinging herself
willy-nilly against the walls as she chased another
shrew into the cottage. As quick as lightning, she'd
scoop it up in her mouth and hurtle upstairs to dump
it in the master's boudoir, if you please!

'Oi!' I'd scream, taking three stairs at a time.
'Fetch him down here *this instant* or I'm phoning
the police!' Then we'd have a comical 'Keystone Cops'
chase: me pursuing the cat, and the cat running
after the squeaking shrew who was legging it for

all he was worth. Once, when I'd cornered one of Sooty's victims, I caught it and haughtily placed it on my palm, and carried it downstairs towards freedom.

Oi! That's mine!

But in the hallway it did an incredible kamikaze double somersault and flipped itself nine inches up into the air, after which it plummeted to the tiles where it let out a blood-curdling squeak – *Eeekk!* – then promptly shot off under the nearest skirting-board, and it was never seen again.

Sooty did a quick double-take and was dumbfounded.

'Now listen here, Madam,' I scolded, stabbing my forefinger down towards her bewildered face, 'if you carry on like that, you'll never be a person in your next incarnation!'

Big deal.

And she swaggered off, with her tail erect and her backside swinging in arrogance. Needless to say, a plethora of scrunched-up shrews, fieldmice, minced voles and bedraggled birds continued to appear in her 'Munchies' biscuit-bowl thereafter.

The shrews started saving up to get a shotgun licence.

As the sun sank behind the horizon at the end of that first hot spring day, I lay down beneath the copper beech tree for a rest before supper. The swaying red leaves seemed to soothe and heal my soul, and my thoughts began to wander . . .

How similar the pattern of life is to that of Nature. In the beginning, there's the spiritual mystery and silence of a human Winter, when a new baby's soul develops in its mother's womb, until the Spring of its life arrives when it's born.

And then comes the child's long and difficult climb upwards through infancy and into adolescence; and then into adulthood where, as a mature person, a Summer peak of strength is reached.

Then there is a gentle mellowing, and a golden spiritual light of Autumn that comes from realms within to flood the soul's last days on Earth, when the physical body grows tired and it welcomes the Winter sleep of death, which is but a fleeting pause in the eternal life-cycle; for after 'death' there comes another Spring awakening, another re-birth, but this time into an everlasting life.

I got up, strolled into the cottage and had a shower, donned a dressing-gown and then ironed a shirt for a meeting I was to take the next day. But while I ironed, my train of thought stayed with how much the unfolding of Man's life resembles the rolling of the seasons: human beings are constantly progressing; we gain wisdom; the old ones pass over, and the youngsters come through to take their places, and Life goes on . . .

Thoughts of Gordon Higginson were furthest from my mind at that time; after he'd suffered a few strokes and had then had a massive heart-attack which sent him across to the Other Side earlier that year, I didn't expect to hear from him again – but he suddenly made contact:

'Hellair,' said a voice, behind me.

'Good God, Gordon. To what do I owe the pleasure?' I put the iron down. No doubt Mr Higginson knew I'd been asked to take part in one of his many memorial services, and that I'd had strong reservations about accepting because I felt it would be a hypocritical action when it was well known that he'd held a low opinion of me.

'If you take part in my services,' his spirit voice said – then he suggested what I might say about him!

'Now look,' I assured him, 'I know how to behave in public, so don't worry.'

But he pressed his case, until in the end I politely invited him to leave the cottage, which he did.

Sooty looked up at me in amazement.

To whom are you speaking, young man?

I got straight on the phone to Eric Hatton, the new SNU President, and explained my awkward position to him. 'The man himself doesn't want me at his tribute, Eric,' I said, 'so I shouldn't be there.' And I wasn't.

But I never dreamed Mr Higginson would visit me again, much later on at a closed home circle I conducted in a private house in Swansea each week. During the silent-time, I caught sight of Gordon squatted down on his hunkers at the right-hand side of my chair. Again, I greeted him with surprise; but he surprised me further.

'I've come to apologize for the way I treated you when I was on earth, Stephen,' he said. 'I didn't realize, then, the spiritual motivation behind your work, as I do now.'

'That's OK,' I said, and I sent him my very best wishes for his new life in the world that he'd served with such dedication.

Back in the gardens at Willowtrees, spring had blossomed and bloomed into a really hot summer, and life at the cottage had been wonderful; the beauty of the surrounding countryside had re-invigorated and refreshed my spirit, got me fighting fit, and had prepared me to tackle another round of British tours.

I travelled right through the autumn months, when deserted night-time city roads had been cleanly swept of red and gold leaves by blustery gales, and Christmas had passed very quietly and peacefully at the cottage.

With not so much as a turkey-leg from the mean vegetarian!

Then winter set in, hard and strong, with its short dark days and long cold nights, and, somehow, Sooty didn't seem to be her usual self. She became listless and had a faraway look in her yellow-green eyes. Her fur started coming out in patchy handfuls, and she just didn't want to do anything. So off we went to the vet; and, even though she was ill and I was very worried about her, what a performance we had.

Getting the ailing 'Bette Davis' out of her travelling-cage proved nigh on impossible. When the vet unlocked the bars and swung them open, Sooty was determined to stoutly defend her honour – and she pushed her two front paws behind the top of the cage door, and splayed her two back legs across the bottom of it, then set her body into a concrete boomerang shape; she was utterly immovable.

'Oh Gawd,' I mumbled, recognizing the danger signals of an impending 'Push-me pull-you' Contest.

'It's no use,' groaned the sweating vet, whose hands were pulling and yanking away at her as if there were

305

no tomorrow. 'I can't shift her. She's as hard as a brick.'

Get that man away from me! I'm not well!

And the more he heaved and puffed, and grabbed and grunted – the more rock-like Sooty became.

I half-heartedly volunteered to help and into the lion's den went my own two hands. Well, we shoved and pushed and tickled until the vet couldn't take it any more. I smiled apologetically, but Bette growled at the cheek of him. 'Is she always like this?' he asked.

'Oh, she's a swine,' I said. 'She's behaving herself today.'

Then we simultaneously launched an attack and gave the cage's occupant a massive yank – whereupon she shot out like a cannonball, whizzed clean across the examination table, banged into the opposite wall, then slid to the floor.

Oowww, I feel terrible now.

Once captured, she became remarkably silent and pliable and submitted to the indignities of the thermometer as though she were his model patient.

'You sneaky old bugger,' cooed the vet, smoothing her fondly; but he didn't know what was wrong with her; so she had antibiotic injections, X-rays, and some blood tests were taken. I was told to collect the results from a vet up north near to Sheila, with whom Sooty was to stay for a few weeks while I took some meetings. When we got to Sheila's, I took a very bedraggled and sorry-looking Sooty immediately to the vet's and learned that her tests had proved negative; furthermore, they had to be done all over again.

It was then that I heard a young spirit-girl's voice speaking beside me in the surgery. 'This cat has cancer,' she said.

My blood ran cold.

What a terrifying comment for a spirit person to make, especially if it was just a guess. I could only pray that the young girl's diagnosis was wrong, while I watched the female vet taking a few skin cultures to test for AIDS, feline enteritis, and cancer – all potential killers. 'Just keep her warm and rub this ointment into her skin each day,' she said kindly, 'and we'll ring the results through soon.'

Sheila promised she'd pray for Sooty's health and that she'd apply her ointments for me while I travelled up into Scotland with Jeff to a dismal little guest-house, for we could now ill afford the better type of hotel; our money was getting tighter, and the large numbers of people attending my demonstrations seemed to be falling slightly.

That night, in the unwelcoming guest-house, I was so worried about Sooty that I couldn't sleep properly, and I prayed again that my spirit friends would do everything in their power to heal her, and to send her peace.

But little Sooty's health wasn't the only concern that kept me wide awake on that chilly night; there was another, more private, one.

My mind was also tormented by the painful, recent memory of the end of a secret romance I'd been having; when it finished it had almost broken my heart in two. It had been an assignation made in stolen whispers, and it had been snatched away before it had had the chance to reach fruition, for my lover was trapped in a strained and harrowing lacklustre marriage which involved young children, whereas I was free.

Such absurd triangles rarely work, of course, and the children's needs, we'd both felt, should always come first. But oh, there were times, such as on that dark night, when my heart felt fit to burst wide open as I lay awake, restless, listless, and dying inside. How I would have loved to gaze again into those deep brown eyes framed by their dark lashes; how I would have loved to hold you close and to have felt, for just one more time, the gentle kiss of your lips upon my neck, and the beating of your heart next to mine.

But none of this could be.

Instead, for endless hours into the hollow night, my heart ached and I dreamed of the warmth of love – but the guest-house pillow beside me was lonely, cold and empty; and the only comforting thought that came to me was that what I was now feeling had been experienced at some time or another by every soul who had ever loved and lost.

This very real pain comes to everyone whose heart has been broken in two.

Box of Tricks

I woke at six
and you'd slipped away in the April dawn
leaving a scent-warmed pillow,
a faded box and a scribbled note:
Destination unknown.
Don't trace me—
gone

no goodbyes
no final kiss
no explanations for this sudden flight:
just six break-words
and that faded 40's chocolate-box
sneak-placed beside me in oblivious night

some blue-time later
I shakily raised the lid
and paralysed my mind

for in it were
my photograph
and my poem-book with its silver pen
and alongside hid my grandfather's watch that never
   ticks
and your diamond ring, I find
finger-worn

all abandoned
in your little box of tricks

21

'I Do Love to be Beside the Seaside . . .'

I awoke just after midday, and I was still thinking
of my broken romance; but I shook my head and
shoulders, got up and dressed, and went down to
the lounge to meet Jeff. He was sitting on a comfy
sofa and watching television. With a silent nod for
'good afternoon', I joined him; and any attempt at
conversation was immediately silenced by a palpable
wave of tension when we heard the BBC news
reporting: 'Britain's crippling economic recession has
further tightened its grip throughout the nation, and
one government source has estimated that since the
recession began somewhere in the region of 60,000
small businesses may have gone bankrupt.'

We exchanged anxious glances, and a note of
seriousness crept into Jeff's voice. 'I'm worried,
Stephen. The tide's turning against us – fast; and
we can no longer ignore what's staring us in the face.
You know as well as I do that the numbers of people
attending your meetings have gradually been going
down; they've been steadily dwindling for months.'

I knew he was right, but I just sat and listened to
him.

'In the past, where a thousand people would come
to see you, now it might only be six hundred, or
sometimes less. Even some big household names,

stars that have made films and have had their own TV shows, have had to cancel some of their performances because tickets aren't moving fast enough. And it looks like things are going to get worse, according to the news.'

I switched off the television, and pulled on my coat. 'Everything goes in cycles,' I said, brightly. 'It's just a phase.' But my smile couldn't mask my concern.

While Jeff strode out to Reception and settled the bills, I picked up the luggage and waited for him, deep in thought. The news had branded its warning in both of our minds; financial darkness could soon shadow Voices Promotions, as swiftly as a thundercloud obscures the sun. Until then, the recession had always seemed so far away and unimportant, but now it presented a very real threat, not only to my spiritual work, but also to my livelihood, for the two were inextricably linked.

When Jeff and I left the building and walked to the car park, he had another grumble. 'People's living expenses are going up and their wages are frozen, Stephen. Everyone'll find it much harder to make the money go around.'

Trying to make light of the issue, I assured him, 'It's just a sticky patch.' And we started loading up the car in the chilly car park.

'Well, you mark my words, we're in for a rough time,' Jeff warned, as he packed the luggage into the boot. 'When money gets tight, the first things to go are the luxuries.'

I stopped what I was doing. 'But I'm not a luxury.'

'You're not a necessity either, like the need to buy bread and clothes, or to pay bus fares and rent.'

My back was as straight as a ramrod while we stood silently in the fine Scotch mist that surrounded the car. 'Look, whatever happens,' I reminded him, 'none of my meetings will ever be cancelled. OK?'

He nodded. 'OK.'

After three heavy bags, six boxes of books and two of cassette tapes had been safely stowed in the car, we got in and I drove off through the rising, strong winds, down-country towards northern England.

The concrete city where we'd been working was soon far behind us and, as we sped past miles of windswept grassy fields and misty hedges, Jeff continued our conversation:

'You know, all the signs of recession are there, Stephen: some theatres have held on to our ticket-monies for six weeks or more – they're banking our cash and reaping the interest, while we're struggling away to make ends meet, and some weeks we've been without wages. It's wicked. Last month I sent two solicitor's letters to try and force venues to pay up.'

There was a long pause while the car moved fast through country roads, and we contemplated the injustices that big businesses sometimes perpetrate on the little man in the street.

'The sky's darkening,' I said. 'It's leaden-grey up ahead, and there's a bank of black clouds gathering on the horizon. We're in for a storm, I think.' And I had the most peculiar feeling that in the coming week there'd be a great deal of misery and uncertainty ahead of me . . .

Above the monotonous drone of the engine as we whizzed along and joined the motorway, Jeff spoke up again, 'You know as well as I do that your meetings cost thousands of pounds to stage. Here's a bit of logic: fewer people in the audience means less profit, which means we can't hire further venues. End of story. It's a vicious circle, and it's tightening up.'

I broke the tension with, 'Yes, but there are more important things than money.'

'Of course there are. I know that. But I've got to eat, and pay my mortgage every month. And so have you.'

After more long pauses for thought, I remarked, 'Never mind . . . Everything's being watched by the Great Power. You know something?'

'What?'

'If God wanted a thousand people to be packed into each theatre to witness the work of the spirit, then all the seats would be filled.'

'Either that,' said Jeff, without hesitation, 'or the empty seats are God's way of telling you to chuck it all in.'

I glanced sideways at him, then revved up the engine. He had a good point there.

Two miles of tall green fir trees blurred past the car windows while I sat quietly and mulled over the problems. What Jeff had said was undoubtedly thought-provoking.

'We both know you're right; but whether or not money becomes scarce, I can't ignore the spiritual impulse that's driven me for nearly twenty years, to give service.' I then expressed to him another of my personal convictions. 'I was born to do this work,' I said . . . 'Whatever happens, I must go on.'

Our journey continued until night had fallen and

we'd passed down through the Scottish borders and crossed into northern England, then I headed for a popular coastal town where another of my meetings was to take place.

A lot of folks whoop with glee at the very thought of a short stay next to the briny, and they claim that English seaside towns in winter are the most magnificent places: they're beautiful and wild, bracing and blustery, those folks say; and they hail them as the ideal places in which to relax and find time to reflect, and to sort out tangled thoughts – but I'm not one of those folks, I'm afraid.

The moment we left Scotland we were surrounded by sheets of drizzling English rain; and the nearer to the coast we got, the more the skies blackened with mountainous clouds. The windscreen wipers worked overtime, swishing vigorously back and forth, but visibility got worse and worse. How many miles we'd travelled through these sheets of rain and high winds I couldn't say, but the miserable journey seemed endless.

When the car hit a patch of cold 'black ice', Jeff and I were bumped up and down as though we were unbelted passengers on a roller-coaster at the fair. And then the bumps suddenly got bigger. 'Oh my Gawd, we've got a flat tyre!' I groaned. 'And just look at the weather!'

I skidded over onto the waterlogged hard shoulder of the motorway, got out, and the high winds immediately blew my raincoat right over my head. I thought I'd gone blind, until I struggled to free myself. Then two massive articulated lorries whooshed past and splattered me from head to foot with dirty slush, and I was drenched. After screaming out a barrage of unrepeatable language, I dragged Jeff out of the warm car and indicated that he should remove the flat tyre while I grumped and groaned and I got the spare from the boot. When I rolled it through the muck towards the front of the car, Jeff was nowhere to be seen – because he was at the back end, unscrewing the wheel-nuts of *the wrong tyre*!

'You bloody twit! Can't you recognize a flat when you see one?' I yelled, hopping up and down like an Indian doing a rain dance, and waving menacing spanners.

'Oops! Sorry,' he smiled; then I did a bit more shouting at the top of my voice – until I'd sorted it all out. It took me twenty finger-numbing minutes before I got us mobile again.

In the steamy car, the atmosphere was as silent as the grave for the next stretch of our journey. I'd always disliked night driving because visibility was often so poor, and now, because I was tetchy and irritable, I'd driven for many miles before I realized something was drastically wrong. Why couldn't I see any road signs? 'Where the hell are you taking us?' I demanded of my navigator, who just sat there wide-eyed and apologetic.

'Well . . . we're going down-country, along this road here,' he said, and I caught a quick glimpse of him tracing a thick purple line down the map with his finger. With a huge sigh that came from my bootstraps upwards, I pulled over on to the hard shoulder again, stopped the engine, switched on the inside light, and explained to Jeff that for the last

315

ten miles he had tried to direct us along the map's purple line which divided one county from another!

How we eventually reached our destination, I'll never know. But somehow we did, and at least we were both in one piece. 'Nothing else could possibly go wrong,' I said.

Jeff peered through the misty windscreen as we moved along a black and deserted promenade, lit only by dim pools of orange light, and tried to spy the cheery windows of the digs he'd booked. 'Good God,' he mumbled. 'Out-of-season by the sea! Who'd be mental enough to come out in dreadful weather like this?'

'We would,' I said; and I parked the car outside a very dilapidated-looking guest-house. My eyes widened in disbelief. 'Is *that* it?' I asked, incredulously.

'I see no other,' was the nonchalant reply.

Instant annoyance bubbled up within me. 'Why on earth did you book us into a dump like that?'

'Well, we're cutting back on expenses. We can't afford swish hotels all the time. This place sounded good in the brochures.' He must have seen the look on my face. 'Well, it's cheap.'

'Oh, and I wonder why?' I replied, wide-eyed and innocently; then I filled with dismay at the sight of the layers of grimy dark-green paint that had peeled off the three-storey terraced dwelling. Jeff did his best to ignore my tut-tutting, and we braved the gusty winds and pelted headlong through the drizzle towards the guest-house passage-way with our luggage. The inside of the digs was as dark and dingy-looking as the outside.

While I stood awkwardly in the damp hallway, my feet sucked at my wet shoes, and I prayed someone would answer the loud bell that Jeff had pressed — three times.

I was freezing cold. 'I must've been mad, letting you talk me into working in a seaside town in winter!' I grumped. There was no reply. Jeff pressed the bell another three times. Where the heck was the landlady?

As if from nowhere, there came the deafening thuds of monstrous footsteps that shuddered the wooden staircases at the top of the house. Down the creaking flights of stairs the landlady was descending, grumbling and muttering away to herself, and making enough noise to raise the dead. Her big feet gumped along the landing directly above our heads, and suddenly she boomed out in a thick northern accent that resounded in the long passage-way, 'Fer Christ's sake, Ah'm comin'! Ah'm comin'! That's enough bell-pressin'. D'ye think Ah'm deaf or summat? Youse'll wear it out!'

Jeff looked at me. I looked at him. Then we both looked towards the landing above us, ready to behold the owner of that foghorn voice.

My eyes nearly popped out of my head when she rounded the corner and waddled down the last flight of stairs to meet us. She was about four feet ten inches tall, but measured at least five feet around her middle. Her heaving breasts threatened to pop the buttons on the ragged black cardigan and smock she'd poured herself into. She halted to catch her breath. 'It's no good. Ah'll 'ave to 'ave a whiff.'

She leaned her considerable chassis against the

creaky bannisters, then lifted her faded pinafore and scratched her pendulous belly. Sheer delight lit up her face. She looked about sixty years old before she'd scratched, but much younger afterwards. Though she was top-heavy, she did her best to bend over to straighten her dark stockings, grumbling, 'These bloody pop-socks'll be the death o' me on these stairs.'

In a magnificent effort, she pulled her floppy slippers to the back of her heels, shoved her feet tighter inside them, and ignored the mounds of flesh that bulged over their frayed edges. 'Right,' she muttered to herself, straightening up, 'Ah'm ready.' Then, patting her mass of mousy-coloured curls, she made her way downstairs, while adjusting two huge sponge curlers that were rolled up in the front of her quiff. Just as her feet thudded on the last step, she puffed at the very long cigarette that hung from her thick lips.

I was so fascinated that I couldn't move. Until then, I'd only seen such characters in scratchy black-and-white English movies; they were a dying breed in the Second World War – but here was one who'd survived into the 1990s.

Jeff coughed, rather nervously, and from the end of the long passage she rattled a huge bunch of keys that clanked against her thighs, and boomed out, 'Fer Christ's sake 'ave a bit o' patience! Ah'm not what Ah was! Ah can't rush roun' like a young 'un!'

While she made a slow approach, I whispered to Jeff out of the corner of my mouth, 'Have we paid?'

'Yes,' he rasped back.

'Oh well,' I sighed in a low voice, 'welcome to Ma Keys – and all the comforts of home.'

We smiled weakly.

'Nah!' she boomed, standing right in front of us, legs apart. 'Ah been expectin' youse two fer a couple o' hours. It's nearly midnight – *very* late – an' Ah'm not used ter bein' kep waitin'!' And she meant it, too. I dreaded to think what kind of punishment she'd doled out to other wicked guests who'd previously annoyed her. Suffocation, perhaps?

Jeff began to stutter an explanation, but she didn't give him a chance.

'Yer 'aven't paid yer dues. Ah want me money now, or yer'll be leavin'.'

I smiled again, but this time more strongly: if we hadn't paid we could leave straight away and find somewhere else to stay – anywhere but here.

'Beg pardon?' – it was Jeff speaking.

She frowned hard, and her double chins wobbled as she raised her voice: 'Ah'm not in the 'abit o' repeatin' meself. Youse two 'aven't paid yer balances on them rooms. Ah'm not stupid; Ah knows what's *what!*' she bellowed amid clouds of swirling cigarette smoke.

Clearing my throat gently, I asked, 'Ahem, I wonder if you might excuse us for a moment, please? Ahem, Jeffrey?' and I gripped his arm and steered him into the nearest corner, where I whispered, 'Let's leg it!'

He rasped back, 'What? In this rain? Are you mad? It's midnight – we'd never find another place now. This isn't London, you know, with all-night hotels on every street corner.'

I grinned over my shoulder at the woman who was shrouded in clouds of smoke – she looked just

319

like a dragon in the mist. She didn't smile back; at least, I don't think she did. But I heard her swinging her bunch of keys around and around – rather menacingly, I thought. I huddled back and whispered to Jeff, 'Well, if she picks a fight – it won't be with me.'

We rejoined our hostess, but despite Jeff's protest that our cheques had been forwarded *and* cashed, Ma Keys would have none of it; and in the end, we paid again, after which she boomed out, 'Follow me!' And like little lambs, we did.

Up the stairs the three of us huffed and puffed, and three flights later we traipsed past a pea-green door and Ma Keys chucked a key at me and said, 'Y're in there!' And she did the same to Jeff, further down the corridor, after which she wheezed her way up into her private apartments near the roof; her great clod-hopping feet thudded and creaked on the floorboards above.

My room, or rather my cupboard, was tiny, bare, cold, and damp. Completely unsurprised, I spread an extra-thin blanket that I'd found in the wardrobe onto the bed, and then threw my spare jacket on top of that. I'd already been warned that my room had no central heating ('Ah've no inklin' what's wrong wi' it. It's allus on the blink on them top floors'), and Jeff's 'apartment' turned out to be a room full of old mattresses that had been piled on top of one another. Even Ma Keys felt she must apologize for this oversight, which she later did; then she flung a different key at him, and grunted heavenwards again.

Neither of us could settle down in our cupboards for the night, but we tried the best we could . . .

A high-pitched digital alarm woke me the next morning at nine o'clock and I was greeted by the persistent sound of big raindrops drumming against the windowpanes. I was numb: my legs and feet were cold, the tip of my nose was freezing – and so were my other bits and pieces. After a mammoth yawn, I jumped into my cold, but dry, clothes and sought out a hot shower to revive me. I trudged down the corridor to the communal bathroom, but decided against a wash when my foot slithered over a layer of thick grime that lined the shower base.

It was then that a powerful and negative psychic feeling swept through my spirit. Added to the strange feeling of dread that I'd experienced the day before, which was still lurking at the back of my mind, I now had an overwhelming sense of foreboding – not about the horrible digs, but about the next two days ahead of me. I was booked to do a live radio interview later that morning at 10 a.m., and my public meeting would take place the following night. As I tried to dismiss this horrible psychic sensation from my thoughts, a cold shiver ran up and down my spine. My head tingled, and pins-and-needles numbed my hands.

More than a little disturbed, I slid quickly out of the bathroom and returned to my cupboard, where I hung a note on my doorknob: *Please do not disturb, or clean – thank you* (because I can't bear anyone fiddling about with my book manuscripts, business papers, or my personal belongings). Then I called for Jeff and we descended to the hallway, where Ma Keys awaited us wearing exactly the same black rig-out, including the two huge sponge-curlers, that she'd poured herself into on the previous night. A big lump of ash dropped from her cigarette onto the carpet. She rubbed it in with her flip-flop.

'Yer've missed yer sausages an' dripping.'

My stomach churned at the thought. 'We don't eat breakfast, thank you.'

'Skinny swines,' she mumbled, and she shuffled away.

As Jeff and I walked to the car he offered me a packet of crisps, but I refused.

'You're not eating properly, you know, Stephen. You can't expect to do a full day's work on an empty stomach.'

'It's the stress!' I said, light-heartedly; but I knew he was right: I felt quite tired; I'd been dieting again for the last two months to keep my weight down, and I hadn't been getting enough nourishing food on tour.

About an hour later, when he and I were waiting in the radio station reception area and listening to my interviewer conducting his show, we were not impressed by his cynical attitude towards his guests; he'd been quite unkind to them, and I thought his manner very rude and rather abrupt.

Jeff said quietly to me, 'Doesn't the presenter's voice sound hard and sharp? Like a jagged piece of tin.'

'Yes. He's being very sarcastic to that phone-caller.'

'He keeps butting in when she's talking; and he doesn't sound as if he cares, either.'

'No he doesn't, and I'm next . . . I have a bad feeling about this,' I said. 'This is going to be awful.' Jeff nodded. 'Why are some presenters so controversial?'

322

'Aggressive interviews are all the rage these days. The media people question everyone's motives now, especially if their claims are off the beaten track, like yours are.' I gave him a hard stare. 'You know exactly what I mean, Stephen.'

'Maybe. But the public don't want to listen to people being verbally mugged; surely, they want to hear the guest's views, his ideas? The public are quite capable of knowing whether or not they agree with them.'

Suddenly the big padded door swung open, and a petite researcher called out, 'Stephen O'Brien! This way, please!' As we marched through to the studio, she informed me, 'It's just a short item today, but don't be put off by your host: he sounds a bit sharp and abrasive but he doesn't really mean it. Still, I think you ought to know that he might challenge you and play the devil's advocate.'

'What a pity,' I said, stepping into the sound-proofed room, where I shook hands with my over-enthusiastic host, sat at the microphone opposite him, then prepared myself to face a live grilling that would be heard by tens of thousands of souls.

Make no mistake about it: you're tuned in to the best radio programme today! Happy listening! And with me I have a special guest. His name is Stephen O'Brien, and he's a psychic. But is he a medium rare? We shall see.

But first things first! My researcher, the delicious Sara, has handed me a severe gale warning – hasn't the old weather been rainy and dreadful in the last few days? Well, there's more of it on the way! Gale-force winds are expected tomorrow, of strength seven or eight, and full shipping information will be given at the top of the hour, straight after the national and international news.

Righto! Britain's famous medium and best-selling psychic author, Stephen O'Brien is in the studio with me. He's written volumes of autobiography, and he fills theatres up and down the country, claiming to re-unite loved ones with their relatives who've died. But does he actually do that, I wonder? Is there an afterlife? Are mediums genuine, or just big cons? Well, let's see! Hello, Stephen.

Good morning.

I have to warn you that I'm a sceptic.

That's OK; it's good to question rather than to blindly accept.

And I will question, too. Now let's get straight on with it. A caller named Daphne rang us to say she thinks mediums are raking in pots of money off the backs of the vulnerable and the bereaved.

Well, she has a right to her opinion, of course. But I don't agree with it. Up and down the country many mediums work in Spiritualist churches, which are charitable organizations, and they often don't even claim their travelling expenses. Mediums offer a service that can provide comfort and hope to a wide cross-section of the public, only some of whom may feel their lives have been shattered by grief. Not everyone who seeks a medium's help is in a vulnerable or suggestible state. In—

Come on! Many are!

I wouldn't agree. Mediums are consulted for all kinds

of different reasons; but anyway, I don't think people would pay them if they failed to produce survival evidence, or spiritual guidance – if that's what the seeker needs.

But mediumship has made you a wealthy man. Don't look so shocked.

I'm far from wealthy.

You can't expect us to believe that of Britain's top psychic star.

. . . Well, I don't think of myself in that way. If a man dedicates his life to any kind of career, or calling, surely he's entitled to be paid, or how would he survive in western society? 'The labourer is worthy of his hire'.

But you can't possibly justify ticket prices of between six and seven pounds just to see you.

Many overheads and expenses have to be paid, and these are met by public monies. In—

Nevertheless, it must be said – and I'm going to say it – that there are a great many frauds in your line of business, charlatans who practise guesswork to startle people. It's called 'cold-reading', I'm told, when they make up strings of lucky guesses as they go along.

I'm sorry, but I don't see mediumship as a business: it's a calling.

But there are charlatans.

I've worked with many sensitives in the last two decades, and I've rarely come across anyone who was fraudulent. Each medium has reached a different stage of development: some have minds that are well attuned to the spirit world, others don't; some sensitives are just starting to learn how to use their psychic faculties; and others have established their

325

abilities so well, that they're reliable channels for communication. So—

Answer my question.

I've alread—

Do you deny there are practising frauds?

Some sensitives are more proficient than others. Very few mediums have ever got away with fraudulent activities. The Spiritualist Movement, within which most of Britain's reputable mediums work, does the best it can to police itself. On the rare occasions when fraudulence was discovered, it was often the Spiritualist Movement that exposed it. Years ag—

That's nonsense, of course.

No, it's the truth. Surely, at some time or other, every profession suffers at the hands of individuals who don't live up to the high expectations demanded of them by their code of ethics? And—

Let's move on! A lady called Laura feels that communicating with the dead is 'Against God's Law', and that 'People like Stephen O'Brien are an abomination in the sight of the Lord'. That's right, isn't it?

Well . . . that's a rather sad statement. I think everything depends on what religion you profess to follow, and how you interpret its teachings.

And a clergyman has just rung in to say that 'If Stephen O'Brien were a member of my church I'd have him excommunicated because mediumship is condemned in the Bible'.

The Bible is only one of many revered religious books in the world – and it's full of accounts of visitations from angels. The translation of the Greek word

Angelos is *Messenger*; so, angels are messengers who come from the invisible world that surrounds us. People have spoken with them since antiquity – long before the time of Jesus. Even Socrates wrote that the spirit-form of one of his 'dead' colleagues sat on his bed one night and talked with him, and—
Come off it! That's pure hallucination.
No. Sceptics always say that. But if I asked you to sit down and hallucinate the presence of your 'dead' mother, or father, and then go on to hold an intelligent conversation with them – could you do it? I couldn't; I've tried it many times – and failed. The psychic faculty has always been widespread throughout humanity, and evidence of another life beyond death is available to anyone who diligently, and intelligently, seeks it.
But people think it's a load of old codswallop.
They don't.
Yes they do!
But I read the other day that recent statistics show that over 80 per cent of the British public believe in an afterlife.
We only have your word for that, of course.
Look – huge sums of money have been used to set up seats of parapsychology in universities around the world: if there isn't an afterworld, then what are all these scientists and professors investigating?
What indeed? I could think of much more productive ways of using that money. Finally: Moira wants to know 'Just how much does Stephen O'Brien get paid for giving out all this rubbish'?

. . .

No answer?

. . . Nobody gets paid for giving rubbish. People are paid to take it away.

It was just as well that this dreadful interview had finished, for I was on the verge of getting up and walking out of the studio. The experience had thoroughly sickened me, and I felt as if I'd been repeatedly bashed around the head with a cricket bat.

Jeff and I got into the car as quickly as possible. 'What a day,' I sighed, my voice barely audible.

'And it isn't over yet, Stephen. Ma Keys told me there's cabaret and singing tonight at the digs.'

The miserable look on my face was equalled only by the dismal rain-swept streets.

When we got back to the House of Hades, Ma Keys met us at the door, grinning all over her chops. She brandished a local newspaper and thrust it at my face. A 'witty' reporter's poisoned pen had asked its readers, 'What is this medium Stephen O'Brien? A miracle worker, or just a con man?'

'Is that you?' she said, chuckling and pointing to my photograph. Then she tottered off down the corridor, muttering away to herself, 'Well, Ah'll eat me own wash-pot!'

I said nothing, but ran upstairs to my room and discovered that the 'Do not disturb' notice had been ripped from my door, and my papers and belongings had all been moved; and (I'm convinced of it) my book manuscripts had been flicked through and read. I was livid, and I locked myself in for the rest of the miserable day.

In the late evening, I crept downstairs to the payphone and rang Sheila to see if Sooty's blood tests and X-rays had come back, and she gave me the good news. 'She's OK, Stephen. The vet says she doesn't have cancer, but she's suffering from a very severe and rare strain of ringworm; and it can be treated.'

I leaned against the wall and heaved a huge sigh of relief. Sooty didn't have cancer. She wasn't going to die. She was all right, which meant that the young spirit girl's diagnosis at the vet's surgery had been proved quite wrong, thank God.

Kindly Sheila said, 'Don't worry about anything. I'll nurse Sooty, and apply her ointment, and administer her tablets until you can collect her after the next leg of your tour.'

'God bless you, Sheila,' I said, at the end of our conversation.

Over the moon about the great news, but still feeling quite narked about the awful radio interview and the damp digs, I made my way back to my cupboard but inadvertently opened the wrong door and entered a dance-bar by mistake. All eyes turned on me, and I had to run the gauntlet through a coachload of senior citizens – mostly women – who were as tight as a miser's purse, and all waving pints of lager and snorts of whisky as they sang and made merry for all they were worth.

I dashed for the opposite staircase just as one drooling old duck made a grab for me and shouted out as I slithered across the dance-floor, 'Good Gawd'l'Mighty! It's my lucky night, girls! Cor, look at them legs! Who is he? Let me get my 'ands on his body! Hold me back; hold me back!'

(And thank God, two of them did.)

My door was locked in a trice, and I quickly undressed and got into bed.

During my prayers, I sensed White Owl's incredibly powerful healing presence, which bathed my tired body in waves of pulsing golden light. He obviously knew how I'd been treated and how it had affected me, and of my concern over being able to keep my public work going. It was good to sense him nearby, for, just lately, all my problems seemed to be surfacing at once.

My guide's big but gentle spirit hands encompassed my weary head, and in a short while his peaceful mind had eased away some of my tensions, and heralded the promise of rest . . .

In my mind I visualized purple-headed mountains, birds singing in pine trees, and a blood-red sun as it sank in the western sky. These calm images eventually lulled me into a deep sleep, during which I dreamed a dream of my beloved Willowtrees cottage. Free as a bird, I flew over the lush green fields of Wales, past ripening corn and small farmhouses, and viewed from some fifty feet in the air my secluded little home – and I longed to be back there, inside it. But—

Loud cymbal-clashes smashed my eardrums and startled me wide awake. With my senses reeling, I didn't know where I was for a moment. Then I heard the ear-splitting *thump thump thump* of huge loudspeakers in the dance-hall downstairs. It was deafening, and the lusty pensioners were having a marvellous time, shouting their lungs out and singing, 'Oh, we do love to be beside the seaside! Oh we do love to be beside the sea!'

It was two o'clock in the morning, and still raining hard. By the sound of the wind, the storm that the radio station had predicted was already well into its stride.

Thump thump thump went the big bass drums, pounding their vibrations into my sensitive throat and chest; every bone in my body seemed to be quivering with the sound. 'Oh, we do like to be beside the sea!' I'd have been so much happier if someone had thrown them *into* it! 'Dear God, is there no mercy?' I murmured.

Thump thump thump for another half-hour went the cacophony, and then at last the jolly senior citizens retired; but they got up throughout the night and stomped over the creaky floorboards to use toilets that were then noisily flushed.

One irritable old dear perfectly expressed my feelings when, in the room next to mine, she shouted to her wandering hubby, 'Oh, for Jupiter's sake, Arthur! Give it *one bloody good squeeze* and have done with it!'

I'd had a dreadful day, and now the happy promenaders were robbing me of my sleep, but what could I do about it?

Nothing.

I was cold, tired and miserable, but I just had to accept this awful situation and try to snatch forty winks between loo-flushes, if possible.

For a long time, I lay wide awake and restless, thinking about all the hassle I'd suffered throughout the day, and wondering just how much it would affect my meeting tomorrow . . .

331

22

The Taming of the Shrews

After a restless night, I was woken by the unearthly sound of rolling thunder, and the pummelling of torrential rain as it smashed against the windowpanes; bleary-eyed, I watched big drops of it as they dripped through a leak in the skylight and splashed onto the foot of my bed.

My eyes felt as if they didn't belong to me: they were dry and gritty, and a banging migraine headache pounded behind them. 'Little wonder,' I thought, 'after what I've been through in the last few days.' Every time I tried to focus my vision, blinding flashes of white light blanched out the miserable room; and outside the skies were lit up by much brighter forked lightning.

When the house-phone rang it practically shattered my skull. It was Jeff. 'It's two o'clock in the afternoon! Are you OK?'

My voice was thick and slow. 'No, I think I died in the night. I feel absolutely awful. There's a little man inside my head . . . and he's making horse-shoes out of my brain.'

'Well, look – swallow a few tablets, and sleep for another few hours. I'll meet you at five o'clock downstairs in the hall, and then we'll drive straight to the theatre.'

I did as he suggested; and two hours later, after slowly shivering into my cold clothes, I met him and we both encountered a dishevelled Ma Keys who, while puffing away at the inevitable cigarette that was glued to the side of her mouth, produced another surprise. 'Read this bit, 'ere,' she said, passing Jeff a newspaper; then she waddled off to the kitchen, where she laughed like a drain.

Jeff handed me the free sheet and, as I scanned the lines, my jaw hit my chest. 'That's right,' he said. 'They've mixed up the dates in the advertisement, and some people probably turned up *last* night to see the meeting, instead of tonight.'

My head throbbed and I stood dumbstruck and numb. 'No point in moaning about it,' I said. 'Let's go; there's a lot to do.' And we set off for the theatre in gale-force 10 winds that rattled and shook my old Ford Fiesta car so much that it was a miracle its tyres kept contact with the rain-drenched roads. I could hardly see through the windscreen – as fast as the wipers removed the deluge, more water poured onto them and blurred my vision.

As we crawled along the deserted promenade, twenty-foot waves smashed against the sea wall and spurted up and over the iron railings; and when bright flashes of lightning lit them, they looked like silver curtains falling from a dark sky.

Jeff seemed subdued. 'I know a bunch of singing pensioners who might be cooled off if they took a little walk along that prom today,' he said; and I realized that he'd also suffered from insomnia. 'Is your migraine gone?'

'No. It's too strong to respond to medication.'

Twenty minutes later, we huddled out of the car and fought our way through the powerful winds and sheets of rain, and ran into the cold venue. It felt quite eerie to stand in the dark theatre wings, when the building was being buffeted by the wind; it sounded as if giant hands were slapping against the walls.

When I lumbered into my dressing-room and switched on the light – which momentarily dazzled my migraine headache – I was greeted by the feeble warmth of a single-bar electric fire which was supposed to heat the room. It sputtered and flashed, and then went out. Jeff said, 'Typical,' then he wandered off to find the technicians so that sound and lighting checks could be set.

After changing into my stage clothes I opened my dressing-room door because I heard Jeff having a disagreement over the equipment we'd booked. The two technicians sounded old and obstreperous. 'Now listen here, mate!' ordered one of them, very arrogantly. 'You haven't booked a radio-mike – so you're not having one. And that's that!'

I peeked round the door and watched Jeff steel himself. 'Mr O'Brien *must* be able to hear the audience's replies – so microphones will have to be fixed up.'

The unshaven electrician grizzled something under his breath, which made Jeff snap back, 'You have ten minutes to provide our requirements. And could you please put a decanter of water and some glasses on this coffee table for the medium?'

The man barked back, 'No rush, sunshine. I'll put the water out when the blokie starts his show.'

334

Jeff's back lengthened; the man had obviously pushed him too far. 'You'll do no such thing, sir. No-one is allowed on stage when Mr O'Brien is working: he stands out here completely alone. The full attention of the audience is focused on him, and him only. I hope that's clear? And by the way, it isn't a show.'

The uncouth man in the boiler suit scratched his six-o'clock shadow, coughed, then spat into his handkerchief. 'Please yourself, mate.'

'That's not the point at all: the public, and the medium, have a right to expect a professional service. Now – we need three microphones fixed up, and ready for a sound check in fifteen minutes, sir. OK?'

As the grumbling electrician stumped away, Jeff called after him, 'Mr O'Brien will make his exact lighting requirements clear to you after a thorough sound-check.' The man ambled his way out of the shadowy auditorium.

Fifteen minutes later, I walked onto the stage and it took the technicians an agonizing forty-five minutes to set the correct tones and levels on the microphones, to my satisfaction. They'd been downright nasty to me, and when I stated my requirements for the lights, the officious man puffed out his chest and yelled back, 'You'll have to make do with what we've got, sunshine. This is an old place: we can't work miracles – that's *your* department, see!' and he gave a coarse laugh, then coughed and spat into his handkerchief again.

I counted five, then spoke my mind. 'These spotlights above my head are much too near;

335

they'll throw deep shadows over my eyes. Those five key-lights can light me from the back of the auditorium ceiling. And from over there' – I pointed – 'I'll have those two follow-spots on full white, fixed to cover as much of the apron of the stage as possible. No coloured lights and no lamps from the side. All right?'

He opened and closed his mouth, twice, and looked as though I'd whammed him in the face with a shovel. 'No it isn't bloody all right. I'm not getting up on ladders at this time of night, mate. I've told you: you'll have to make do with what's been fixed up.'

I cast Jeff a knowing glance, and he returned it: he knew he'd have to settle the dispute, for I walked off the stage. Later, when he came into my dressing-room to say he'd sorted out the bother, neither of us was in high spirits, and he suggested a bleak possibility.

'Stephen, I think we've reached a watershed . . . We'll have to close down Voices Promotions if the economic recession deepens. We can't continue to spend huge sums of money to organize poorly attended meetings; our finances will be bled dry.' His voice was quiet and sensible. 'There's no alternative.'

'The government keeps promising that the recession's ending, but that's—'

'—Absolute rubbish!' Jeff snorted.

My migraine thumped away and seemed to keep time with the bursts of sheet lightning that flooded through the high windows. I rubbed my brow and became pensive; I felt so weary and disheartened that all I could say was, 'Perhaps we should apply one of my old adages.'

'Which one?'

'When in doubt – *wait*.'

Jeff nodded, and we agreed to carefully monitor our cash-flow over the next few months, before deciding whether or not to close down the business. Our conversation was abruptly ended by the grumpy technician who poked his head around the door. 'The press are here for the gaffer!' he cried, and then he was gone.

Out on the stage I met a bright young woman and a middle-aged man with a camera. She was bubbly and sharp-witted, but I sensed something unpleasant in his character. The woman said, 'Sorry to bother you, but we didn't think you'd mind if I did an interview and we took a few shots for the regional paper.' It wasn't a question: it was a statement.

I wondered what she'd say if I replied that it did bother me, very much in fact; but instead, I sank down wearily on the stage, extended a tired hand, and greeted them both. 'We're in the middle of setting up for tonight's meeting.' She smiled but completely ignored my remarks, and eagerly opened her notepad. 'So this'll have to be quick,' I added, 'because we're very busy right now.'

'Oh, it won't take long,' she said, breezily – but I knew that wasn't true. For the next twenty minutes she gave me as thorough a grilling as I'd had at the radio station on the day before, and asked many probing questions; some of them were silly, and one or two of them were downright impertinent. But I hid the pain of my headache and slapped on a brave face. Under the circumstances I think I tolerated this unwelcome intrusion quite well – but when she smirked and came out with, 'Do you have any girlfriends or boyfriends at the moment?' I immediately stood up and curtly replied:

'Look, I don't feel well; I'm very tired and I'm under a lot of stress. This interview is now over. Concluded. Excuse me – but I have a lot to do.'

My last shred of patience had vanished, but before I could turn on my heels the sly photographer had crouched down beyond the footlights, and I saw my shadowed face clearly reflected in his camera lens. Instantly I raised a hand and shielded my head, and with my other palm I blocked his line of vision. 'Don't take that shot!' I commanded.

He was visibly shaken. 'Why not?' he barked back.

'Because of the shadows. Because I'd have looked like Vincent Price in a Hammer Horror movie.'

His hackles rose in anger. 'I've photographed more important people than you, mate! You're a nobody to me. I've photographed Royalty, and I know what I'm doing!' he exclaimed.

'And so do I,' I said firmly. 'I'm tired of people using me and my mediumship to get a cheap laugh. I'm not a sideshow exhibit. My work is serious. I'm sorry – but this interview is over.' And I stalked away from them, leaving the situation in Jeff's capable hands.

Backstage, for the next thirty minutes, I listened to the thunder-crashes as they rolled around the dark skies, and the wind as it howled around the building. I was annoyed, and I paced stupidly back and forth. My spine was prickling. Why had I been so irritable? It couldn't have been just my headache. Nor my lack of sleep. Bursts of white light obscured my vision.

I thumped the nearest table-top. Every fibre of my being was bone-weary, tired, and my body felt too heavy to carry. I knew I hadn't been eating properly – maybe that's what had made me so tetchy.

There was no way I could get myself to relax; so instead, I tried to blot out this world and to contact the next. But when I exercised my psychic awareness, I was sorry that I had; for my mind went spinning like radar and revealed that the small audience who had now gathered in the theatre felt lost in the cavernous auditorium – and this made them emanate a depressingly negative and heavy psychic atmosphere. I knew then that the meeting would undoubtedly be a difficult one, and my morale sank even further.

A coded knock came on the door. I unlocked it and Jeff crept in looking like a youngster who'd been sent to the headmaster's study for judgement. 'I checked the sound and light for you. The reporter's gone, and the crowd's in . . . but there aren't—'

'I know!' I snapped, testily.

'Oh.' He looked at the floor.

I shook my head. 'I'm sorry,' I said, turning to the mirror and noticing the dark circles under my eyes that showed clearly through my stage make-up. 'It's not easy, you know . . . for me.' I slumped into a chair. 'I've had a gut's-full of the cynics and their sneering remarks; and people who think that they can treat me like some kind of freak.'

He tried to be helpful. 'But they're not all like that.'

I rested my head in my hands, sighed, then looked up. 'I'm well aware of that. But I'm the one who has

339

to deal with the people who *are* like that. Then I'm supposed to shake off their aggression, dust myself down, then walk out onto the stage and produce survival evidence for two and a half hours – as if nothing's happened. Well, it's not on.'

Stillness filled the room.

Jeff was sympathetic, but firm. 'It's bound to be tough. Whoever said it'd be easy every time?'

A grunt left my throat.

'Try to keep calm, Stephen. The people are waiting. Just do the best you can.'

I rubbed my eyes to stem the searing pain of my blinding headache. 'Oh I know, I know . . . Don't worry, I'm going out there. I'm going on, and I'm going to work. But it's much harder to receive clear messages when my mind's this troubled. And the audience "felt" so negative.'

'You've always taught that mediums should never rely on the public's co-operation: if the people are listless – *you've* got to work that much harder to make the night a success. There's no easy way to solve it.'

'I know that,' I said, defiantly.

Jeff looked serious. 'Why don't you take a tablet?'

'Pointless.'

Another silence.

'Have you got a link yet?'

'No. I haven't heard a thing. The psychic power's very low out there.'

During the pause that followed I turned to the mirror and tried to cover the dark circles under my eyes with make-up. When I looked up again, Jeff had silently left the room.

As the minutes ticked away towards 7.30, the start of the meeting drew nearer and I felt physically sick. Perhaps overwork had caused this terrible sense of nervous exhaustion.

Just before curtain-up, I glanced in the dressing-room mirror again and I saw, as if through different eyes, that I was far too thin and undernourished. My cheeks were hollow and my chin seemed to jut out over my collar. Perhaps I was suffering from 'the vegetarian's disease' – a vitamin-B deficiency, as I'd done once before, a few years previously. The B-complex is essential for a healthy nervous system. Maybe that was my problem – a faulty diet. 'Oh, to hell with it!' Then I became too irritable even to think.

Suddenly the tannoy speaker crackled out, 'Beginners, please. This is your call, Mr O'Brien.'

Apprehension swept over me.

I straightened my tie. I had to go on stage. But the sides of my head throbbed so much that I thought they were going to burst wide open. For a few moments I closed my aching eyes, took some very deep breaths, and listened to the persistent hammering of heavy raindrops as they bounced off the theatre's flat roof. The wind was still shrieking madly along the promenade outside. I opened my eyes and sighed heavily. My name had already been called – I had to take the stage.

Nervously, I stood behind the red crushed velvet drapes that had seen much better days; a number of rips in the fabric were discreetly held together by sticky-tape . . . I swayed on legs that wobbled like jelly, and for a moment I blacked out – but woke

341

instantly to find myself clutching at the curtains for support.

I steadied myself with both hands . . .

Jeff whispered across from the wings, 'Are you OK? Are you ready?'

Lifting my eyebrows and breathing very deeply, I replied, 'Yes . . . I'm OK . . . And I'm never ready – but let's get going.'

The psychic conditions around me were so depressing, and not at all conducive to contacting the Other Side. I couldn't even sense White Owl's presence. In the stillness and darkness of those few tense moments before the meeting begins, moments which the audience never sees, I prayed that my guide would be able to intervene somehow, to put matters right, and to make the meeting successful.

After working with him for nearly twenty years, I knew there was only one thing I could do now: *trust*.

Jeff introduced me, I smiled when the curtains parted, and the small crowd bravely applauded. Then began one of the most difficult theatre meetings I'd ever taken, where the audience seemed determined to be unresponsive and unco-operative. Though I could barely sense the presence of the spirit people, they seemed more alive to me than the audience was.

For the benefit of the public, and especially for the press (who I knew were reporting the event), I took great pains to clearly explain, before I attempted to relay communication, why I stood before them as a sensitive, and what I hoped to achieve during the evening.

'A medium's task is to serve the spirit people and their loved ones on Earth,' I said through the microphones. 'I haven't come here tonight to convince anyone of anything, or to convert anyone to my way of thinking. God forbid. We're intelligent beings and we can find our own pathway to the Truth. No, a medium's job is to serve. My work is about love and service, and not about proving anything at all.'

This was greeted by the usual blank stares that I'd come to expect from crowds who didn't really want to participate in the proceedings, but merely wanted to watch a clairvoyant at work. Not surprisingly, clear spirit messages were difficult to hear, and some of what I did receive was greeted by a marked lack of enthusiasm.

But I plodded on valiantly through the first half, while the rain hammered down on the roof above the people's heads, and my temples pounded in rhythm with it. It was difficult enough to keep my concentration going, but I was further put off my stroke by two female reporters sitting in the gallery, who were scribbling away in their notepads like fury – but only when my messages were refused, or their details needed to be checked.

I tried not to let them affect me. I had a job to do, and I was determined to do it – and I just about managed to relay some uplifting contacts that had maddeningly 'faded-in' and 'faded-out' of my consciousness. But the psychic atmosphere was so 'thick' and 'dense' that my mind felt as if it were being dragged through sticky black treacle . . .

Polite applause opened the interval, and I felt terribly downhearted and disappointed as I slumped off the stage and into my dressing-room. As soon as I was out of the spotlights I let slip my public face, and my eyes burned hot under their lids. But no tears fell; I was much too experienced a demonstrator to allow myself to be swamped by that kind of emotionalism; I was much too well-disciplined and professional. But in silent privacy, I clasped my hands together and prayed so intensely for greater success in the second half that I lost track of time, and before I knew it I was called again to the stage.

A few minutes later than usual, I steeled myself, stepped back onto the platform, and started a short question-and-answer session. When a hand waved in an exaggerated way in the gallery and I said politely, 'Yes, what's your question?', I realized I was addressing one of the reporters, who snidely asked:

'Can you tell me why the first name you gave out tonight is the most common surname in the phone book?'

There was a stunned silence.

What had she just said? And why had she used that sarcastic tone? Her manner had upset me more than the rudeness of her remark – it had been packed with unpleasant implications.

With a shaky voice, I replied, 'I wasn't aware that the name of "Crawford" occupied that place.'

'Well it does,' she said, smugly; and I didn't need to be psychic to recognize this as an accusation of fraudulence.

Anger bubbled within me, just below the surface of my smile. How I controlled it, I'll never know; but my stomach muscles were shaking when I asked her to, 'Tell us *exactly* what you're saying.'

There was no reply; all we heard was the chords of distant thunder that penetrated the auditorium.

My face reddened at the thought of her planning to disrupt the meeting in such an impolite way, and I was annoyed about the mocking tone of voice she'd used. My blood was up.

'Why don't you say what you mean, in plain English – openly?' I said, my voice quivering.

Dozens of people turned their heads and stared at her, and she felt embarrassed enough to cover her face with both hands. The public sat poker-backed in their seats, and charged the atmosphere with their attention, but my patience evaporated and I swung into action, and asked the audience:

'Who received spirit messages through me in the first half, please? Would you make yourselves known?' Several people raised their hands, and I took a deep breath and gripped the microphone stand to try to steady my weak legs. 'Do any of you know me personally?' I pointed to each of them in turn, and they all said 'No', they didn't. 'Did the messages I gave you contain any correct information, any facts that I couldn't possibly have known?' I asked.

The recipients chorused 'Yes'. I pointed to a woman who was waving her hand, and she shouted out loud towards the press, 'I don't know Stephen, but he told me I'd been looking at photos of a new baby today, with my mother. Here are the snapshots of the baby' – and she took them out of her handbag and held them up for all to see. 'My mother brought these over only this afternoon, and we were looking at them together. My mum isn't here tonight – and there's no way Stephen, or anyone else, could have known that.'

A murmur of agreement rippled through the crowd.

I turned towards the press in the gallery and challenged them defiantly with, 'If you want to print a story – why don't you publish that evidence?'

One or two brave people applauded, but I'd been a public medium for nearly two decades and I was experienced enough to know that a thorough hatchet-job would be written and printed in her newspaper that week.

Shaking with annoyance at this realization, and burning with shame because of my unprecedented outburst, I found it extremely difficult to continue the second half of the meeting – but I stayed where I was, and carried on giving messages as best I could under the circumstances.

An hour later, I had completed my job of service. I left the stage and, when alone in my dressing-room, I was so dejected and miserably unhappy that my spirit felt as if it weighed a million tons. My body ached and my chest was tight. I felt as though I were suffocating. Too tired to stand, I flopped into a chair, and my trembling hands covered my lowered head.

My promise to serve the next world had been all but crushed within my spirit. My vision blurred, and I couldn't think straight.

What on earth had come over me lately? Why had I challenged someone from the stage? It had been so unlike me. Stephen O'Brien wasn't himself. And where were my spirit friends now? Had I failed them? Had they abandoned me? Or was this some kind of important soul-test that I had to go through, alone?

Loud thunderclaps boomed overhead, right above the theatre roof. Sheet lightning flashed in the sky and lit up the dressing-room, and gale-force winds rattled its small windows in their frames as Jeff silently appeared in the doorway.

I shall never forget the look of astonishment on his face when I told him quietly, but with conviction, 'I can't take much more of this. I'm giving it all up.'

23

Dialogue with Death

The walls of Willowtrees cottage seemed to warmly embrace me, to soothe and nurture my spirit as I rested within them. And Sooty, my dearest little friend, joined me in a long spell of recuperation through the winter months. By day, we sat before a roaring log fire and didn't step outside onto the thick frosty ground, except to gather fallen branches from the woods nearby for firewood; and by night, we curled up under the warm duvet and listened to chilly winds moaning through the bare branches of the trees outside my bedroom window. We cuddled each other, happy in the knowledge that we'd shunned the world. My sole means of communication was the telephone, and that was used only when necessary.

During many quiet evenings, I sat before the flickering firelight and gradually realized what had caused my problems. It had been the last four years of strenuous touring, and the mental fatigue I'd got from writing books and articles on which I'd often worked way into the early hours of the morning, pushing myself to meet publishing deadlines; my appearances in many and frequently stressful media features had played a major part, too, as had the complete concentration I'd given to my essential business responsibilities: to run

348

Voices Promotions efficiently had always required masses of nervous energy. All these factors had combined with an inadequate diet to batter my body and nearly break my spirit. I'd been overworked and malnourished, and I knew my recovery to full strength would take time.

It would be easy enough to rest and feed my body, but what would alleviate my spiritual pain?

To find the answer, I did some serious thinking . . . and realized that in the past I'd foolishly allowed the pressure of public demand for my mediumship to trap me like a caged bird. In future, whenever I would say 'No', I'd have to really mean it. Right now, I longed to spread my wings and fly into freedom. But I couldn't, because I'd committed myself to a life of service. This knowledge ached deep inside me, and I could practically hear my soul begging to complete its spiritual mission: it wanted to bring people comfort and new hope; it wanted to serve. But what of me, the physical man? My body was so tired and weary that I didn't know what to think, or what to do next.

'When a man's down,' I sternly reminded myself, 'he must fight his way back up again. He can be guided, helped and encouraged – that's true enough – but the struggle is his alone.'

Under my own power, I'd have to climb up out of the darkness, and move towards the light. Didn't the spirit world teach that life was about growth, evolution, movement and change? They maintained that the only way the character can be purified and strengthened is by meeting, and dealing with, life's challenges, head-on. 'Every soul,' my inspirers had often told me, 'must drink from the cup of happiness and also taste the wine of sorrow.'

And so my thoughts tumbled round and around and each winter night, when the cottage doors had locked out the bitter weather, I contemplated my situation, and reviewed my life. As a young man of twenty, I had 'married' myself to a spiritual Cause, and had faithfully served it ever since. But strangely enough, even though this Cause had proved to be an exacting mistress, I felt no bitterness towards her. Instead, there was warm gratitude for the many wonderful spiritual experiences she'd threaded into my life. A great many people had suffered much more hardship and soul torment than I had, I reminded myself. 'There's always someone worse off than yourself,' my mother had alway said, and no-one could question the truth of that. But I still couldn't shake off the dreadful sense of world-weariness that plagued me.

For several soul-searching weeks, the only comfort I obtained was from watching the perfect relaxation of Sooty who, when curled up and purring contentedly each night upon my bed, was a champion in the art of letting the world go by.

A man can learn a lot from his cat.

Nevertheless, during those weeks of painful reflection, I couldn't have cared tuppence if I'd died in the night. Perhaps that's why death paid me a call.

For a few weeks or more, in the small hours of the morning, I'd been startled awake by the terrifying feeling that my heart and lungs were about to burst; I sensed they'd stopped working for a matter of seconds during these 'attacks', and momentarily I would lose consciousness. Then I'd quickly regain awareness and sit bolt upright in the bed. During the frightening pause while I gasped like a fish out of water, my mouth would work and gape – then a sudden rush of air would surge into my lungs to kick-start my breathing again. While my body tried to relax and settle down into a steady rhythm again, I'd wipe my brow, lie back in the bed, and listen to the pulses thudding in my throat.

This strange condition occurred so frequently that I wondered if my death was approaching. I wasn't afraid to die, but my friends nagged me to get a medical examination, which I did – for the sake of peace and quietness.

The officious doctor made his diagnosis. 'Put your shirt back on. You're a remarkably fit young man,' he snapped at me, folding away his cold stethoscope. 'If all my patients were as healthy as you, Mr O'Brien, I'd be out of a job.'

I knew, then, that my condition was a psychic one; the mind definitely affects the health of the body, and vice versa – and my heart had been 'broken' in so many ways of late, and had been psychically stressed beyond endurance, that now I was paying the price.

Weeks later, on an icy winter's night, after another breathing 'attack', I received a chilling visitation from the spirit world. Restless and uncomfortable, I was lying in bed, still wide awake and very far away from sleep at just turned two o'clock in the morning when it happened. Even Sooty, who was snuggled up under the duvet near my feet, must have sensed something was up, for she couldn't settle.

351

My restive thoughts started to wander – country nights are so black and still . . .

Then, through the open door of my bedroom, I looked across at the landing towards the dark rectangular hole in the floor, which is the top of a narrow stairwell that leads down into the hallway, and psychically felt that something strange was happening, downstairs . . . Sooty stirred, and as I gazed through the shafts of moonlight that fell across the stairwell, I sensed a sudden change in the psychic atmosphere.

'Oh, my God . . .' There was a stranger in the cottage. A burglar. Downstairs. Standing in the hallway, at the foot of the stairwell . . .

I covered my mouth with my hand. What should I do? I was alone and naked in bed, and I felt terribly vulnerable. I glanced quickly around the bedroom – and there was nothing metal or heavy with which to protect myself. What could I do? My thoughts started whirling. With a suddenness that startled me, I raised myself up onto my elbows, and stared out through the doorway, and I'd just focused on the dark hole in the floor, when I sensed it—

Someone . . . something . . . was climbing the stairs, quietly, very deliberately, one step at a time. My throat was bone dry, my face a tight mask. In seconds I would see the intruder. But before I could move a muscle, the burglar's head rose up slowly through the hole in the floor, and it was shrouded in a black hood of some kind. And then his slender shoulders appeared, and his body continued to rise, until the full length of his back was visible. He was covered in black robing.

With a massive sense of relief, I released the breath I'd been holding. The visitor was not a burglar, but a spirit-form whose eerie figure now hovered on the landing, no more than ten feet away from me. Then it slowly turned around and faced me.

Only its face was visible within the dark folds of the long cape that shrouded it from head to foot. In the moonlight, its skin seemed pale and whitened, and its eyes were sunken in their sockets and ringed with dark circles.

In slow motion, the shimmering figure glided across the landing, until he stood right next to my bedside, about six feet tall. I was aware that he was a bringer of news – and I sensed his news was Death. He looked directly into my face and, in deep tones, said to me, 'I will return here soon.'

I shivered and immediately rejected him, saying out loud, 'I've wanted to die many times, God alone knows. For years, I longed to go Home. But not now . . . because there's so much more I can achieve, before I go.'

Instantly, the hooded messenger vanished, as if the light of his image had been switched off, and the surprising thought occurred to me that despite the way I'd been feeling of late, I'd rejected the idea of death – and I'd chosen to live.

(But if only I could have known, then, that months later my beloved friend Sooty would be the soul who would suddenly be called Home, I'd have loved and cherished her all the more.)

Seconds after the figure had vanished, I wrapped myself warmly in the duvet again and wondered where my spirit guide was, now, when I needed him.

But all I got from White Owl was a fleeting glimpse of his face, seen through a golden misty light. These were some of my darkest hours; why on earth was he smiling?

I decided that nothing seemed to make sense any more; so, what was the point in trying to work it all out? To hell with it. To hell with everything. What will be, will be. I turned over, and drifted off into a troubled sleep . . .

The following evening, because I dreaded going to bed in case the choking phenomenon should repeat itself (though in fact, I was never to experience it again), I sat for a long time and tried to relax in the small conservatory, lit by the orange rays of the setting sun. At least here I could still my mind in preparation for deep sleep by watching the tops of the giant trees swaying hypnotically in the evening breeze. I had a lot on my mind, but despite this I felt blissfully alone – and strangely at peace with myself.

The winter world seemed hushed silent, as if frozen in time, and my mind had floated far away from any thought of contact with the Other Side, when the spirit world decided to pay me another call. All around me there came the psychic sensation that someone was drawing near – but this soul had an emotional, spiritual presence, so different from the one last evening. Without doubt, a gentle woman was close by, and she'd brought a presence with her that soothed my spirit.

In the stillness that followed, she delivered to my spirit a wonderfully powerful healing treatment, after which she identified herself by repeating an endearing phrase from the past that touched my soul.

'Now then,' she said gently – and I instantly recognized my dear friend and tutor, Mrs Palmer.

Suddenly the years rolled away, and my throat clogged with gathering tears as I whispered to her, 'Oh, Mrs Palmer, thank you for helping me.' Then I sensed her own emotions rising, and knew she couldn't reply because of their intensity.

My lips trembled at the thought of the happy memories we'd shared all those years ago during my apprenticeship, and my whispering voice shook when it said, 'You were so kind to me when I was young, Mrs Palmer; when no-one else cared. Twenty years ago, when you were lying in that hospital bed, and I knew you were dying, I wanted to tell you so many things, about how grateful I was, but the words wouldn't come. I was too young, then, and too frightened of what you might think . . . But I can tell you now.' And with a deep breath, I gathered my thoughts together, and said, 'You were like a mother to me, Mrs Palmer . . . and I love you.'

Emotionally, she whispered into my mind, word for word, the wisdom she'd spoken to me when I was a younger man, as she lay dying upon a hospital bed.

'Think of all those who are suffering in the world, and what the Power of the Spirit can do for them, through someone like you . . . Stay the way you are, Stephen – don't change. Always be humble, and serve God's children who are in spiritual need.'

And in that moment, I knew my own mother was standing next to Mrs Palmer, and I sent my love

355

to her, too, as the presence of these two special ladies faded from my mind.

I could no longer see the glorious sunset, or the swaying trees, because my vision was entirely blurred. Teardrops rained down my face, and I made no effort to wipe them away . . .

For several days that wonderful visitation lingered in my mind and I felt so privileged to have received it. Daily, Mrs Palmer's poignant and emotional remarks returned to make me think again, and I reflected on them many times in the wintry days ahead, for she'd reminded me of my promise to serve. But still, I couldn't reach a firm decision about whether or not I should continue my public work.

Winter turned into spring and when summer arrived with a burst of colourful flowers that nodded and danced in the cottage gardens, one bright day Jeff called to discuss our future business plans. We sat around a table under a giant parasol in the garden, and sipped orangeade. Jeff said he had something important to tell me.

'Great news today. Things are finally on the mend and the tide's turning back in our favour. The next ten tour dates are just a few weeks away and I checked the ticket sales this morning – and guess what?'

I shrugged my shoulders.

'They're going like hot cakes! Three meetings have already sold out! The recession's far from over, I know, but something's happened to change our luck. It doesn't seem to be affecting us so badly now. So there'll be no more empty halls! Isn't that great?'

'Yes,' I replied calmly, sipping my drink.

'Just think of it: packed-out venues – loads more people will be able to hear your message again.' He grinned. 'Things are on the up-and-up! That means our wages'll be secure now, and my mortgage can be paid on time for a change. And no more losses at the box office. It's great news.'

'Yes, it is,' I said, putting on my sunglasses to take away the glare of his smile.

'There's no need to close down the business now. Voices Promotions can keep on running. And you're halfway through writing *Angels by my Side*, aren't you?'

'Yes. Book four's going well.'

My complacency seemed to agitate him, so he leaned forward into the sunlight and his 'business head' started talking.

'Look, Stephen, there's a lot of work to be done, and we can't hang about. You're back to your old self again now; you've had plenty of time to relax and get fit; you've corrected your vitamin deficiency, and you've had weeks to make up your mind. So, shake a leg. What about next year?'

Leaves rustled in a gentle breeze, and my eyes glazed over as I stared at some birds perched in the sunny treetops.

Jeff leaned across the table and spoke more firmly. 'Theatres have to be booked, *now* – to reserve dates for next year. And other matters need urgent attention. Several press and TV features must be confirmed. I can't keep these people waiting much longer. Just say the word and I can get on with my

357

job. They need answers straight away – and so do I.'

This threw me into a turmoil. What should I do?

Silently, I refilled my glass from the water decanter, then sipped my orangeade . . .

'You'll have to wait, Jeff.'

'But—'

'Please – ' I said, raising a hand to silence him. 'Look, would you do me a big favour, and take care of Sooty for me while I go away?'

His eyebrows lifted. 'Where are you going?'

'I've been so hassled lately, I forgot to tell you of a long-standing engagement I took on – ages ago – to teach in England for a week. It'll be very pressured work, with lots of lectures, demonstrations and workshops.' I sighed heavily. 'God knows, I'm not looking forward to it, and I don't want to do it. I'd rather stay here, be peaceful, and enjoy the sun. But I've got to go, tomorrow for seven days.'

Jeff laughed out loud. 'For a minute there, I thought you were heading for the hills!'

He took the now healthy Sooty home with him when he left, and promised that he'd stall the acceptance of the interviews and bookings for another week. 'But *only* for a week, mind!' I was warned. I thanked him, and mentally prepared to drag myself away the next morning.

Before dawn, I was sad to take my leave of Willowtrees, and had to force myself to drive to the conference in England. I loathed the thought of dealing with the boisterous students, because I knew from experience they would constantly demand my individual and undivided attention – no matter how I felt.

When I arrived at the big hotel, I was immediately struck in the face by disturbing news: I'd specifically asked the Spiritualist organizers not to book me any consultations with the public, because of the stress and strain this would place me under, but the ignorant bunch had ignored my request – and I was coldly informed that 'Twenty people have booked private sittings with you during the week, and we've no intention of cancelling them now.'

I was so annoyed, so tensed up, that I was speechless. I felt like that trapped bird again, who couldn't even stretch his wings.

But what could I do? There was no way out of a commitment.

So, I slapped on a brave face, steeled myself, and then got on with it.

24

Golden Spiritual Light

We were the only people in the room: I, an anxious and tired man; and she, a kindly old woman who seemed quite certain of the road she'd travelled in her seventy-odd years.

We sat facing each other, almost knee to knee, in the elegant hotel lounge. The dear lady was short and plump, with a milky-white face crowned by fine silver hair that shone like a halo in the shafts of sunlight streaming through the bay windows. She looked like a wise old angel, wrapped in a faint scent of lavender that wafted over her pale pink dress.

I rubbed the tiredness from my eyes, put on my best smile, tried to mentally remove my own irritating problems, and prepared myself to get on with the job of service, even though I was in no mood to work.

When I pressed my psychic awareness into action, I immediately sensed the silver-haired lady was surrounded by a host of invisible friends; I also got a clear picture of her character: she was just the kind of loving grandma everyone would want to hug; her sparkling blue eyes were wrinkled by happy laughter-lines, and her kind face radiated the grace that only wisdom and maturity can bestow. And yet . . . and yet, despite her peaceful expression – somewhere within her, something was wrong . . .

My sensitivity searched a little deeper, and discovered that she was not at peace. God alone knew I could recognize that easily enough; if anyone had ever felt robbed of tranquillity, I was that man. But I dismissed my own grumblings, and tried to discover what was haunting my sitter's soul, what was moving through it like a ravenous wolf stalking its prey.

My clairvoyant vision scanned the woman's mental aura for an answer. Was she afraid? . . . No. Was she anxious? . . . Yes; that was it. She was deeply distressed; but why?

Like silent radar, my mind swept through the atmosphere around the woman . . . and then I felt it: an appalling sense of grief, a devastating sense of despair that was jabbing at her heart with needle-point fingers. She was bereft of her greatest love, and I felt the agony of her grief, as if it were my own pain, as if infected wounds on my body were being gnawed by sharp rat's teeth.

This woman's heart had been broken, the same way that mine had been after my mother's death when I was a lad; a death that had propelled me along a road of service full of joys and heartaches, and had now placed me face to face with that silver-haired woman, on that summer morning.

Grabbing the polished sides of my Regency chair, I shuffled myself around on it until I was comfortable, then my weary voice mechanically stated, 'I'm going to tune my mind into the astral realms, and try my best to hear what your loved ones are saying.'

The woman nodded gracefully and smoothed her soft pink dress, which filled the air with sweet lavender perfume again, then she folded her hands on her lap, smiled, and waited.

I closed my eyes to all earthly impressions, banished from my mind the anxiety about my future, and mentally reached out to touch the next world, and I was successful.

'We have a communicator. I sense a very gentle man with us this morning,' I began. 'Though I don't see him, I know he's standing here on my right-hand side, and he thinks the world of you, my dear. His love is very powerful.'

I opened my eyes and saw she was smiling.

'This man suffered in agony for more than thirty years before he passed over, but never once did he complain of pain or sickness.'

(My communicator's astonishing courage and endurance deeply impressed me, and made my own difficulties pale into insignificance.)

'And he brings a most odd sensation with him,' I continued, 'as though he's a mature soul, and yet – quite young at heart.'

For the first time, the lady ceased to resemble a statue and leaned forward into the orange columns of sunlight between us. She nodded gently; then she was perfectly still again, and I hoped she wasn't going to be the kind of awkward sitter who remains silent and so far removed from the proceedings that she might as well not be present.

I gathered my strength, and emphasized, 'This man is desperate to reach you, and he begs me to stress these words: "I am fully alive now, and one hundred and fifty per cent fit and well."'

His excitement was bubbling so strongly that I asked him out loud, 'Please calm down a little.'

He did.

'And he mentioned someone just then, but it's such a commonplace name. He said "John".'

By now I was convinced that my mediumship was having one of its 'off days' and that nothing of great importance would be forthcoming, for this was the first factual evidence I'd relayed and I wasn't impressed by it. But when I glanced across at the old lady, I was surprised to see that she was silently crying: small teardrops were trickling down her face, and glinting in the sunlight as they splashed onto her hands in her lap.

I was quiet for a while, for an old woman's tears are always very humbling. Then I went on:

'This gentle man says, "We didn't have much time together; and what we did share was scarred by my pain, which never let up for a moment."'

Then something strange happened to my right hand; manipulated by spirit power, it was twisted into what looked like a bird's stiff talons with sharp pointed fingers that curved upwards and inwards; they were rigid, and when I touched them they were colder than stone. As soon as this spirit-transformation was complete, the 'claw' rested itself on my right knee.

Startled, but controlling my surprise, I said, 'This must be significant.' Then the strange hand we'd both been staring at, instantly resumed its normal shape, thank God. The dear lady was fascinated, as indeed I was, but still she said nothing; so I took a deep breath, and relayed more of her communicator's words:

'Thanks for staying with me. I know how much guts it took: I'll never forget the courage and spirit you showed.'

My sitter was obviously moved, but I wished that she would explain the significance of these 'trivial' messages, especially the meaning of the silly word her man kept repeating, over and over again throughout the sitting. He kept saying, 'Mew, mew, mew . . .'

But she didn't offer an explanation, so I carried on.

'He tells me, "I don't know what I'd have done without you; but don't worry about me any more because I'm happy, and living with my father".' And I added, 'If he could be here today, physically, he'd throw his arms around you and embrace you. "She fought the good fight. Thank her for everything she did, Stephen," he says. "And tell her I didn't die. I'm alive, and I visit her each day."'

I shivered with warmth and emotion, leaned into the rays of sunlight between us and encompassed both of the woman's thin wrists with my palms, as instructed by her man, and explained, '"You used to hold me like this," he says. "And I want to return the kindness – and all the love you gave me."'

The woman's wrinkled fingers slipped through my hands and then closed lovingly around them. Her arthritic thumbs stroked my skin, as I heard her communicator speak that strange word again, 'Mew, mew, mew,' followed by '. . . I love you so much.'

These final words of his must have touched the

dear lady's heart, for they made her pleasant voice murmur with such depth and sincerity, 'Yes, I know he does; and I'm very happy.'

She patted my hands again, then dried her eyes.

I received nothing more from her man, so she stood up on bent legs, turned around, hobbled across the elegant thick-carpeted lounge, and clicked the big door shut behind her.

For a few moments I sat in bemused silence. Here was I, a soul in desperate need of guidance and positive direction for his own tangled life, guidance which I'd not received, but the spirit people had just used me to comfort a stranger and ease her emotional burdens.

Frustrated, I moaned to the empty room, 'Life just isn't fair.' Then I reproached myself for being so selfish, and, clasping my hands tight in prayer, I closed my eyes and thanked the Great Spirit for using me to help the mature lady and her man, after which I silently left the room.

But for the rest of the week, while I rushed around and gave exhausting lectures and teaching workshops, I was haunted by the emotions of those two kind people – and yet I was puzzled. The messages had seemed quite unremarkable, banal even, so why had they generated such a tide of love in the three of us? And only one common name had been given: John – there was nothing earth-shattering about that, and the communicator hadn't even told me who John was, or revealed his own identity.

Dark thoughts of 'not enough detail' in my mediumship loomed up in my mind, and I was disappointed with my psychic abilities. Why couldn't the communicator have added his surname? Surely that wasn't too much to ask? And why had the sitting been so short?

I heaved a great sigh and dutifully reminded myself that the spirit people are in charge of formulating and relaying the evidence, and not the medium; and that they deliver whatever *they* think will be helpful to the recipient. 'It isn't their objective to satisfy your ego, Stephen,' I told myself.

Still, I did wonder about asking the silver-haired woman for some kind of explanation, but thought better of it when, one morning, while dashing out of one class and heading for another I spied her sitting alone on a plush bay-window seat, gazing out at the flowerbeds surrounding the hotel. She seemed so remote, so far removed from the bustle and noise of the other students that I didn't want to break her cocoon of smiling thought; so instead, I hurried away down a corridor to take my next lecture.

It seemed that every class on my schedule was destined to be full of boisterous and over-attentive people, and after each exhausting day's work I couldn't wait to flee from the burning stare of eighty pairs of eyes. I think every student selfishly tried (and managed) at one time or another to commandeer my exclusive attention and tuition. You didn't have to be psychic to see that I was exhausted and that I had other pressing appointments, but many of the students displayed a remarkable talent for recognizing only their own needs, and they cornered me wherever and whenever they could.

Sometimes, people can be very thoughtless.

By eleven o'clock each night, I was thoroughly whacked out and I rushed upstairs, locked my bedroom door, and crashed into bed.

But I couldn't sleep soundly at all: the decision about my future had to be made soon – and this Sword of Damocles hanging over my head made it impossible for me to rest. Each night, my prayer was that I would find the strength to steer my life aright, and also that the stressful teaching course would come quickly to its end.

But a watched pot never boils, as they say, and the week dragged on . . .

However, when the final day did at last arrive, I shuffled my weary feet into the reception hall, my whole body bending forward under the weight of a massive suitcase which I plonked down on the parquet floor.

I was knackered. I didn't care if my baggage scuffed the expensive wood; as a matter of fact, I wouldn't have given a toot if the bomb had dropped. I'd worked myself skinny all week and I was desperate to flee from so many questioning minds. Even when people are trying to be kind, they can still be very demanding, and I wanted to run miles away from them. All week I'd longed to go home and rest.

Home. What a wonderful thought . . . My beloved Willowtrees. Privacy, silence, and precious seclusion. Ancient trees and perfect peace. Night after night, how I'd dreamed of standing again on the rich earth at Willowtrees cottage, my haven of rest, where there are no other human beings, just birds singing brightly in the woods, and the joyful company of my lovely Sooty. At Willowtrees I could 'put my face in a sling' for a few weeks, and let the tiresome world go by . . .

Raucous laughter snapped my thoughts like a dry branch — loud people of all ages were wishing one another well, cackling like egg-bound hens, exchanging hugs and addresses, and shouting 'See you next year!' and 'Promise us you'll write!' Then they ploughed through the big doors like hordes of lemmings, eager to catch their planes, trains, taxis and cars.

I don't know how I managed to smile, shake hands, and wave them all off — but I did, even though my heart wasn't in it.

When the lobby was blissfully empty, I straightened my back and clumped my heavy feet towards Betty, the cheerful receptionist who was waiting at the desk.

My voice was hoarse. 'So long, Betty,' I said; then, just as I swung my cases up from the floor to generate some forward momentum to flee from the building, out of nowhere a strange bundle of lilac mohair, topped with a woolly hat, planted itself in front of me and barred my way. I nearly knocked the poor woman over. 'Oh, I'm sorry,' I apologized, dumping my bags back onto the floor, as from the depth of the fur there came the pleasant voice of the silver-haired lady.

'That's all right, Stephen. Can you spare a minute?' she asked, her rosy cheeks flushed and glowing.

Strangely enough, I was really glad to see her, and my attitude brightened. 'Of course I can,' I replied.

'Only I didn't thank you earlier in the week, when I should have. You see, I was rather emotional;

368

I'm just a silly old woman. Please forgive me.'

I smiled warmly, 'Really, there's no need.'

'Oh, Stephen,' she continued, taking both my hands in hers and squeezing them tight, 'he brought such wonderful evidence to me in our consultation. You don't know it, but you linked me with my darling son.' Her lips quivered with emotion as she spoke. 'My boy was only thirty-seven when he died, but he was incredibly brave . . . he was my only child, and he had such a hard life. He was severely handicapped, you see, Stephen, both physically and mentally.' The words jammed in her throat, and large teardrops welled in her eyes, trembled on her lashes, then ran freely down her face and into the corners of her mouth.

'Here,' I said, offering a tissue. 'Please don't be upset.'

'Oh, I'm not upset,' she said, dabbing her eyes, 'I'm overjoyed. I can't remember the last time I was this happy; and I slept as soundly as a bell last night, after my boy's messages – and I haven't done that for years. Upset? Good Lord, no! I feel like a new person.'

She gazed into my silence.

'Stephen, I must tell you something. You gave me my son's name: John. I nursed him every day of his life. He was in constant agony for thirty-seven years; day in, day out. He suffered so much because the doctors couldn't fully suppress the pain.

'His right hand was crippled, utterly useless, it looked like a bird's claw, just as yours did when it changed in the sitting. But the worst of my memories that John mentioned was the legal wrangling. I'm a widow, you see, and the authorities wanted to take him away from me. They wanted to institutionalize John, but I stood my ground and wouldn't let them.'

Her eyes shone, and her voice lowered. 'They said I was too frail to look after him on my own – but I showed them the door and growled after them, "He's my son," I said; "I carried him inside me for nine months. I birthed him and I've loved him all these years! So you can get out of my house," I shouted at them – "Right *now*!"'

She sniffed into the paper tissue, then gathered her memories together with a huge sigh that seemed to rise from the depths of her soul.

'And then . . . oh God . . . then I battled on for years, you see, on my own. I was totally alone; nobody cared whether John lived or died, only me. But I was adamant: they weren't going to lock up my boy and turn him into just another statistic. I was determined he wouldn't go into some strange place without his mother to see him each day.' And she emphasized, 'I promised my son I'd help him, always – and I've never broken that promise, Stephen, never – in my life. Promises shouldn't be broken. Don't you agree?'

I nodded thoughtfully, and the lady went on, 'In the Second World War I did my bit for my country; I'd stood my ground against the tyranny of Hitler, so I was damned if some jumped-up pen-pushers, who wouldn't know love if it hit them in the face, were going to get the better of me, or make me give in. After all, some things are worth fighting for.'

She wiped away more falling tears. 'And my John knew that: in the sitting he referred to the pressures the authorities had put on me, and how hard I'd battled to keep him when he said I'd "fought the good fight". No, I didn't give in; I'm made of stronger stuff than that. I understood every word.'

A quietness descended between us. The woman blew her nose, and then I spoke.

'Thank you for telling me,' I said, moved by her courage, love, and determination. 'It all makes sense now.'

'Stephen, you brought me my boy; and for that I can never thank you enough. I fed him, changed him night and day, and washed him; I did everything for my beautiful boy, because he couldn't do a thing for himself. But I didn't mind,' she said. 'No, I didn't mind one bit, because I'm his mother – and I love him with all my heart.'

I clasped her small arthritic hands and said, 'A kindness is never forgotten.'

'Yes, that's true enough . . . and I shall treasure your messages; they mean the world to me; especially' – her voice caught in her throat – 'especially since John died only two weeks ago.'

I didn't know what to say to her.

When I did speak, I said quietly, 'If I've helped to reunite you with your son, then my trip from Wales has been well worthwhile.'

'Oh, you've done more than that: you've given me comfort and hope, and a reason to go on living. John couldn't speak properly, you see . . . the words just wouldn't come. God love him, he could never say "Ma"; so, to him, I was always "Mew," which is what he called me several times in the sitting.'

At last, the puzzle was solved.

'And it was so wonderful to hear that he's happy and living with his Dad, that he's fit and well in a new body now, and able to walk and talk like everyone else. And when you were speaking for him, for the first time I sensed him standing next to me.'

She straightened her small frame, beamed a smile, and said, 'May God always be with you.'

Then she stood on tiptoe, kissed my face, and threw her arms around my neck in such a sincere hug that I closed my eyes and returned her embrace; and it was then that I felt the invisible, but gentle, power of this dear soul's love flowing from the middle of her heart right into the centre of mine. It flooded my spirit until I felt that even the woman herself was strangely no longer present – she'd vanished, and I was caught up in a vivid psychic vision:

And all at once, it seemed to me that I was standing alone, lost in a vast expanse of windswept moorland that was bathed in a strange and glowing golden light. The strong fresh tang of wild heather was on the breeze, and the sun was a brilliant ball of light in the sky, and the moor beneath my feet was firm and strong. And in my hands I held a snow-white dove; I could feel its little heart beating beneath its silky feathers under my fingers. And for me, the dove symbolized Peace, and the Freedom and Power of my spirit.

Then, with an upward curve of my arms, I released the bird into a brilliant sky, and in a rush of feathers it flew way up into the blue.

I felt proud to stand and watch it go. It was alive, and free – and so was I.

And a voice within me seemed to say, 'None of

God's creatures are chained or bound, for their souls can fly.'

In that moment, I knew beyond doubt that like the dove I was for ever loved by the One who created me; that His silent guidance had never once forsaken me; and that no matter where I went, or what I did, I could never be cut adrift from His loving presence. I knew, too, that all the challenges I'd encountered had taught me valuable spiritual lessons which had developed and matured my soul. My battles had made me strong. And even if storm clouds should gather on the far horizon, no harm could ever befall my true self, the spirit within me.

Standing on that moor, I was wrapped in clouds of Golden Light; and I knew then that the Gift of Golden Light was the Gift of God's Love. And the Golden Light of Love is so freely given by Him to all of His children, whoever they are, and wherever they may be.

Then suddenly the spell broke as the old woman released me – and in an instant I was back in the hotel lobby, watching the silver-haired lady turn on her heels and then, leaving behind her the sweet scent of lavender perfume, she marched briskly from the building and out into the sunny grounds.

For a minute or two, I felt I didn't want to move.

Then slowly, I retraced her path to the wide stone steps outside. Sudden gusts of air billowed into my face, and caught in my throat; and a skylark called out its greeting to a brand new day. But, glancing around the car park, I couldn't see my little lady in the lilac mohair coat and hat, for she'd boarded her coach, and had gone.

It was then that I remembered the echoing words of my tutor, Mrs Palmer, who years ago had said, 'God will always comfort the lonely.'

She was right; He always will.

I stood tall, opened my lungs and filled them with clear, fresh air, then with a lighter step I walked across the deserted lobby back to the big desk, to check out. Cheery Betty, the middle-aged receptionist, was waiting.

'Gawd blimey, is that a smile on your face, Stephen? That can only mean one of two things: either you're having a nervous breakdown, or you've lost your marbles,' she joked.

I chuckled readily.

'Well, Mr O'Brien, you know what I always say: if anyone can survive a week's slog trying to turn a bunch of psychics into proper mediums, and then stroll up to this desk without his solar plexus hanging out and dragging over his boots like an old cow's udder – he must be a bloody good medium!'

'Or loopy,' I quipped, and we laughed. I signed out, confessing to Betty, 'It was a very stressful course . . . but it was satisfying' – and I glanced at the big oak doors through which the old lady had just left.

'Stephen, it's a wonder you're still standing, son. I've watched you all week; you've worked like a thing possessed!'

'I have,' I said, stepping between my suitcase and hand-luggage just as a man's loud voice shouted from the telephone booth at the opposite end of the lobby, 'Stephen O'Brien! A long distance call from a Mr Jones in Wales!'

When I picked up the receiver, Jeff's voice was urgent:

'Where've you been? The phone hasn't stopped ringing all week down here. I can't delay these theatre managers another minute, Stephen. They want confirmation of tour bookings for next year.' His voice was tense.

'I see.'

'Well, what do I do? Those radio and TV shows must have your decision, too. What do I tell them?'

The hollow chimes of an antique grandfather clock standing next to me slowly struck twelve midday, and drowned out any possibility of a reply.

'Stephen! They need answers; and so do I,' Jeff declared on the stroke of twelve. 'What do I say?'

There was a pause, and then I replied calmly:

'Confirm the venues, and book the interviews. I'll be back in Wales this afternoon.' And I heard Jeff laughing as I plonked the receiver on its cradle.

I strode briskly over to Betty at Reception and pecked her rosy cheek goodbye. She smiled at me, and winked. Then I lifted up my heavy luggage and made my way to the massive oak doors, where I stopped and gazed at the beautiful day.

'Aye, aye, Mr O'Brien! And what's that silly grin for?'

I looked back at Betty over my shoulder. My voice was bright and cheerful. 'Oh, I was just thinking,' I said. 'There's so much to do . . . and I can't wait!'

And the next instant, I was wrapped in golden sunlight.

For further information on all aspects of the life and work of Stephen O'Brien, including obtaining by Mail Order his bestselling books, tape cassettes, autographed pictures, full-colour souvenir programmes, inspirational greeting cards and a full range of other quality items – please write enclosing a stamped addressed envelope to:

VOICES MANAGEMENT
(Dept B5)
PO Box 8
SWANSEA
SA1 1BL
UK

Voices Management regrets it cannot reply without a stamped addressed envelope, and correspondents are respectfully advised not to mail irreplaceable items, for neither Voices, nor Mr O'Brien, can accept responsibility for the loss or damage of any unsolicited manuscripts, poems, sentimental objects and photographs, or cassettes, etc. posted by the public.

Please keep your letters brief, and be patient when awaiting replies, as Stephen receives vast quantities of mail.

Thank you.